COMPETENCY-BASED CAREER PLANNING
FOR REFERENCE AND USER
SERVICES PROFESSIONALS

ALA Editions purchases
fund advocacy, awareness,
and accreditation programs
for library professionals
worldwide.

COMPETENCY-BASED CAREER PLANNING
FOR REFERENCE AND USER SERVICES PROFESSIONALS

JO BELL WHITLATCH

BETH S. WOODARD

Chicago 2020

© 2020 by the American Library Association

Extensive effort has gone into ensuring the reliability of the information in this book; however, the publisher makes no warranty, express or implied, with respect to the material contained herein.

ISBN: 978-0-8389-1780-0 (paper)

Library of Congress Cataloging-in-Publication Data

Names: Whitlatch, Jo Bell, author. | Woodard, Beth S., author.
Title: Competency-based career planning for reference and user services professionals Jo Bell Whitlatch, Beth S. Woodard.
Description: Chicago : ALA Editions, 2020. | Includes bibliographical references and index.
Identifiers: LCCN 2018050751 | ISBN 9780838917800 (paper : alk. paper)
Subjects: LCSH: Reference librarians—In-service training. | Library education (Continuing education) | Career development.
Classification: LCC Z682.4.R44 W48 2020 | DDC 025.5/2—dc23
LC record available at https://lccn.loc.gov/2018050751

Cover design by Karen Sheets de Gracia. Image © abbiesartshop/Adobe Stock. Text design and composition by Dianne M. Rooney using Charis SIL and TitlingGothicFB Normal typefaces.

♾ This paper meets the requirements of ANSI/NISO Z39.48–1992 (Permanence of Paper).

Printed in the United States of America

24 23 22 21 20   5 4 3 2 1

contents

LIST OF FIGURES *vii*

FOREWORD *ix*

ACKNOWLEDGMENTS *xi*

INTRODUCTION
    Introducing the RUSA "Professional Competencies" *xiii*

one Access *1*

two Sources *23*

three Collaboration *33*

four Information Literacy *49*

five Marketing and Advocacy *83*

six Assessment *101*

seven Future Services *121*

CONCLUSION *151*

APPENDIX
    Professional Competencies for Reference and User Services Librarians *153*

BIBLIOGRAPHY *161*

ABOUT THE AUTHORS *173*

INDEX *175*

figures

0.1	Managing One's Own Learning	*xviii*
0.2	Development Assignment Plan	*xxi*
0.3	Library of Congress Individual Development Plan	*xxii*
0.4	Transferring Learning into Practice	*xxvii*
1.1	Checklist of Elements for Inquiry Analysis	7
1.2	Self-Assessment Checklist for Follow-Up	8
1.3	Behavioral Observation Scale for Follow-Up	8
1.4	Reference Assistance to Users: Diagnosing the Stage of the Information-Seeking Process (ISP)	9
1.5	Self-Assessment Checklist for Interest in Individual's Information Need	10
1.6	Self-Assessment Checklist for Listening/Inquiring	11
1.7	Checklist for Evaluating Secret Patron Transactions	12
1.8	Interviewing Test	12
1.9	Reference Text Project Rubric	19
1.10	Self-Assessment Checklist for Searching Behaviors	21
2.1	Checklist for *Readers' Advisory Service in the Public Library*	27
2.2	Book Annotation Format	28
2.3	Information-Seeking Process Assessment for Web Pages or Other Information Presentations	30
2.4	PRIMO Selection Criteria	31
3.1	Sample Permission Form	35
3.2	Questions for Interviewing Effective Group Leaders	37
3.3	How Collaborative Are You?	38
3.4	Self-Assessment Rating Scale for Collaboration	39
3.5	How Effective Are Your Meetings?	41
3.6	Reflection on General Community Relationships	44

- **3.7** Evaluating Potential Partners *45*
- **3.8** arXiv Partnership Evaluation Rubric *47*
- **4.1** Reference Desk: End-of-Shift Checklist *56*
- **4.2** Types of Instruction in All Types of Libraries *57*
- **4.3** Roles for Instruction Librarians: A Checklist for Developing Proficiencies *59*
- **4.4** Techniques for Engaging Students in Learning *62*
- **4.5** Summary of Suggested Strategies for Student Engagement *63*
- **4.6** Checklist for Presentation Skills Adapted from the "Proficiencies for Instruction Librarians" *67*
- **4.7** Presentation Feedback Form *70*
- **4.8** Universal Design for Learning Guidelines *72*
- **4.9** Erlinger's Seven General Assessment Types *76*
- **4.10** Reflecting on Your Practice of Active Learning *78*
- **4.11** Using Evidence to Assess Your Development Efforts *80*
- **4.12** Time Allocation in a Class Session *81*
- **5.1** SIVA: The Marketing Mix *87*
- **5.2** Marketing Assessment Checklist *95*
- **5.3** Marketing Evaluation Checklist *97*
- **5.4** Advocacy Assessment Checklist *100*
- **6.1** Basic Problem-Solving and Decision-Making Skills *103*
- **6.2** Process for Seven Steps in Practitioner Research *103*
- **6.3** Understanding and Applying Basic Information Service Evaluation Methods *106*
- **6.4** Checklist for Evaluating Information Resources *108*
- **6.5** Reference Electronic Database Questionnaire *109*
- **6.6** Checklist for Assessment of Competencies in Evaluating Information Resources *110*
- **6.7** Observation Forms for In-Person, Telephone, and E-Mail Surveys *111*
- **6.8** Reference Activity Counts *114*
- **6.9** Assessment of Service Delivery Evaluation Competencies *115*
- **6.10** Assessment of Evaluation Behaviors for Information Interfaces in Area of Responsibility *116*
- **6.11** Assessment of Competencies in Evaluating Information Service Providers *119*
- **6.12** Assessment of Competencies in the Components of a Performance Management System *119*
- **7.1** Annual Record of Active Learning Activities *138*
- **7.2** Map Out Your Mentoring Network *140*
- **7.3** Force Field Analysis *142*
- **7.4** Comparing Critical and Creative Thinking *143*
- **7.5** Fishbone Diagram: Stress at the Reference Desk *144*
- **7.6** Ease/Impact Model *145*
- **7.7** Decision Matrix Example *147*
- **7.8** Application of Knowledge *149*

foreword

OVER TWENTY YEARS AGO I HAD THE good fortune to be hired and trained by Beth Woodard as a reference services graduate assistant at the University of Illinois. She prepared her new charges as thoroughly as a week of training would allow before placing us at the busy information desk to answer questions during the transition to a new library catalog and our first set of web-based article databases. We weren't left to sink or swim because Beth had also carefully planned out weekly meetings with training topics and included career development as an integral part of our training.

A few years later Beth moved into a library-wide role as a training coordinator, and I stepped into her role of training the reference graduate assistants. I started with the excellent training framework that Beth had designed over the years and then modified it. During my time at Illinois I trained over seventy graduate assistants for the main reference department and led further training for hundreds more across the campus libraries. Beth has been thinking about and training librarians in professional competencies for decades, and I owe most of what I know about training and career planning to her tutelage.

Jo Bell Whitlatch also had a foundational impact on my career, even though we have only met a few times in person. Her book *Evaluating Reference Services* made its way from our reference department shelves to a semipermanent home in my office and was a guiding light as I developed both training for and the assessment of reference services at the University of Illinois. Her research was pivotal to my research by providing both insight and inspiration.

The influence of Beth and Jo Bell exemplify the impact that both mentors and researchers can have on the career development of librarians. I feel lucky in having found so much guidance at an early stage in my career. Librarians' individual experiences vary greatly both within the master's degree program and afterward, and this is where *Competency-Based Career Planning for Reference and User Services Professionals* has a vital role in providing a framework and useful exercises for career planning in public services librarianship across all types of libraries.

Whatever we think we know going into our training, or our first job in libraries, or our second or fifth job in libraries, there is always more to know, and another level of expertise to reach or another skill to develop. There are myriad "What I didn't learn in library school" articles and blog posts, but a career is always a lifelong learning process, and much is learned on the job or otherwise outside of the classroom.

Being a public services librarian is broader than I imagined when I was studying for my MLIS degree. Marketing and assessment were not subjects that I thought much about as I trained for my future career, but in my very first job I found myself promoting a grant-funded project to the upper administration and marketing our project's services to library faculty. Another of the grant's requirements was to perform an assessment of the project's impact. Careers can develop in both planned and unexpected ways, even for the same person. My job nearly twenty years later contains even more marketing and assessment. I've had to master planning a wider range of public services beyond reference service. I have worked at different types of libraries with diverse patrons representing a range of cultural and academic backgrounds. The competencies in this book have applied to all of my positions, albeit as varying proportions of my day.

The RUSA "Professional Competencies for Reference and User Services Professionals" encapsulate the range of skills and expertise that are required of a public services librarian. In this book, Whitlatch and Woodard combine their research acumen and experience to deliver a practical, well-grounded set of tools that expand on the RUSA "Professional Competencies" and can help you develop your own career plan. My favorite aspects of this book are the many tools for self-assessment. Reflective practice enables us to learn from our own experiences—both those we assess as "good" and those we experience as "bad"—in order to continually improve. Structured self-assessment such as the checklists in chapter 2 situates our self-reflection within agreed-upon best practices, and moves us beyond feelings of inadequacy or success by facilitating more nuanced assessment and guided follow-up.

If this book had been written when I was training graduate students at Illinois, it would have been a cornerstone for designing their training, and a recommended book for them to use after graduation. Often supervisors plan training that is very specific to their libraries, but this training may either assume particular existing competencies or does not connect to a broader set of skills that will serve the employee in future jobs. When approached this way, the work can feel more like a set of tasks and less like a career. I know that at times my own approach was focused on immediate mastery of a tool or local policy, and for the training to be most effective I would need to "back up" to the underlying principles. The RUSA "Professional Competencies" connect us to the profession of librarianship and help create a trajectory for lifelong learning, which is what we should want for everyone working in our libraries. *Competency-Based Career Planning* also has value for managers and supervisors in developing position descriptions, training plans, and in promoting professional development for their staff at all levels.

This book will provide a foundation and inspiration for your own career as a reference librarian. It is a work to take with you throughout your career and use not just as a new librarian but as a mid-career librarian, a manager, and to recommend to librarians that you mentor.

M. KATHLEEN KERN
Director, Miller Learning Center
University of Georgia Libraries

acknowledgments

WE WISH TO ACKNOWLEDGE THE DEDI- cation and hard work of our fellow members of the RUSA Professional Competencies for Reference and User Services Librarians Task Force, chair Nancy Huling, Larayne J. Dallas, and Robin Kinder. We especially thank chair Nancy Huling for her leadership and dedication to the importance of competencies for reference and user services librarians. We also wish to thank our RUSA colleague of many years, Kathleen Kluegel, for her continual support and encouragement over many years.

JO BELL WHITLATCH
and BETH WOODARD

introduction
Introducing the RUSA "Professional Competencies"

THE WORLD OF INFORMATION IS CHANG-ing rapidly. The challenges in accessing, organizing, and managing today's rapidly evolving information formats are growing every day. In reference services, the rapidly changing information environment challenges new, mid-career, and senior librarians. How can reference librarians keep their professional knowledge and skills on the cutting edge in our global information society?

Reference librarians need to be in charge of their own careers. Employers, educational programs, and professional associations can help with this, but the bottom line is that reference librarians need to be proactive when it comes to their own professional development. A good place to start is with the ideas outlined in this book. By using the practical suggestions in this book for updating and assessing their skills and knowledge, librarians will be able to reflect on their strengths and develop strategies to enhance their abilities, thereby leading to a more satisfying and enjoyable career.

The primary goal of this book is to introduce a document developed by the Reference and User Services Association (RUSA), which is a division of the American Library Association (ALA). This document is called "Professional Competencies for Reference and User Services Librarians" (hereafter the RUSA "Professional Competencies") and was published in 2017. (See the Appendix at the end of this book for the full document.) This document is a model statement of the competencies that are essential for successful reference and user services librarians. The statement builds upon the ALA's "Core Competences of Librarianship" and specifically on section 5, "Reference and User Services." In this book, we examine the RUSA document's practical potential for librarians to enhance their skills, achieve more successful individual performance, and explore their development opportunities. Reference and user services librarians are those who assist, advise, and instruct users in accessing all forms of recorded knowledge through both direct and indirect service to patrons. In this book, librarians will learn how to use the RUSA "Professional Competencies" to assess their professional skills and abilities, create and implement individual plans for professional development, and assess their progress in enhancing their professional skills and abilities. The RUSA "Professional Competencies" are grouped into seven categories that encompass key areas for reference and user services librarians. These categories are access, sources, collaboration, information literacy, marketing and advocacy, assessment, and planning for the future.

Each category has a separate section in the RUSA "Professional Competencies" document, and the section's title is phrased in terms of a broad behavioral competency. For example, the title of section 5A is "Accesses Relevant and Accurate Recorded Knowledge and Information." Each section then has one or more subheads that cover more specific behavioral competencies; in section 5A the subheads are "Offers Services Responsive to Individual Expressed User Needs" and "Organizes and Designs Services to Meet the Needs of the Primary Community."

The organization of the seven main chapters in this book follows this same scheme. In chapter 1, "Access," which covers the competencies enumerated in section 5A of the RUSA document, there are two main subheads: "Offers Services Responsive to Individual Expressed User Needs" and "Organizes and Designs Services to Meet the Needs of the Primary Community." Each of these main sections has three subsections whose titles are characterized by the phrases "Competencies for," "Development Methods for," and "Assessing Development Efforts for." These sections respectively treat the competencies, development methods, and assessment methods for a specific competency. The "Development Methods for" subsection discusses strategies for enhancing the librarian's competencies, and the "Assessing Development Efforts for" subsection describes methods for determining the effectiveness of the librarian's individual development efforts.

The sections below will briefly outline the importance of the seven categories of the RUSA document.

A. ACCESS

A key value of the librarian profession is providing access, which is connecting users with appropriate information. We connect people with information and knowledge by guiding them in selecting the information that best meets their individual needs. The primary focus of this category is on understanding the information needs and information behavior of primary users and developing the skills to effectively meet those information needs. Access includes organizing and designing services that recognize the importance of user time and convenience, remove barriers to service, and assist users in coping with user information overload.

B. SOURCES

The evaluation, selection, retrieval, and presentation of information sources for the benefit of our user communities continue to be an important function of reference. We identify and present highly recommended, carefully evaluated, diverse sources in many formats. We promote the use of these sources by creating a wide variety of guides and instructional materials.

C. COLLABORATION

Collaboration competencies focus on building partnerships and promoting teamwork. Although librarians have always worked together, collaboration has assumed new importance in a world that has witnessed phenomenal growth in information, new knowledge, and sophisticated technology, all within a relatively short time frame. Because of the expansion of information and the increasing variety of ways to access it, librarians must work in partnership with users, colleagues, professional organizations, agencies, and other groups to ensure that users receive the information service they need at the time of need and in the most suitable format. Librarians must actively pursue collaborations that enhance services for their users. Also, librarians need to recognize and respect the role played by the user in the information interaction.

D. INFORMATION LITERACY

For librarians and library users, the basic skill sets for finding, evaluating, and using information in all formats are critical for successful reference and user services. Successful service requires understanding and integrating information literacy concepts across the full range of services; engaging individuals through effective presentation and communication strategies; and creating a learner-centered environment.

E. MARKETING AND ADVOCACY

Marketing is much more than publicizing the library's services. It involves systematic planning, and implementing and controlling the different services that are intended to bring together users and library services and resources. Marketing involves understanding why, how, when, and from whom users obtain the types of educational and recreational information that libraries typically supply. A planning process is essential in order to identify and promote these services to users. Promoting the value of library services requires understanding and applying marketing theory and practices; developing, implementing, and evaluating an ongoing marketing plan; and promoting the value of libraries by educating our communities about the essential role that libraries play in society.

F. ASSESSMENT

Evaluation and assessment are also very important values for the survival of the library profession, since they assist in creating and refining professional practice and in developing new, innovative services. Evaluation and assessment programs should ask not only how good the service is, but also whether the service provided is the right one.

G. PLANNING FOR THE FUTURE

Core knowledge is acquired as part of basic professional education. However, that knowledge must be continuously updated. Lifetime learning, as manifested in the practice of remaining current in the domains of knowledge for reference and user services, is crucial for the development of future services. Planning, implementing, evaluating, and enhancing innovative services and resources are also essential.

WHAT ARE COMPETENCIES?

A competency is a combination of "knowledge, skills, abilities, and behaviors that are required for job success in most professional organizations" (Association for Talent Development, 2014). So a "competency" is a skill, knowledge, ability, or behavior that is used on the job. Core or foundational competencies are the distinctive competencies that are important to the organization. They are behaviors that excellent performers exhibit more consistently and effectively than average performers. The effective assessment of competencies depends on observed behavior.

Because they relate to performing specific tasks, competencies depend on context. In this book, our context expands beyond an individual institution or work organization. The context is the collective group of reference and user services professionals. The RUSA "Professional Competencies" focus on the unique set of skills and knowledge that is required to effectively negotiate two complex systems—the ever-expanding world of information resources and the information-seeking needs of a wide variety of user groups.

Concerns about changing technology, global competition, and the quality of the workforce have led to the discussion and development of competencies in many professions in the last two decades. Rapidly changing technology and increased global competition require a more flexible workforce and a greater emphasis on individuals taking responsibility for their own continual learning and self-development. The discussion and development of competencies for reference and user services librarians has occurred within this broader societal context. Initially reference competencies were often described in vague terms, such as "conduct a good reference interview" or "provide excellent reference service." But such statements provide no basis from which we can create learning programs and measure our success in obtaining or enhancing competencies. Therefore, these are not effective competencies statements.

BEHAVIORALLY BASED STATEMENTS

Competency statements must be easy to measure or interpret. Specific competency statements, defined in behavioral terms whenever possible, facilitate the creation of, and assessment of, professional development plans. Behaviors can be observed, described, and verified. Librarians will find that a behavioral or performance-based perspective makes working with competencies more meaningful. To assess your learning, you should evaluate how well you are able to apply the competencies—the skills, knowledge, and abilities—to specific tasks, and also evaluate your success in performing those tasks. To determine whether a competency statement is behaviorally based, ask yourself: Can you observe the individual performing a certain task and determine whether the required skills, knowledge, or abilities are at a level that results in successful performance of the task?

COMPETENCIES AS STANDARDS

Competency statements can be viewed as specific standards that support the values, mission, and goals of a library, information service, or professional organization. For example, the mission of the ALA is to provide leadership for the development, promotion, and improvement of library and information services and the profession of librarianship in order to enhance learning and ensure access to information for all (American Library Association, 2008b).

As part of its mission, the strategic plan of the ALA highlights advocacy as a strategy to provide "a vision of innovation, focus on the impact of libraries and librarians, enable the future of libraries, and promote libraries as centers of community engagement, lifelong discovery and learning" (American Library Association, 2008a).

In support of the ALA's mission and advocacy strategies, the broad, general goals of individual libraries or information service organizations might be to "conduct a good reference interview" or "provide excellent reference service." Competency statements can be developed from goals that set specific behavioral standards on how to achieve these general goals, which support the mission of organizations.

WHY SHOULD WE CARE ABOUT COMPETENCIES?

Establishing and maintaining distinctive professional competencies are essential for the survival of all professions, including that of library and information science. Developing and maintaining distinctive competencies are one of the hallmarks of a profession. Therefore, clearly defined and distinctive competencies form the core definition of a professional. The right of professionals to determine how their work will be accomplished is generally accepted by society because of the professional expertise (the distinctive competencies) and the commitment of professionals to regulate themselves through professional associations, which set general performance standards for professional practice, establish codes of ethics, and so on. Max Weber regarded professions as a model of collegiate authority in which leaders are the first among equals (Scott, 2014).

LEADERSHIP

We need to develop leaders at all levels of library and information organizations. In the library profession in recent years, more emphasis has been placed on leadership through activities such as outreach and partnering with organizations in the community. Today librarians continue to move away from focusing mainly on internal library operations and instead emphasizing collaborative partnerships with client groups beyond the library organization. *Summer Matters,* a book about the partnership between the Chicago Public Library and the Museum of Science and Industry (McChesney and Wunar, 2017), notes the importance of professional development in their collaborative project. In the public library, professional development allows librarians to grow their skills and practice in order to create the best outcomes for those they serve. Professional development opportunities also ensure that staff are able to respond to their users in the most effective way.

Leadership is an important professional competency. The report "Museums, Libraries and 21st Century Skills" (Institute of Museum and Library Services, n.d.) includes a section on "Leadership and Responsibility."

Library administrators and staff still frequently view leadership only as a managerial role. However, management and leadership are related, but distinct, concepts (Phillips, 2014). A leader is "the person who leads or commands a group, organization, or country: the leader of a protest group | a natural leader" (Heery and Noon, 2017). In contrast, a manager is "a person responsible for controlling or administering an organization or group of staff" (*Oxford Dictionary of English*, 2010). However, frequently leaders are not managers who command a group. Leadership is placed in the "Administration and Management" section of the ALA "Core Competences of Librarianship" (American Library Association, 2009) rather than in the "Foundations" section. The addition of "leadership" to the ALA "Core Competences" was a last-minute amendment at the 2009 ALA Council meeting (Hicks and Given, 2013). In addition to acknowledging the importance of leadership for managers, acknowledging leadership as a foundational competency in the ALA "Core Competencies" would better serve all future library professionals. Thus, "Museums, Libraries and 21st Century Skills" lists leadership as one of the skills that all citizens should have. Leadership skills do not include the managerial skills required to

---

21ST CENTURY SKILLS
Selected Definitions—Life and Career Skills

Leadership and Responsibility

GUIDE AND LEAD OTHERS

- Use interpersonal and problem-solving skills to influence and guide others toward a goal.
- Leverage the strengths of others to accomplish a common goal.
- Inspire others to reach their very best via example and selflessness.
- Demonstrate integrity and ethical behavior in using influence and power.

BE RESPONSIBLE TO OTHERS

- Act responsibly with the interests of the larger community in mind.

Initiative and Self-Direction

BE SELF-DIRECTED LEARNERS

- Go beyond basic mastery of skills and/or curriculum to explore and expand one's own learning and opportunities in order to gain expertise.
- Demonstrate initiative to advance skill levels towards a professional level.
- Demonstrate commitment to learning as a lifelong process.
- Reflect critically on past experiences in order to inform future progress.

SOURCE: Institute of Museum and Library Services. n.d. "Definitions," in "Museums, Libraries and 21st Century Skills." https://www.imls.gov/issues/national-initiatives/museums-libraries-and-21st-century-skills/definitions.

administer or control a group. Thus, as a professional and citizen, every librarian should develop the 21st-century leadership skills as a core competency.

LIFELONG LEARNING

Maintaining distinctive professional competencies requires taking responsibility for lifelong learning. Libraries, as employers, do need to provide more funding for specific job-related skills that will assist librarians in maintaining and enhancing their distinctive professional competencies. Today, however, professional growth and development is primarily a personal responsibility. "Museums, Libraries, and 21st Century Skills" includes under the "Life and Career Skills" heading being a self-directed learner. Self-development, with the individual taking primary responsibility for choosing what, when, where, and how to learn, is likely to be the most important skill set of the future for all librarians. How much responsibility do you take for your own learning and development? Use the competencies in figure 0.1 to assess the extent to which you practice these self-development competencies.

Specific, distinctive competency statements provide benefits for individual professionals, an individual library or information service organization, and the profession as a whole. When competencies are clear, individuals know what it takes to succeed.

Competency	Self-Assessment
Maintaining an active interest in self-development and responsibility for furthering one's own learning	Identifies areas for development annually and taking identified best methods ____ Yes ____ No
Defining and updating career goals	Updates written career goals annually ____ Yes ____ No
Evaluating one's own strengths and weaknesses	Uses organizational or professional competency statements to assess ____ Once a year ____ Less often ____ Never
Modifying behavior based on feedback from others on one's performance and the self-analysis of one's experience	Seeks feedback on performance ____ Frequently ____ Occasionally ____ Seldom Prepares analysis of professional development annually and shares with manager. Solicits feedback. ____ Yes ____ No
Continually seeking opportunities for learning and training	Scans environment for development opportunities on the job and through formal and informal education ____ Continuously ____ Occasionally ____ Seldom

SOURCE: Competency statements are from J. Bryant and K. Poustie. 2001. Competencies Needed by Public Library Staff. Gutersloh: Bertelsmann Foundation, p. v.

FIGURE 0.1 *Managing One's Own Learning*

This in turn leads to greater career satisfaction, both in terms of the intrinsic rewards of doing a job well and of recognition by others. Organizations will also benefit through the enhanced quality of products and services.

BENEFITS OF COMPETENCIES FOR INDIVIDUALS

For individual professionals, the major benefits of developing distinctive competencies are:

1. Identifying gaps in their skills, abilities, and knowledge
2. Creating professional development plans to enhance their professional skills, abilities, and knowledge
3. Seeking organizational and professional support for well-defined and focused development plans
4. Identifying job assignments that will enhance their professional skills, abilities, and knowledge
5. Enhancing their job success, quality of performance, and job satisfaction
6. Developing distinctive expertise and being recognized by others for their unique expertise within the organization or the profession as a whole
7. Assisting in preparing for job advancement and promotion within the organization or the profession as a whole

BENEFITS OF COMPETENCIES FOR ORGANIZATIONS AND THE PROFESSION

For the organization and the profession, the major benefits of developing distinctive competencies are:

1. Reinforcing and enhancing a shared understanding of the work
2. Establishing uniform performance expectations
3. Ensuring consistency of performance across all professionals
4. Identifying needed areas for staff development and training
5. Assisting in counseling or coaching individuals for improved performance
6. Assisting in recruiting the best-qualified people
7. Providing public statements about what competencies the public can reasonably expect
8. Identifying common gaps in the skills of organizational/professional members
9. Assisting in establishing common goals and understandings
10. Providing a better fit between people and their task requirements
11. Establishing guidelines for organizational success

THE RUSA "PROFESSIONAL COMPETENCIES" AND PROFESSIONAL DEVELOPMENT PLANS

The RUSA "Professional Competencies" define the knowledge, skills, and abilities for librarians who perform reference and user services roles. Although the RUSA "Professional Competencies" provide general guidelines for development, librarians should also create an individual development plan that focuses on development priorities.

Association for Talent Development (ATD) Competency Development Model

A professional development plan that is especially relevant to developing and enhancing competencies is the Association for Talent Development's (ATD) new plan for training and development competencies. Of most value is the ATD Competency Model's Job Aid: Action Planning for Individuals (Association for Talent Development, 2014), so that you can identify strengths and weaknesses in your existing competencies. This ATD job aid also provides an outline of the main steps: (1) reviewing the foundational competencies and rating their importance for you; (2) listing your priorities for development of the various competencies; (3) reviewing the areas of expertise and selecting those that are most important to you; and (4) listing your priorities for development in foundational competencies and areas of expertise.

In applying the ATD Competency Model, you should use the RUSA "Professional Competencies" to serve as your focus for areas of expertise, rather than the ATD training and development competencies. For training and development professionals when considering foundational competencies, the ATD model lists business skills, global mindset, industry knowledge, interpersonal skills, personal skills, and technology literacy. Certainly, many of these foundational skills would be relevant to all librarians.

Action Plans

Another useful tool is the action plan. In this approach, a participant defines appropriate outcomes and the steps to achieving them as a result of the training program. Obstacles are anticipated as well. Viewed as a self-motivational tool, the action plan helps keep the person on track for implementing changes.

Janet Shapiro (n.d.) in her "Action Planning Toolkit" notes that most action plans consist of the following elements:

- a statement of what must be achieved (the outputs or result areas that come out of the strategic planning process)
- spelling out of the steps that have to be followed to reach this objective
- some kind of schedule for when each step must take place and how long it is likely to take (when)
- clarification of who will be responsible for making sure that each step is successfully completed (who)
- clarification of the inputs/resources that are needed

The title of Catherine Hakala-Ausperk's (2010) article "Invest in Yourself!" summarizes the main theme of this introduction very concisely. Although her article is primarily aimed at developing managers, we would encourage all librarians and library staff to invest in themselves by taking charge of their careers. Hakala-Ausperk advises you to design a training program for yourself in order to achieve growth in a particular area, develop a strategy that will focus your learning, and get better at what you do and grow professionally throughout your career. At the beginning of each year, she advises you to start with two or three goals—things you would like to accomplish. Make a plan to achieve these goals and monitor your progress every three months. Next, measure your progress and celebrate your successes along the way. And we would add to her advice: learn from your failures.

Growth and development frequently require taking some risks and trying new experiences, which may not always be as successful as you originally envisioned. However, reflecting upon experiences, which may result in failures or partial success, can often provide you with greater learning opportunities than your easy successes. Figures 0.2 and 0.3 provide forms to get you started in designing your own plan.

Goals for Action Plans. For specific goals (often called objectives) to be more useful, they should be written in the SMART format, where S = Specific, M = Measurable, A = Attainable, R = Realistic, and T = Timely (Mindtools, n.d.). A specific goal has a much greater chance of being accomplished than a general goal. A specific goal should answer these six "W" questions:

- Who: Who is involved?
- What: What do I want to accomplish?
- Where: Identify a location.
- When: Establish a time frame.
- Which: Identify requirements and constraints.
- Why: Identify the specific reasons, purpose, or benefits of accomplishing the goal.

For example, a general goal would be, "Get in shape." But a specific goal would be, "Join a health club and work out three days a week."

For goals to be measurable, you should establish concrete criteria for measuring your progress toward the attainment of each goal you set. When you measure your progress, you stay on track and you reach your target dates. To determine if your

COMPETENCY TO BE ADDRESSED

_____
_____
_____

(HINT: Start by reviewing the RUSA "Professional Competencies" and considering, possibly in consultation with others, your first priority for enhancing your knowledge and skills)

Timeline: _____

Possible Strategies* to Achieve Growth in Skills and Knowledge in the Selected Competency

Reshaping your job: _____
_____

Temporary assignments: _____
_____

Outside activities: _____
_____

People to consult:
  Peers: _____
  Your manager: _____
  Others: _____

Plan of support: _____
_____

Plan for feedback: _____
_____

Necessary resources: _____
_____

*NOTE: Evaluate the strengths and weaknesses of each possible strategy you list in terms of support from significant others that you will need to do the developmental assignment, and consider McCauley's (2006) list of job characteristics that stimulate learning opportunities: unfamiliar responsibilities; new initiatives; solving existing problems; dealing with employee problems; managing work with high stakes and/or visibility; managing work that is broad in scope and/or large in scale; managing relationships with groups outside of the organization; influencing key people when you do not have authority over them; working across cultures; and working with diverse groups.

FIGURE 0.2 *Development Assignment Plan*

Employee Name/ Employee ID:	Current Position Description Number / Title / Series / Grade:	Organizational Unit:	Appraisal Period Date:
			(Example: 05/03/2012-05/02/2013)

The Library seeks to model a high-performance culture that encourages, supports, and invests in the development of its staff. Professional development is an ongoing process to ensure that employees are staying current, if not one step ahead in their fields and mission-critical competencies.

This plan is intended to:

- Encourage each employee to take ownership of his or her career development
- Provide an administrative mechanism for identifying and tracking development needs and plans
- Assist in planning employee training and development activities
- Align employee development with the mission, goals, and objectives of the Library and the Service Units (SU)
- Allow supervisors to develop a better understanding of their staff's professional goals, strengths, and development needs
- Provide a basis for discussion periodically and tracking progress throughout the year

Additionally:

- Development goals will assist the employee in becoming stronger in his or her current role or expanding on strengths currently demonstrated—these are goals for improving over the next year
- Development goals also will relate to preparing the employee for future roles or foreseeable changes in existing roles
- Specific training activities should be entered and tracked electronically through the "My Plan" portion of the Online Learning Center
- Goals expressed in the plan should be viewed as flexible and are subject to resource constraints
- Resources that can be used by both the employee and supervisor to create this IDP include: position description, performance plan, performance appraisal, performance targets, annual objectives, SU strategic plans, unit priorities, and the Library of Congress Strategic Plan 2011–2016

	Goal (Describe the observable competency, knowledge, skill, or ability you would like to enhance or develop)	Target Completion Date	Core Competency Addressed (optional)	Category 1) Position essential 2) Career development 3) Persona development	Developmental Activities (Examples: shadowing, detail, just-in-time learning, conference, online or classroom training, reading, Toastmasters, coaching, mentoring)	Progress Made/ Next Steps
1						
2						

FIGURE 0.3 Library of Congress Individual Development Plan

	Goal (Describe the observable competency, knowledge, skill, or ability you would like to enhance or develop)	Target Completion Date	Core Competency Addressed (optional)	Category 1) Position essential 2) Career development 3) Persona development	Developmental Activities (Examples: shadowing, detail, just-in-time learning, conference, online or classroom training, reading, Toastmasters, coaching, mentoring)	Progress Made/ Next Steps
3						
4						
5						

Employee Signature and Date: _____   Supervisor Signature and Date: _____

NOTE: This form supports individual employee development. For more information, contact your SU point of contact for WPM or Alison Pullins, HRS/WPD at (202) 707-1130 or apul@loc.gov.

goal is measurable, ask questions such as: How much? How many? How will I know when it is accomplished?

Goals should be realistic and attainable. Goals should be neither out of reach, nor below standard performance. An attainable goal may stretch an individual or team, and help individuals or groups grow and expand to match their goals. Planning steps wisely and establishing a time frame that allows you to carry out those steps are necessary for goals to be attainable. An attainable goal will usually answer the question: How can the goal be accomplished?

To be realistic, a goal must represent an objective toward which you are both *willing* and *able* to work. A goal can be both high and realistic; you are the only one who can decide just how high your goal should be. But be sure that every goal represents substantial progress. A high goal is frequently easier to reach than a low one because a low goal exerts low motivational force. Some of the hardest jobs you've ever accomplished actually seemed easy simply because they were a labor of love. Additional ways to know if your goal is realistic is to determine if you have accomplished anything similar in the past, or to ask yourself what conditions would have to exist to accomplish the goal. To conduct additional analysis of how realistic a particular goal is for you, Faithe Ruiz (2017) has developed a personal SWOT analysis to use.

Timeliness. A goal should be grounded within a time frame. With no time frame tied to it, there's no sense of urgency. A commitment to a deadline helps a team focus their efforts on completion of the goal on or before the due date. This part of the SMART goal criteria is intended to prevent goals from being overtaken by the day-to-day crises that invariably arise in an organization. A time-bound goal will usually answer the questions:

- When?
- What can I do six months from now?
- What can I do six weeks from now?
- What can I do today?

"T" can also stand for "tangible"—a goal is tangible when you can experience it with one of the senses, that is, taste, touch, smell, sight, or hearing.

ENHANCING YOUR PROFESSIONAL COMPETENCIES

How can reference and user services librarians maintain and enhance their professional competencies? Professional development activities are sometimes divided into three broad categories: (1) development activities that emphasize job experience; (2) development activities that focus on developing and maintaining relationships; and (3) formal methods of education and training. Although librarians are more likely to think of "professional development" activities as participating in conferences, attending workshops, and enrolling in formal courses and degree programs, often the most accessible and least expensive development opportunities are local ones.

ON-THE-JOB EXPERIENCES

Much of the growth and development for professionals is created by rich on-the-job experiences, which provide the potential for updating current skills and learning new ones. Professional development can thus be pursued using "development in place" (McCauley, 2006). Development in place does not require a major job shift or a move to a different organization; however, it does require adding new responsibilities to your present assignment or taking on temporary tasks. Also, developmental assignments might include challenges outside the workplace, for example, in community nonprofit or social organizations.

A key component that is present in developmental assignments is work that requires learning new knowledge and skills and which provides opportunities to perform challenging and difficult tasks. Attebury (2017) studied the professional development experiences of academic librarians and found that when librarians reported transformational experiences, none of the experiences involved routine on-the-job activities. Developmental assignments can include activities such as shadowing, internships, interviews with experts, mentoring, reading, research, developing training courses, and teaching skills to other staff. Cynthia McCauley's handbook *Developmental Assignments* (2006) is intended to help people seek out and design their own developmental assignments. She provides many strategies for broadening your practical experiences by reshaping your job, adding a temporary assignment, or seeking a developmental challenge outside of the workplace. According to McCauley, the key job characteristics that stimulate learning are opportunities to experience:

1. Unfamiliar responsibilities
2. New initiatives
3. Solving existing problems
4. Dealing with employee problems
5. Managing work with high stakes and/or visibility
6. Managing work that is broad in scope and/or large in scale
7. Managing relationships with important groups outside of the organization
8. Influencing key people when you don't have authority over them

9. Working across cultures
10. Working with diverse work groups

When seeking developmental assignments, you need to evaluate the assignment in terms of these key job characteristics.

One section of *Developmental Assignments* is focused on developing competency-driven assignments through use of the Center for Creative Leadership's Model of Leader Competencies. However, the RUSA "Professional Competencies" reflect many of these same key characteristics, particularly those related to developing collaborative partnerships; building and maintaining relationships; communicating effectively; responding to diversity in user needs, communities and preferences; and planning, implementing, and evaluating innovations. In the competency-driven assignment, the assignment must provide the opportunity to practice a specific skill.

In the reference field, studies over past years have demonstrated the value of practical experience in learning new skills. For example, Luo (2009), in a study on chat reference training, reports that "hands-on experiences" received the highest rating of all training techniques. The next most effective method was asking questions of real chat reference users. In a classic study on effective training methods, Gers and Bolin (2000) report that in order to be effective, reference interview skills training needs to focus on model reference behaviors, include sufficient practice, and incorporate peer coaching. Librarians truly do value learning by doing.

Therefore, people who want to develop all types of skills cannot wait around and hope that management will assign them some interesting responsibilities, which will allow them to grow. Rather, people should approach their managers and negotiate growth opportunities. Annual goal-setting as part of a performance evaluation often provides an opportunity for this, but you can take advantage of many other opportunities in the course of your daily activities as well. You could ask your boss to delegate one of her responsibilities to you with feedback on how you're doing on a regular basis, or you could trade responsibilities with a colleague and provide peer coaching to each other. If the organization has a job rotation program, you could participate in the program, actively seeking feedback on your performance from each department or unit. In her study of professional development experiences, Attebury (2017) found that on-the-job learning is one of the most inexpensive and convenient approaches and provides long-term, interactive, and self-assessment opportunities.

RELATIONSHIPS

Development activities that focus on developing and maintaining relationships include attending professional conferences, informally engaging in peer instruction on the job, coaching by managers or with peers, reading the professional literature, participating on discussion lists, and writing or editing articles in the professional literature. In Attebury's (2017) study, meaningful and transformational professional development experiences were related to long-term activities and interactions with peers and fellow learners.

FORMAL EDUCATION AND TRAINING

Formal methods of education and training can include certificate or degree programs, courses, seminars and workshops offered by employers, educational institutions, and professional associations. Often the formal methods of education are costly because of registration fees and travel. However, new learning formats such as online education may decrease costs and make formal education opportunities more affordable.

Because the authors endorse the view that the hallmark of a professional is taking responsibility for his or her own development, informal methods of education, development through experience, and learning through relationships will be emphasized throughout this book. A wide variety of professional updating activities are available, and recommended methods for enhancing certain competencies will be discussed in each of this book's seven chapters.

ASSESSING YOUR DEVELOPMENT EFFORTS

Assessment is an important form of self-development. As part of assessment, individual librarians identify their own strengths and weaknesses. Thus, assessment techniques can help individuals determine their competency level and develop a plan for what they want to achieve. Self-evaluation—critical reflection on one's own skills, abilities, and knowledge—is valuable in figuring out what is required for a career that will be personally satisfying.

The RUSA competencies are defined specifically so that performance can be evaluated. Competency can only be inferred from performance. Therefore, one needs to focus on the types of performance that will assist in making judgments about individual competence. Generally, evaluating competency—the extent to which a task or set of tasks can be performed—is best done in a real-world setting. Evaluation should be linked to goals and therefore should compare performance with the competency goals.

Multiple methods of assessment are valuable, and the methods selected should be those that are the most direct and best-suited to judging performance related to a specific competency.

The major methods for assessing professional competence are through supervisor evaluation, self-evaluation, peer evaluation, testing or on-the-job performance, outside consultants or external reviewers, and special projects. Other methods, which may have potential but are less commonly employed, are evaluation by subordinates and evaluation of individual librarian performance by patrons. The 360-degree feedback appraisal method suggests that those receiving the service and those being supervised should be queried as part of performance evaluations. This appraisal method (Law, 2016) is "a system that provides employees with all-round performance feedback from colleagues, manager(s), customers, and others. Crucially, it also compares the individual's self-perception with performance ratings supplied by others."

Self-Assessment

Accurate assessment of performance strengths and weaknesses is key to setting learning goals and identifying the most vital competencies for professional growth. In the future, an important component for knowledge professionals will be self-assessment—that is, reflecting upon and assessing your performance regularly and using the results of the assessment to strengthen your performance. Self-assessment is regarded as a basic foundation for a self-regulating professional (Mann, 2010). Practicing self-assessment encourages people to take responsibility for their own learning.

A worksheet (figure 0.4) for the self-assessment of learning can be used to reflect upon your transfer of learning in workshops into everyday life and practice. In addition, the worksheet can easily be modified to help reflect upon transferring your learning in developmental assignments to your regular daily work activities.

Assessments by Supervisors and Others

However, self-assessments are subject to individual bias, which often results in an inability to judge one's own performance accurately. Therefore, librarians must also take responsibility for incorporating assessment information from external sources, such as managers, customers, and peers, in order to achieve a more reliable picture of their overall performance. One source which can be useful in generating feedback from others is Coaching Ourselves (www.coachingourselves.com/), which is committed to self-development and self-directed learning. In this format, a team gets together over lunch every couple of weeks to reflect upon their experience on a particular topic.

One could also solicit the help of the supervisor in developing a follow-up questionnaire that can be administered at a later date, after a month, for example. In developing the questionnaire, consider using formats such as checklists, rating scales, incomplete sentences, and short essays. Other questions

LEARNING EVENT: _____ Date:_____

How is the content of the learning event relevant to my professional development goals?
_____
_____
_____

What did I learn that might be useful in my professional practice?
_____
_____
_____

What aspects of my professional practice do I hope to change as a result of what I learned?
_____
_____
_____

What opportunities can I identify to apply what I have learned to my professional practice?
_____
_____
_____

I plan to discuss these ideas with: _____

Did workplace colleagues attend this learning event with me?   ___Yes   ___No

   If yes, what ideas do colleagues think might be worth implementing in the workplace? _____

How will I share ideas from the learning event with my colleagues who did not attend?
_____
_____

Do you think colleagues will be interested in incorporating some of these ideas into their professional practice?
____ Yes ____ No

For the new ideas presented in the learning event, list resources (media, reading, etc.) to explore:
_____
_____

Did the learning event include any tools useful in transferring learning into practice?   ___Yes   ___No

   If yes, please describe: _____
_____

Will the learning event have another session, after I have had an opportunity to integrate the learning into practice and reflect upon the results?
____ Yes ____ No

FIGURE 0.4 *Transferring Learning into Practice*

you might consider are asking about what is remembered the most, what skills are currently being used, and what success you've had. This offers a follow-up for application questions.

Each chapter in this book will include recommended self-assessment activities, such as writing up notes from group discussions, fact-finding, practical exercises, short verbal and written reports, short presentations on a topic, and providing concrete examples of how one's skills were applied in the workplace. Because professionals are expected to take responsibility for their own development, they also need to take the primary responsibility for assessing their progress in obtaining and enhancing their professional competencies. Therefore, the authors of this book will focus primarily on self-evaluation or self-assessment activities.

CHAPTER **one**

Access

SECTION 5A: ACCESSES RELEVANT AND ACCURATE RECORDED KNOWLEDGE AND INFORMATION

This chapter is about developing and assessing your knowledge, skills, abilities, and behaviors associated with section 5A of the RUSA "Professional Competencies," a section entitled "Accesses Relevant and Accurate Recorded Knowledge and Information." The topics covered are the librarian's responsiveness to user needs and the organization and design of reference services. This chapter focuses on understanding users' information-seeking behavior.

OFFERS SERVICES RESPONSIVE TO INDIVIDUAL EXPRESSED USER NEEDS

Competencies for Offering Services Responsive to Individual Expressed User Needs

The typical behavioral strategies suggested in the RUSA "Professional Competencies" that demonstrate the librarian's competencies related to responsiveness are:

- Applies the "Guidelines for Behavioral Performance of Reference and Information Service Providers" (Reference and User Services Association, 2013)
- Recognizes, honors, and responds appropriately to diversity and cultural differences
- Determines the situational context of individual information needs
- Engages in discussion and expresses interest in individual experiences related to information needs
- Understands and applies the laws and policies governing confidentiality and rights to privacy
- Consults with the user to identify the most appropriate resources in the context of accuracy, authority, interest, and content level
- Respects the right of individuals to pursue their research preferences
- Assists the user in evaluating, managing, formatting, storing, using, or displaying information
- Consults with the user to select appropriate technology for providing answers, balancing the nature of the information being provided with user preferences
- Applies knowledge of state-of-the-art information retrieval technologies and systems to assist the user in identifying and obtaining information
- Identifies opportunities for instruction that empowers users to improve their own information-seeking abilities

Development Methods for Offering Services Responsive to Individual Expressed User Needs

Underlying responsiveness is the ability to listen to users with both understanding and empathy. Librarians need to continue to shift from a focus on question-answering to assisting users while understanding the context of the information-seeking needs from which their queries arise. In a classic text, *Seeking Meaning,* Carol Kuhlthau (2004) notes that an important professional skill for librarians is the ability to diagnose when mediation and instruction are important in the user's process of information-seeking. Another essential professional skill is the diagnosis of the most appropriate type of mediation or intervention. Is the best intervention directing the reader to a source, a selected group of sources, or coaching assistance on the search process, such as searching sources in a specific sequence?

When thinking about how to improve one's responsiveness to user queries, the most important area to examine first is one's ability to conduct a reference interview. None of the other aspects come into play unless the librarian understands the individual's information request. According to RUSA, "the reference interview is the heart of the reference transaction." The RUSA "Guidelines for Behavioral Performance of Reference and Information Service Providers" provides a set of specific guidelines to aid librarians during the reference interview. These guidelines state that the most important aspects of the reference interview are the librarian's visibility/approachability, interest, listening/inquiring, searching, and follow-up (Reference and User Services Association, 2013).

Visibility/Approachability and Interest. Strategies that help increase approachability and openness include making the service and individuals providing those services visible to approaching individuals, whether they "approach" the service in person or virtually, with emphasis on eliminating physical barriers, reducing clutter and distractions, and maintaining the privacy of the reference transaction.

A librarian who is poised and ready to engage approaching patrons obviously appears much more approachable than someone who has a nose in a book or attention focused on a computer screen. The acknowledgment of individuals waiting for service, and the use of verbal greetings as well as nonverbal encouragers such as eye contact, an open stance, and smiling, let the patron needing assistance know that the librarian's attention is on the individual requiring assistance. Other aspects to consider is whether the librarian remains visible to patrons as much as possible, or is mobile and roves through the reference area to approach patrons and offer assistance where they have an information need instead of forcing them to approach a desk.

In demonstrating interest in users and their questions, the librarian strives to build and maintain a positive climate for communication. Creating rapport is not the answer to all the challenges we face, but it does provide a simple technique for improving relations (Stock, 2009). Sometimes this rapport is easy to establish, while at other times we have to work at developing it so that we can communicate effectively. These rapport skills include matching the patron physiologically, as well as matching his or her language use.

In matching the patron's nonverbal stance, the librarian should watch his or her overall posture, for example, leaning backwards, standing up, crossing and uncrossing of limbs; gestures, for example, shaking a finger; rate of breathing, and facial expressions, for example, smiling, frowning, and rate of blinking. The librarian indicates interest by facing the patron while speaking or listening, and by signaling an understanding of the patron's needs through verbal or nonverbal confirmation, such as nodding head, making brief comments, or asking questions. In virtual settings, maintaining the link via frequent updates lets the patron know that he or she still has your attention. While many of us do these activities naturally, it takes others some practice to learn to do this, without behaving in a mimicking manner.

Voice-matching is also a useful way of developing rapport, and includes some of the following verbal cues: volume, tempo, rhythm, pitch, tone, length and choice of phrases and sentences, choice of key words and phrases (including jargon), use of language to indicate thinking style, and use of language to indicate key drivers or motivators.

Matching common experiences may not be feasible in a short reference interview, but asking about the user's experiences, such as learning their opinions, exploring their feelings and attitudes, clarifying a misunderstanding, assessing or appraising, and picking up small but significant points of view demonstrate that you are actively involved and interested.

Enhancing your awareness of your own skills, or lack thereof, in reference interviews is another matter. This requires putting yourself in the user's shoes and looking at your own actions. Examining your own reactions in customer service situations, outside of libraries, is a starting point to thinking as a patron who is "receiving" services rather than a librarian who is providing them. One technique for looking at your responsiveness competencies is to start with your own experiences as a user. Examine your past experiences with services of all types, such as someone installing your cable, starting a new phone service, opening a back account, buying a television set, or visiting a restaurant, grocery store, theme park, or a bookstore. What made those experiences good or bad? Was it the knowledge, skills, or behaviors of those service providers? What did they do or not do that influenced how you felt about the experience? In making your list, divide these characteristics into good and bad ones. Once you've compiled your list, compare the characteristics to the RUSA (2013) "Guidelines for Behavioral Performance" and you'll likely be surprised at the overlap between the behaviors of commercial service providers and reference librarians.

Some mechanisms for enabling reflective observation of your own performance might be to have yourself videotaped (in doing so, don't forget to notify the patron that this is happening), record your telephone interactions (again, with appropriate notification and permission), ask a trusted peer to give you feedback, examine virtual transcripts, or keep a journal or log regarding your observations about each shift at the reference desk, noting particularly successful interactions (what worked) and unsuccessful ones (what didn't work).

Reading the "Guidelines for Behavioral Performance" will give you the background information you need for the concepts underlying approachability and interest, but there are many other possible sources for this information, including the ORE Online website (Ohio Library Council, 2017), the Minnesota Opportunities for Reference Excellence

(MORE) site (Minitex, 2015), and the many books and journal articles on the reference interview referenced by Kern and Woodard (2016). Several videos are available regarding the reference interview and improving your responsiveness competencies, including some from the Library Video Network (https://www.kanopystreaming.com/category/supplier/library-video-network).

Other options include discussing your observations with your peers, and articulating the principles out of your common experiences. The ORE Online site suggests that you walk around the reference area of your library and see if it encourages approachability by providing an appropriate setting, maintaining privacy, eliminating physical barriers, reducing desk clutter, and lowering distracting noise levels.

Ross and Nilsen (2013) provide several exercises to improve your approachability, including role-playing, experimenting with the use of name tags, visiting other libraries to ask reference questions, studying the signage system in your library, trying to lean slightly toward the other person during the conversation, and focusing on one interviewing skill at a time.

Another possibility is conducting virtual field trips to the websites of other library reference services, posing as a patron in those online reference environments, and analyzing the transcripts of those encounters.

Listening and Inquiring. A reference staffer can improve her listening and questioning skills by reading materials about the reference interview as indicated previously, or by watching a video which describes the process, again as suggested above.

In general, most resources advocate the use of open questions in the reference interview, which encourage users to state their information needs in their own words. Open questions give control to the patron to determine where the interview is going. Closed questions, which have a limited number of known responses, are typically used when trying to relate the user's request to the library system and its methods of organizing, retrieving, and providing information.

But it is one thing to know the difference between an open-ended question and a closed-ended question, and still another to be able to apply this knowledge to the appropriate situation. Ross and Nilsen (2013) include sample open and closed questions, but then they go on to provide sample reference interactions with guided questions to look at the types of questions being asked. Generally, reference librarians then reflect the responses of users to make certain that their understanding is correct. Ross and Nilsen also provide several examples that paraphrase or summarize user statements or reflect user feelings.

In some instances the reference transaction cannot go forward because the user's emotions are getting in the way of resolving a problem. The user may be angry, frustrated, or difficult. Regardless of whether the problem is real or imagined, instigated by the library or by outside factors, the emotion must be acknowledged before progress can be made to solve the problem. Unfortunately, this is not a skill that most reference staff members have in their repertoire. Most people want to jump to solving the problem, which typically makes the problem worse. Listening empathetically is especially important in these situations, and acknowledging the feelings of the patron is the important first step. Learning how to state the problem empathetically can go a long way towards getting the patron ready to talk about a solution to the problem. The WebJunction site (https://www.webjunction.org/) has many resources that deal with customer service topics, including angry patrons and difficult patron behavior.

There is no substitute for practice in acquiring these skills. In learning how to conduct a reference interview, individuals need to practice in environments that are "safe," such as a classroom or workshop setting where the consequences of incorrect execution are minimal, or in the actual workplace with guidance from a coach or mentor. One-on-one practice, which starts with getting to the patron's real information need instead of emphasizing how to answer the question or the end result, is a much more comfortable environment for most individuals. Comfort level with a group is required before actual role-playing, where pairs of individuals act as patrons and reference staff in front of a group, can take place. Another good option for role-playing is to have individuals in pairs practice on getting to the real question, but not in answering the questions. This is a particularly useful exercise when the individuals don't have a lot of experience working as a service provider.

There are a number of good sources on general listening skills. For example, the Mindtools (n.d.) website's section on "Communication Skills" has videos, quizzes, and other materials on communication topics, such as active listening and empathetic listening. The WebJunction site (https://www.webjunction.org/) also has courses and presentations on communication techniques and listening skills. These sources have some limits in terms of practicing listening skills. For example, one cannot practice empathetic listening in a solo environment. For learning to improve empathetic statements, role-playing a scenario with an angry patron is one of the best techniques. At first, have the role-players only respond to the patron's emotions and expressed problem. Once the role-players have mastered this task, then they can go on to practice in dealing with the problem portrayed.

Involving the Patron. In order to maintain responsiveness throughout the reference transaction, the reference service provider must involve the patron throughout the interview and the searching process. The interviewer must find out what sources the patron has already tried, explain the search strategy and sequence, explain how to use sources when appropriate, work with the patron to narrow or broaden the topic as appropriate, and ask the patron if additional information is needed after the initial result has been found. The interviewer should offer pointers and detailed search paths (including URLs or names of sources) to find the answer, and should accompany the patron in the search, using appropriate technology (such as co-browsing, scanning, faxing) to help guide the patron through the library's resources. Ross and Nilsen (2013) discuss four basic steps for the inclusion of patrons: acknowledge, describe briefly, explain briefly why, and indicate the time required. In instructing users, it is important to guide them, but leave them in control.

Borrowing from the National Association of Social Workers' (2017) "Code of Ethics," we endorse respecting the client's inherent dignity and worth by promoting socially responsible self-determination. In the "Code of Ethics," social workers seek to enhance clients' capacity and opportunity to change and to address their own needs. Librarians respect the patron's right to self-determination when they encourage users to become full participants and influence their own outcomes. Improving this aspect of performance as a librarian implies a high level of self-awareness of how one interacts with the patron.

Organizing or Chunking. Content can be "chunked," or broken down into more manageable units, by using headings, lists, and other means of grouping to make the information more easily digestible and more easily remembered (Fichter and Wisniewski, 2016). Typical chunking strategies include spatial, narrative or sequence, procedural, logical, classifications, and other types of sorting such as cause and effect, similarities and differences, forms and functions, and advantages and disadvantages. We'll explore some ways these strategies can be applied in library settings.

During the reference interview process, a librarian uses questioning techniques to solicit answers that help her analyze the user's information need, generally starting with "what, where, when, and who" questions and not directly by asking "why." For a good discussion on the use of "why" questions in reference situations, consult Ross, Nilsen, and Radford (2009, 101). These questions can be used to clarify and redefine issues/problems, provide cues for determining the goals of the problem situation, find out what additional data and analyses need to be conducted in order to better understand the causes of the problem, and redefine solutions. The use of these questions strengthens the librarian's skills in analysis and helps her to avoid leaping to thinking about solutions.

An alternative organizing structure for the reference interview is offered by the Minnesota Opportunities for Reference Excellence (MORE) website (Minitex, 2015), which includes "Six Pieces of Evidence": purpose, deadline, type and amount, who, where, and the basic question; and several worksheets useful for reflecting on and reviewing important reference interview practices.

Some libraries have found that creating checklists for librarians to use when conducting the reference interview facilitates the analytical process. One example is the enquiry analysis form (figure 1.1), which guides the staff member through a series of questions.

Simply breaking down the components in bibliographic verification questions is a great tool to practice analytical skills. When a patron presents a bibliographic citation that is not immediately findable in your library, it presents an opportunity to apply your problem-solving skills. To solve

Section	Record (or consider recording) . . .
The enquirer	Name
	Organization
	Address
	Postal code *(worth recording this as a separate field in case you ever want to do market research based on your enquirers' location)*
	Landline phone
	Mobile
	VoIP identifier
	E-mail
	Instant messaging or chat
	Fax *(unlikely these days—but you never know)*
	Special contact instructions *(e.g., try mobile first; e-mail second; call between specific times; don't mention the subject of the enquiry to whoever picks up the phone)*
	[Try to get at least two contact points in case the preferred one isn't working when you need to report back and the deadline is looming. If you're taking enquiries using a web form, make sure the contact information goes into a "compulsory" field, which the enquirer has to fill in before the enquiry will be accepted.]
The enquiry	Narrative description *(as much detail as necessary)*
	Deadline *(date and—if necessary—time)*
	Enquiry taken by . . .
	Enquiry transferred to . . . *(there could be several of these)*
Enquiry analysis	Who? What? When? Where? Why? How?
	What will the final answer look like?
	Focus, dynamism, complexity, viability
	Who really needs to know this?
Search strategy	Root terms, broader terms, narrower terms, related terms
	Search methodology *(how you choose and logically link your search terms)*
	Sources tried
	Search results *(what you found—and where)*
	The answer

Sign-off	Who completed the enquiry
	Who delivered the answer (*may not be the same person*)
	Degree of success in answering it: complete; partial; compromise
	How satisfied the enquirer was (*not necessarily the same as how successful you were in answering it*)
	If the enquiry was referred to someone else—whether within your organization or outside it—then who?
	How long it took to answer (*hours and minutes*)
	When completed (*date and time*)
	Delivered on time? If not, why not?
	Follow-up actions (*add new information to FAQs, Know-How files or Starter Sources; consider newly discovered sources or services for purchase or subscription*)
SOURCE: Tim Buckley Owen. 2017. *Successful Enquiry Answering Every Time: Thinking Your Way from Problem to Solution.* 7th ed. London: Facet, p. 43.	

FIGURE 1.1 *Checklist of Elements for Inquiry Analysis*

each puzzle means analyzing the question for what information is known, and the possible problems, such as incomplete or incorrect information, or title changes. Often the patron is willing to have the librarian work on the query and get back to him. This situation allows the librarian to think about how to break down the question over the course of several days and attempt different strategies.

Improving Follow-up. Ross, Nilsen, and Radford (2009, 79–82) discuss the concept of negative closure in the reference interview as an important concept for improving your follow-up skills. The inclusion of the patron (as discussed earlier) and instruction techniques can improve this tendency to close the reference interview prematurely. Research has shown that asking follow-up questions at the end of the reference interview is one of the most important things you should learn. These questions invite the user to ask for additional help if needed, and invite the user to indicate if the kind of assistance that was needed was what he really got.

Assessing Development Efforts for Offering Services Responsive to Individual Expressed User Needs

The "Follow-Up" section of the RUSA "Guidelines for Behavioral Performance" can be adopted for use as a checklist, which will assist you in reflecting upon how well you are practicing the recommended follow-up behaviors. This section on general follow-up behaviors is presented in figure 1.2 as a sample checklist.

Another more challenging, but more specific type of checklist is the Behavioral Observation Scale (BOS). Critical incidents, which define the varieties of behaviors ranging from very good to very poor performance on follow-up, need to be collected by a team of people providing reference services. Building upon these critical incidents, statements are created describing the range of desirable and undesirable behaviors. The resulting BOS scale is used to assess how frequently each type of behavior occurs. Figure 1.3 provides a sample BOS scale on follow-up. How often do you exhibit each of these behaviors when assisting users?

Figure 1.4 is a checklist that allows librarians to keep a log of individual reference interactions and self-assess the degree to which they understood the stage of the information-seeking process and applied the most appropriate type of assistance. This form could also be used to analyze reference transcripts that have been collected via chat or e-mail.

Because these competencies involve listening with full attention and understanding, an important method of assessment should be self-reflection. How responsive were you when assisting individual users with their queries? A checklist (figure 1.5) is

Behavioral Standard	Almost Always	Frequently	Sometimes	Almost Never	Not Applicable
Asks patrons if their questions have been completely answered.					
Encourages the patrons to return if they have further questions.					
Roving is an excellent technique for follow-up.					
Consults other librarians or experts in the field when additional subject expertise is needed.					
Makes patrons aware of other appropriate reference services (e-mail, etc.).					
Makes arrangements, when appropriate, with the patrons to research a question even after the reference transaction has been completed.					
Refers the patrons to other sources or institutions when the query cannot be answered to the satisfaction of the patron.					
Facilitates the process of referring patrons to another library or information agency through activities such as calling ahead, providing direction and instructions, and providing the library and the patrons with as much information as possible about the amount of information required, and the sources already consulted.					
Takes care not to end the reference interview prematurely.					

FIGURE 1.2 *Self-Assessment Checklist for Follow-Up*

Behavior	Never	Seldom	Sometimes	Usually	Always
Asks patrons if question was answered.					
Encourages patrons to come back, but does not ask if question was answered.					
Provides sources with no follow-up or encouragement to come back.					

FIGURE 1.3 *Behavioral Observation Scale for Follow-Up*

1. State the question the user initially asked you:

   _____
   _____
   _____

2. Describe the background on the requirements of the user task. Include the personal interest of the task to the user, the time the user expects to allot, and the availability of the appropriate level of information:

   _____
   _____
   _____

The stage of the ISP is: _____

	Primary Aspect	Secondary Aspect (if applicable)
Initiation *(recognizing need for information)*	_____	_____
Selection *(seeking background on general area)*	_____	_____
Exploration *(seeking information to become adequately informed)*	_____	_____
Formulation *(forming focused perspective on topic)*	_____	_____
Collection *(gathering most relevant information on focused topic)*	_____	_____
Presentation *(completing search and assignment)*	_____	_____

3. Summarize the information you provided to the user at the end of the reference transaction:

   _____
   _____
   _____

Was it primarily:

_____ Discussion with the user on how to browse potential sources for a possible topic?

_____ General orientation to sources on a broad topic?

_____ Offering the "right" source for background information?

_____ Guidance to a group of highly relevant sources for a topic?

_____ Offering a group of relevant sources and a recommended sequence for their use?

_____ Making an appointment to provide extensive assistance/consultation in the process of seeking information that leads to sources, sequence, and strategies?

4. For this reference transaction, how well did the information you provided match with the needs of the user, given the user's stage in the information-seeking process?

   _____
   _____
   _____

SOURCE: Based upon the concepts of Carol C. Kuhlthau: Carol Collier Kuhlthau. 2004. *Seeking Meaning: A Process Approach to Library and Information Services*. 2nd ed. Westport, CT: Libraries Unlimited. See also http://wp.comminfo.rutgers.edu/ckuhlthau/information-search-process/.

FIGURE 1.4 *Reference Assistance to Users: Diagnosing the Stage of the Information-Seeking Process (ISP)*

Behavioral Standard	Almost Always	Frequently	Sometimes	Almost Never	Not Applicable
General: Focuses complete attention on the patron and his/her information need					
In Person: Faces the patron when speaking and listening					
In Person: Maintains or reestablishes eye contact with the patron throughout the transaction					
In Person: Signals an understanding of the patron's needs through verbal and nonverbal confirmation, such as nodding of the head, offering brief explanations, or asking additional questions to better understand the patron's query					
Remote: Acknowledges user questions in a timely manner					
Remote: Maintains regular online or voice contact with the patron to convey interest and provide assistance that the query is still viable and a response is forthcoming					
Remote: Signals an understanding of the patron's need					

FIGURE 1.5 *Self-Assessment Checklist for Interest in Individual's Information Need*

a useful instrument for reflecting and assessing the extent to which you actually use the responsiveness competencies when assisting users, whether in-person, on the telephone, by e-mail, or via a virtual reference service. A peer or a trusted observer can also use the checklist to advise you on the extent to which you actually demonstrate these competencies while assisting users.

Sections of the RUSA "Guidelines for Behavioral Performance" can also be adopted for use as checklist, which will assist you in reflecting upon how well you are practicing the recommended reference behaviors. The guidelines' section on "Listening/Inquiring" behaviors is presented (figure 1.6) as a sample checklist to illustrate how these guidelines can be used as a self-assessment tool.

"Secret patron" transactions are exercises in which an (anonymous) individual poses an information query to several different reference services and sees how well they are able to satisfy her information need. Figure 1.7 is a useful checklist for evaluating secret patron transactions from the patron's viewpoint regarding the five basic aspects of the reference interview: setting the tone, getting the question straight, keeping me informed, providing information, and follow-up.

We also suggest evaluating your own interviewing skills. The checklist in figure 1.8 is particularly useful in helping you think about your verbal and nonverbal behaviors and reviewing all of the information you should obtain from each reference interview so as to provide the best possible service. Ross and Nilsen (2013) discuss interviewing in more depth, as well as issues that are unique to telephone, e-mail, chat, and texting interviews. They also identify the six common causes of communication accidents: not acknowledging the user, not listening, playing twenty questions (Is it this? Is

Behavioral Standard	Almost Always	Frequently	Sometimes	Almost Never	Not Applicable
Communicates in a receptive, cordial, and encouraging manner.					
Uses a tone of voice and/or written language appropriate to the nature of the transaction.					
Allows the patrons to state fully their information need in their own words before responding.					
Identifies the goals or objectives of the user's research, when appropriate.					
Rephrases the question or request and asks for confirmation to ensure that it is understood.					
Seeks to clarify confusing terminology and avoids excessive jargon.					
Uses open-ended questioning techniques to encourage patrons to expand on the request or present additional information.					
Uses closed and/or clarifying questions to refine the search query.					
Maintains objectivity and does not interject value judgments about subject matter or the nature of the question into the transaction.					

FIGURE 1.6 *Self-Assessment Checklist for Listening/Inquiring*

it that?), interrupting at inappropriate times, making assumptions, and not following up (pp. 130–31).

ORGANIZES AND DESIGNS SERVICES TO MEET THE NEEDS OF THE PRIMARY COMMUNITY

Competencies for Organizing and Designing Services to Meet the Needs of the Primary Community

The typical behavioral strategies suggested in the RUSA "Professional Competencies" that demonstrate competencies related to the organization and design of services are:

- Creates physical and virtual environments that encourage the use of all available services

- Designs services that reflect the demographics, cultural diversity, and special needs of the community

Development Methods for Organizing and Designing Services to Meet the Needs of the Primary Community

Planning and organizational skills, ability, and knowledge play an important role in the organization and design of services. Another very important factor is knowledge of the information needs and behaviors of the primary clientele of the information service. Services need to be organized and designed to best fit with the information-seeking behaviors of the primary clientele. A public library located in Florida in a retirement community would

1. Setting the Tone

    The librarian greeted me personally and used my name

    It was clear that he/she was interested in my query and ready to provide assistance

2. Getting the Question Straight

    The librarian clarified my question using:

    > An open probe
    > A closed probe
    > Both open and closed probes
    > Did not clarify my question

3. Keeping Me Informed

    He/she asked me whether I wanted to see how to find the answer

    The librarian's responses were clear, easy to read, and free of library jargon

    The librarian kept me informed about his/her progress in finding an answer, providing a time estimate when needed

    He or she let me know what he/she was doing, e.g., still looking, pushing a web page, escorting, etc.

    The librarian provided help with any technical difficulties

4. Providing Information

    He/she identified authoritative information appropriate for my need and interest

    The librarian gave me time to determine whether the information found actually answered my question to my satisfaction. He/she:

    > Didn't rush me by pushing too much information.
    > Cited the source of the information.
    > Asked if I wanted to be shown more sources.
    > Recognized if my question needed to be referred elsewhere or could be more effectively answered through e-mail.

5. Follow-up

    Asked if the information found answered my questions to my satisfaction

    Asked if I had any other questions

    Encouraged me to use the service again

    Thanked me

    I was asked to evaluate my experience with the service

    My other comments about the reference transaction are . . .

SOURCE: Buff Hirko and Mary Bucher Ross. 2004. *Virtual Reference Training: The Complete Guide to Providing Anytime, Anywhere Answers.* Chicago: American Library Association, p. 116.

FIGURE 1.7 • *Checklist for Evaluating Secret Patron Transactions*

First, for each reference interaction, test your basic interviewing skills.

Do I . . .

1. Acknowledge each patron with a friendly greeting?
2. Make initial eye [*or if remote, word*] contact with each patron?
3. Try to maintain or reestablish eye contact [*or if remote, word*] with each patron?
4. Focus my complete attention on the patron and his/her information need?
5. Allow the patron to fully state his/her information need before responding?
6. Signal an understanding of the patron's needs through verbal and nonverbal confirmation (e.g., nodding my head, offering brief explanations or attentive comments, asking additional questions)?
7. Rephrase the question or request and ask for confirmation to ensure accurate understanding?
8. Use a relaxed tone of voice and/or written language appropriate to the patron and the nature of the transaction?
9. Verify that my understanding of the question is correct?
10. Use closed or clarifying questions for areas that are not clear?
11. Ask open-ended questions to encourage the patron to expand on the request or present additional information?

Then, review the success of each interview.

Did I acquire the key aspects of the patron's information need?

Did I learn . . .

1. The purpose of the request—why the information was needed and what the patron plans to do with the information?
2. The deadline—the last date by which the information will be useful?
3. How much information the person needs and what format would be most useful?
4. What the patron already knows about the subject?
5. What sources the patron has already consulted?
6. What the patron really wants to know?

FIGURE 1.8 • *Interviewing Test*

be expected to have a mission, services, and targeted populations in the community far different from those of a public library in a college town where the average age is twenty-five years.

Assessing the information needs and behaviors of the primary clientele means seeking answers to the following questions:

Who are the regular users of the organization?

Are the regular users of the organization representative of the population groups that the organization is supposed to be serving?

What needs are the users attempting to fulfill through the use of organizational services and/or resources?

How do these users typically search for information?

What are the major barriers that account for users' failure in locating desired information?

Learning Who Your Users Can Be. In order to design services to meet the special access needs of primary users, you need to know as much as possible about the community your library serves. Demographic information for geographic communities is readily available from census data (www.census.gov). This can include information about users' education levels, kinds of jobs, employment rates, economic background, and age distribution. Communities that are defined by their institutional focus typically have their own ways of gathering population statistics. For academic institutions, typically this means examining institutional characteristics, looking at admission data, retention and graduation rates, learning how many of your students have personal computers from the housing and student services statistics, and examining multi-campus surveys such as the National Survey of Student Engagement, as well as other institutional data.

For public libraries, one of the best opportunities is to work with other city, county, or state agencies in developing performance measures and a government plan to collect the necessary data to evaluate the performance of all government agencies that serve the public. The International City/County Management Association (icma.org/) includes some excellent case studies and publications under the topic: "managing local government performance." Excellent articles can also be found on Governing.com (www.governing.com/manage/) by searching on "citizen involvement."

Learning Who Your Users Are. In order to understand who actually uses your library from the pool of possible users, you must gather your own data. Typically, these are gathered from user studies conducted within the library, such as interviews of users or focus groups, or via surveys of library users. Examples of these surveys include the Impact Survey (https://impactsurvey.org), which public libraries can use to better understand their communities and how people use their technology resources and services; and LibQual (www.libqual.org), which aims to assist libraries in collecting and interpreting user feedback systematically over time. Addional information on user surveys is provided in chapter 6 of this book.

Understanding How People Look for Information. There have been numerous studies conducted on how users look for information. The OCLC (www.oclc.org), the New Media Consortium (www.nmc.org), and the PEW Internet and American Life Project (www.pewinternet.org/) have conducted a number of these studies, and their web pages are good starting points for reading.

There are also a number of excellent studies that look at how people use web pages. The Nielsen Norman Group's "Writing for the Web" website (https://www.nngroup.com/topic/writing-web/) lists several studies of how users read on the Web, and gives suggestions on how writers should write for them. Courses, training seminars, reports, and books are also provided on the site.

Access via the Internet is also a concern for users with special needs. The website of the Association of Specialized Government and Cooperative Library Agencies (www.ala.org/ascla/), in its "Resources and Professional Tools" section, provides a wide range of information for serving special populations, including accessibility toolkits and resources on web accessibility. Another excellent resource is the University of Washington's "DO-IT: Disabilities, Opportunities, Internetworking, and Technology" site (https://www.washington.edu/doit/).

Exploring How Your Users Look for Information. You should examine your assumptions about how users seek information. Just getting down on paper how it is that you think users seek information will be helpful, because until you articulate these assumptions, you cannot prove or disprove them.

You can conduct your own research into these assumptions. IDEO's (https://www.ideo.org/) Design Kit website (www.designkit.org/) presents mindsets, methods, and case studies to actually observe human behavior and develop a deep understanding of how people interact physically and emotionally with products, services, and spaces. The critical point is not to rely solely on your assumptions about user experiences, but to experience as closely as possible what the customer does. If you cannot put yourself in the place of a novice or first-time user, then actual first-time users will have to be questioned. The Design Kit includes an easy research method called "The Five Whys" that will help you understand the deeper motivations and assumptions that form the basis of a person's behavior.

There are a number of excellent resources for improving the usability of your library's web pages, including books, web pages, tutorials, and courses. The website "Usability.gov: Improving the User Experience" (https://www.usability.gov/) provides an overview of usability, extensive practical information on usability research and evaluation, and the visual and content design of web pages, including advice on writing for the Web, such as:

- Consistency in wording and organization
- User orientation (using familiar words and concepts, and providing users with location information and a quick return home)
- Minimalist design
- Using brevity, meaningful headings, and bulleted lists
- Ability to be scanned (minimize scrolling)

Usability studies can provide a detailed portrait of library users, their information-seeking behavior, and their information needs. Simply gathering various ideas is not usability testing. Usability testing suggests that you observe and measure the performance of representative users in real-life tasks, collecting both quantitative and qualitative data. Measurements of accuracy, speed, and recall should be taken. For qualitative data, subjects can record their own opinions using both multiple-choice and open-ended questions, or observers can record their observations or record them with video and audio.

Making Sure That New Services Are Consistent with the Library's Mission, Goals, and Values. Before designing and organizing services, it is important to establish the mission of your organization. A vision statement describes an ideal future state, and a mission statement outlines the organizational initiatives necessary to achieve that vision. Ideally, mission statements also guide an organization in setting its goals, strategies, and tactics (Jones, 2014). A mission, goals, and values are important because making a difference for your clients comes from making thoughtful choices and focusing your efforts (Downey, 2016). Downey suggests that goals and values matter more than missions. Missions may motivate, but they tend to be expansive and are rarely effective in setting priorities and focus. Goals are clear, achievable steps to help achieve the long-term vision and mission. Values state what is fundamental and achievable about the way you work.

Successful organizations also provide proof about how their services support the organization's mission, by focusing on relevant and important outcomes.

Designing Services. The book *Library Service Design* by Marquez and Downey (2016) will be very useful to librarians for developing their skills in designing new or innovative reference services or redesigning current services. The authors' work is drawn from usability heuristics; library service design heuristics are described as rules of thumb tailored to library environments (Marquez and Downey, 2017, 7–8). The library service design methods are discussed in the broader context of usability research in an article by Susan Farrell (2016). In their book *Getting Started in Service Design,* Marquez and Downey (2017) have identified library usability heuristics and worksheets, which help evaluate library services using the following heuristics:

- Clarity of purpose and function
- Meeting current needs and expectations
- Consistency of service delivery
- Consistency of communication
- Context-appropriate
- Acceptable interaction costs (or ease of use)
- Empowers user autonomy
- Reasonable duration and tempo
- Welcoming
- Accessible

Underlying service design is a mindset (Marquez and Downey, 2017, 4–6) that incorporates the following ideas:

Cocreating—service providers and users working together

Making the intangible, tangible—creating visualizations of the steps

Confirming with the evidence—gathering evidence of what users actually do

Focusing on user needs and expectations—understanding how and what people think about your services

Thinking holistically—viewing library services in the larger context

Having empathy—attending to all parts of the user's experience

Being open-minded—exploring all ideas, and paying attention to evidence and possible solutions

Being willing to evolve—realizing that users' beliefs and expectations continually change

The best method for developing expertise in service design is to employ "development in place" (see the discussion of this in the section entitled "On-the-Job Experiences" in this book's introduction). To get started, identify a current service with a real problem to be solved, and then follow the phases that Marquez and Downey (2015) outline:

1. *Pre-Work:* Identify the problem, project scope, teams, and activities.
2. *Observation:* Collect data on the people using library spaces and resources.
3. *Understanding/Thinking:* Delve deeply into user motivation and behavior.
4. *Implementing:* Test proposed solutions.
5. *Maintenance and Continuing Feedback Loop:* Establish a department responsible for ongoing service and evaluation.

Getting Started in Service Design (Marquez and Downey, 2017) is a workbook which builds upon earlier publications: for each project phase, the workbook suggests many possible service design tools to use and includes detailed instructions for the use of each tool:

Pre-Work tools: service inventory, ecology map, stakeholder map, surveys

Observation tools: space analysis, service safari, interviews and contextual inquiry, discussion groups, observation, work like a user

Understanding/Thinking tools: scenarios/expectation mapping, journaling, customer journey mapping, mobile ethnography, prototyping, focus groups, graffiti wall

Implementing tools: blueprinting

Maintenance and Continuing Feedback Loop tools: blueprinting

Everall and Logan (2016) conducted a study of an outdated reference desk using library service design concepts. By using several service design tools, they were able to do just enough research to allow a prototype of a new desk service to be produced, which could be refined after initial implementation. They attribute the success of the project to the prototyping approach, which resulted in more staff engagement and less resistance to change.

Additional useful information for designing services is available in WebJunction's "Topic Areas" (https://www.webjunction.org/explore-topics.html): for example, "Transforming Library Spaces for Community Engagement and Workforce Services." WebJunction's "Course Catalog" (http://learn.webjunction.org/), which lists self-paced courses and webinars on such topics as customer service, readers' advisory, reference, young adults and teens, and older adults and seniors, also provides good background information on best practices for these services. For designing virtual reference services, RUSA provides two useful guides:

- "Guidelines for Implementing and Maintaining Virtual Reference Services" (Reference and User Services Association, 2017)
- "Virtual Reference Companion" (Reference and User Services Association, 2012)

Understanding Users' Special Needs. Librarians need to be aware of specific resources that can help individuals who are in unique situations or in special circumstances. Individuals with disabilities, for example, may need special equipment such as larger screens or TTY capabilities; special software that enlarges or describes visuals online for the blind or visually impaired, such as the Illinois Accessible Web Publishing Wizard for Microsoft Office (cita.disability.uiuc.edu/presentations/awpw); or special formats, such as videos with closed captioning for the deaf or hard of hearing. Also important is a knowledge of translation services or basic language-learning resources in communities where large numbers of the population have another primary language. Librarians need to maintain an awareness of the resources in the local area that can supplement what the library can provide, such as interpreters or readers.

Videos that are useful in learning about diversity issues include the following from the Library Video Network (https://www.kanopystreaming.com/category/supplier/library-video-network): *Differences Make Us Stronger: Diversity in the Library; People First: Serving and Employing People with Disabilities;* and *And Access for All: ADA and Your Library.*

Updating Searching Strategies. One of the most important services that libraries provide is assisting both staff and users in employing a competent and complete search strategy by selecting search terms that are most closely related to the needed information, verifying spelling and eliminating errors in search terms, and identifying sources that are appropriate. There are a number of good online tutorials that can help users improve their searching skills. Webquest (http://webquest.org/index-resources.php) offers several resources on search techniques, including "Step Zero: Before You Search, Four Nets for Better Searching," which takes users through four techniques to improve their ability to use Google's advanced search form, and "Specialized Search Engines." The UC-Berkeley Library offers search tools, including maximizing Google searching (https://guides.lib.berkeley.edu/GoogleTips).

Because these resources are constantly being updated, and are sometimes removed from service, the best approach to finding appropriate searching tutorials is to examine websites that constantly monitor such services. One such website is PRIMO: Peer-Reviewed Instruction Materials Online Database (primodb.org), a project of the ACRL's Instruction Section. Another useful website is Search Engine Watch (http://searchenginewatch.com).

Other possible approaches include looking at your local community college or adult education programs for computer classes, or asking a friend who is computer-proficient to spend time with you. Since computer searching requires typing skills, improving your keyboarding skills is a must. Good keyboarding programs are available on DVD and can be purchased, rented, or used at your library

The most important aspect to improving searching skills is practice, practice, practice, because mastering a skill takes patience and determination. Working with actual reference questions and being able to discuss them with coworkers can improve your ability to think about a user's question in a different way.

One common exercise is to develop a list of quick reference questions that can be answered using the latest edition of the *World Almanac*. This exercise is a great reminder of the types of questions that can be answered in everyday sources, and it challenges staff members to be creative in their search strategies.

Another strategy that an individual can undertake is to compare similar types of online databases or different formats of the same reference tool. For example, a patron comes with the question, "I'm doing a paper on the use of gene therapy in breast cancer and I've tried Medline, but everything is too technical. What else can I use? I need articles in magazines or journals." Comparing Medline with other, more general sources can be beneficial in terms of learning the content of the two sources, but also in comparing access points.

Presenting Information. Designing reference services requires that a librarian be familiar with a number of different ways of presenting information to the user. Presenting information in written form, either in print form as bibliographies, handouts, or bookmarks, or via the Web as in web pages or tutorials, requires that one know how to best present this information. Similarly, presenting information orally via book talks, by guiding book discussion groups, or by leading instructional sessions requires a knowledge of how to present as well as knowledge about the best ways to construct the presentations.

Videos on designing and organizing services from the Library Video Network (https://www.kanopystreaming.com/category/supplier/library-video-network) include *Leading the Change: Breaking New Ground, Marketing Your Library, Merchandising Strategies, Serving Teens in Libraries,* and *Storytelling with Puppets and Props.*

The WebJunction "Course Catalog" (http://learn.webjunction.org/course/index.php) provides a number of self-paced courses and webinar recordings on providing services, for example: "Accompanying the Young Reader: Helping to Choose Appropriate Books"; "Bilingual Story Times: Reaching through the Language Barrier"; "Service Excellence in Challenging Times"; "Beyond the Welcome Sign: Tailoring Immigrant Services for Success"; and "Readers' Advisory Services."

Book displays, booktalks, book discussion groups, and book lists are all services that librarians provide to patrons to expand their awareness of individual books and to provide opportunities to talk about books.

According to Saricks (2005, 139), a book display "consisting of a small group of books and a descriptive sign is one of the most effective ways to promote and market parts of our collections," with displays of twenty to thirty books being the most successful size. Book displays of similar items might provide reader's advisory ideas for the person who wants to read more of a particular author or genre; displays can also be coordinated with special events like Black History Month, or they can highlight special local collections.

Booktalks are another service that library staff may be asked to provide as programs for community groups. A book discussion group is a service that many public libraries provide to their patrons, giving them an opportunity to read with others and providing a forum for discussion. Good websites for book discussion leaders are often found at the websites for

- publishers, for example: Simon & Schuster Bookclubs (www.simonandschuster.com/bookclubs), which features author videos, reading book guides, book club picks, and other resources
- bookstores, for example: Powell's Bookstore (www.powells.com/) under "Staff Picks"
- websites for readers and book recommendations, for example: Goodreads (https://www.goodreads.com/)

Also, there are a number of good resources on the Web for booktalks, including the following:

- Booktalks—Quick and Simple (www.nancykeane.com/booktalks)
- BookTalk.org (https://www.booktalk.org/)
- ALA Book Club Central (www.bookclubcentral.org/)

Assessing Development Efforts for Organizing and Designing Services to Meet the Needs of the Primary Community

Before beginning a new service or expanding an existing one, an institution should assess whether or not the action is consistent with its current mission, values, goals, and objectives and vision. Some questions to answer before starting a new service are provided in the text box.

New services are often small projects or experiments. An excellent strategy for assessing the

> **Questions to Answer before Starting a New Service**
>
> For a new service or even a major service expansion, here is a checklist that you can run through:
>
> - Does this action support our mission?
> - Does it support or conflict with our organizational values?
> - Does it support our strategic planning goals and objectives?
> - Does the action wind up with net income or net cost? If it is a loss center, can we afford it?
> - Is this something that we can do well?
> - Is this action something that I can personally support?
>
> Source: Peter Brinckerhoff. 2003. *Mission-Based Marketing: Positioning Your Not-for-Profit in an Increasingly Competitive World.* Hoboken, NJ: John Wiley & Sons.

success of the new services is outcome-based evaluation. Outcome-based evaluation focuses on evaluating the benefits of services to people; how have the new services changed people's skills, knowledge, behavior, or status? The Institute of Museum and Library Services (2017) provides excellent resources on outcomes evaluation, including examples of small projects.

The "Virtual Reference Companion" (Reference and User Services Association, 2012) provides a model of the information that should be provided for planning, implementing, and evaluating a new virtual reference (VR) service. The introduction invites librarians who are both planning and managing a VR service to "learn some of the things you may want to think about when starting a VR service, what skills those staffing the service should hold, and what types of technologies are relevant. Once you are ready to implement your service, gain information on marketing and assessing it, as well as other important topics." The "Skills and Training" section of the "Virtual Reference Companion" lists four general skills, which are discussed in detail under each skill and include suggested improvement and development methods such as practice, observe, review; seek a guide; role-play; read transcripts from virtual reference sections; observe other virtual reference providers; be a secret shopper at another institution; and participate in informal discussions with colleagues. For evaluation methods, the "Virtual Reference Companion" recommends the following methods: create a best practices checklist or rubric; read and score previous virtual reference transcripts in order to measure service quality and identify skills needing improvement; use small groups to review the transcripts to identify both best practices and areas needing improvement; and read feedback from user surveys in order to understand the user's perspective.

A peer review of chat transcripts by the University of Kansas Libraries' Reference Services (Valentine and Moss, 2017) promotes development by allowing current reference team members to rate themselves on a list of five characteristics derived from the RUSA "Guidelines for Behavioral Performance": correctness, completeness, grammar, courtesy, and instruction. The Reference Services staff discuss a few transactions in order to suggest alternate ways to approach and answer a question. Most of the staff realized that these peer reviews were opportunities to learn how to provide better services to users. Another study using the RUSA "Guidelines for Behavioral Performance" at Sam Houston University developed a rubric (figure 1.9) to assess librarians' performance in providing SMS/text message reference services. The purpose of the rubric is to provide librarians with feedback on their virtual reference skills such as listening/inquiring, interest, searching, and follow-up. The rubric can be used by individuals for self-evaluation, as part of small-group peer review, and also by researchers, as was the case in this study (Cassidy, Colmenares, and Martinez, 2014).

The "Searching" section of the RUSA *"Guidelines for Behavioral Performance"* can also be adopted for

	Accomplished–3	**Developing–2**	**Beginning–1**
Listening/ Inquiring The reference interview is the heart of the reference transaction and is crucial to the success of the process. The librarian must be effective in identifying the patron's information needs and must do so in a manner that keeps patrons at ease. Strong listening and questioning skills are necessary for a positive interaction.	1. Communicates in a clearly receptive/cordial/ encouraging manner. 2. Uses concise language, abbreviations, if appropriate, limiting responses to one text message (or 160 characters) per patron query. 3. Uses open-ended questioning techniques, if appropriate, to encourage the patron to expand on the request or present additional information. Some examples of such questions include: • Please tell me more about your topic. • What additional information can you give me? • How much information do you need? 4. Uses closed questions if appropriate to refine the search query. Some examples of clarifying questions are: • What types of information do you need (books, articles, etc.)? • Do you need current or historical information?	1. Communicates in a receptive/cordial/ encouraging manner. 2. Uses concise language, abbreviations, if appropriate, limiting responses to no more than two text messages (or 320 characters) per patron query. 3. Does not use open-ended questioning techniques even when appropriate to encourage the patron to expand on the request or present additional information. 4. Uses closed questions to refine the search query. Some examples of clarifying questions are: • What types of information do you need (books, articles, etc.)? • Do you need current or historical information?	1. Communicates in an abrupt manner. 2. Does not use concise language, sending responses that exceed two text messages (over 320 characters) per patron query. 3. Does not use open-ended questioning techniques even when appropriate to encourage the patron to expand on the request or present additional information. 4. Does not use closed questions to refine the search query.
Interest A successful librarian must demonstrate a high degree of interest in the reference transaction. While not every query will contain stimulating intellectual challenges, the librarian should be interested in each patron's information need and should be committed to providing the most effective assistance. Librarians who demonstrate a high level of interest in the inquiries of their patrons will generate a higher level of satisfaction among users.	1. An automatic response acknowledges user questions submitted outside of library operation hours (hours during which the library is open). 2. Provides an initial response to the patron in 30 minutes or less during library operation hours (hours during which the library is open). 3. Responds to follow-up questions, if appropriate, in 30 minutes or less during library operation hours (hours during which the library is open).	1. No automatic response acknowledges user questions submitted outside of library operation hours (hours during which the library is open). 2. Provides an initial response to the patron in a timely manner, between 30 and 60 minutes during library operation hours (hours during which the library is open). 3. Responds to follow-up questions, if appropriate, between 30 and 60 minutes during library operation hours (hours during which the library is open).	1. No automatic response acknowledges user questions submitted outside of library operation hours (hours during which the library is open). 2. Provides an initial response to the patron after more than 60 minutes during library operation hours (hours during which the library is open). 3. Responds to follow-up questions, if appropriate, after more than 60 minutes during library operation hours (hours during which the library is open).

(cont.)

FIGURE 1.9 *Reference Text Project Rubric*

FIGURE 1.9 *Reference Text Project Rubric* (cont.)

	Accomplished–3	Developing–2	Beginning–1
Searching The search process is the portion of the transaction in which behavior and accuracy intersect. Without an effective search, not only is the desired information unlikely to be found, but patrons may become discouraged as well. Yet many of the aspects of searching that lead to accurate results are still dependent on the behavior of the librarian.	1. Names the sources to be used, when appropriate. 2. Works with the patron to narrow or broaden the topic when too little or too much information is identified. 3. Recognizes when to refer the patron to a more appropriate guide, database, library, librarian, or other resource. 4. Offers detailed search paths or links/URLs to needed electronic resources. Excessively long links have been converted to a shorter link (for example, using Tiny.URL). 5. If appropriate, detailed directions to physical resources are given, for example: - Call #s and Floor #s - Room #s	1. Names the sources to be used, when appropriate. 2. Indicates that the patron needs to narrow or broaden the topic when too little or too much information is identified. 3. Recognizes when to refer the patron to a more appropriate guide, database, library, librarian, or other resource when appropriate. 4. Offers detailed search paths or links/URLs to needed electronic resources. 5. If appropriate, general directions to physical resources are given, for example--either call #s or floor #s, but not both.	1. Does not name the sources to be used when appropriate. 2. Does not work with the patron to narrow or broaden the topic when too little or too much information is identified. 3. Does not refer the patron to a more appropriate guide, database, library, librarian, or other resource when appropriate. 4. Does not offer detailed search paths or links/URLs to needed electronic resources. 5. Even if appropriate, directions to physical resources are not given.
Follow-up The reference transaction does not end when the librarian leaves the patrons. The librarian is responsible for determining if the patrons are satisfied with the results of the search, and is also responsible for referring the patrons to other sources, even when those sources are not available in the local library.	1. Encourages the patron to return if they have further questions by making a statement such as "if you don't find what you are looking for, please come back and we'll try something else" or similar. 2. Makes the patron aware of other reference services, if appropriate (email, instant chat, phone, etc.) 3. Makes arrangements, when appropriate, with the patron to research a question even after the reference transaction has been completed. 4. Refers the patron to other sources or institutions when the query cannot be answered to the satisfaction of the patron. 5. Takes care not to end the reference interview prematurely.	1. Does not encourage the patron to return if they have further questions. 2. Makes the patron aware of other reference services, if appropriate (email, instant chat, phone, etc.). 3. Does not make arrangements, when appropriate, with the patron to research a question even after the reference transaction has been completed. 4. Does not refer the patron to other sources or institutions when the query cannot be answered to the satisfaction of the patron. 5. Takes care not to end the reference interview prematurely.	1. Does not encourage the patron to return if they have further questions. 2. Does not make the patron aware of other reference services even when appropriate (email, instant chat, phone, etc.). 3. Does not make arrangements, when appropriate, with the patron to research a question even after the reference transaction has been completed. 4. Does not refer the patron to other sources or institutions when the query cannot be answered to the satisfaction of the patron. 5. Ends the reference interview prematurely, before answering or addressing all parts of a question.

RUBRIC NOTES FOR SEARCHING: 1. Librarian answers that were clearly inaccurate to the scoring group received the "Beginning" (1) score. 2. Close-ended questions that required little or no searching on the part of the librarian received the "Accomplished" (3) rating.

SOURCE: Cassidy, Erin Dorris, Colmenares, Angela, and Martinez, Michelle. (2014). So text me --- Maybe: A rubric assessment of librarian behavior in SMS reference services. *Reference & User Services Quarterly* 53(4), 310-12.

use as a checklist, which will assist you in reflecting upon how well you're practicing the recommended searching behaviors. The "Searching" section's list of general searching behaviors is provided in figure 1.10 as a sample checklist.

Tutorials on search strategies often have practice exercises or quizzes. DigitalLearn.org provides self-directed tutorials for users to increase their digital literacy and for librarians to share resources, tools, and best practices. One useful tutorial they provide is a class on search engines (Sze, n.d.). These practice exercises are particularly effective in assessing your skill as an effective searcher after completing the tutorial. Other useful sites are the

Behavioral Standard	Almost Always	Frequently	Sometimes	Almost Never	Not Applicable
Finds out what patrons have already tried, and encourages patrons to contribute ideas.					
Constructs a competent and complete search strategy. This involves:					
Selecting search terms that are most related to the information desired.					
Verifying spelling and other possible factual errors in the original inquiry.					
Identifying sources appropriate to the patron's need that have the highest probability of containing information relevant to the patron's query.					
Explains the search strategy and sequence to the patrons, as well as the sources to be used.					
Attempts to conduct the search within the patrons' allotted time frame.					
Explains how to use sources when appropriate.					
Works with the patrons to narrow or broaden the topic when too little or too much information is identified.					
Asks the patrons if additional information is needed after an initial result is found.					

FIGURE 1.10 *Self-Assessment Checklist for Searching Behaviors*

(cont.)

FIGURE 1.10 *Self-Assessment Checklist for Searching Behaviors (cont.)*

Behavioral Standard	Almost Always	Frequently	Sometimes	Almost Never	Not Applicable
Recognizes when to refer patrons to a more appropriate guide, database, library, librarian, or other resource.					
Offers pointers, detailed search paths (including complete URLs), and names of resources used to find the answer, so that patrons can learn to answer similar questions on their own.					

Purdue Online Writing Lab's (2018b) "Searching Online: An Overview," which also includes practice exercises; the "Best Search Tools Chart" (Infopeople, 2017), which references tutorials; and the MERLOT II website (https://www.merlot.org/merlot/index.htm), an open educational resource of teaching and learning materials. By utilizing MERLOT II's "Learning Exercises Advanced Search" (MERLOT II, 2018) you can locate learning exercises, such as "Searching the Invisible Web" created by Lesley Farmer (2016).

Another valuable method of assessment is to use checklists to evaluate e-mail and reference transcripts of users' questions that you have personally answered. Individual librarians can store these transcripts electronically. Later, across a large number of transactions, you will be able to reflect upon the degree to which you have demonstrated the competencies in the RUSA "Guidelines for Behavioral Performance" and how you might in the future improve your question-answering practices. The checklists for follow-up (figure 1.2), interest (figure 1.5), listening/inquiring (figure 1.6), and searching (Figure 1.10) in this chapter can be used to self-assess your success in actually meeting the behavioral guidelines in these areas. Also, Ward (2003) has developed a "Reference Interview Evaluation Sheet" for virtual reference transcripts that covers many of the elements in the RUSA behavioral guidelines on approachability/interest, searching, and follow-up, and allows for more explicit reflection in the area of question negotiation.

CHAPTER two
Sources

SECTION 5B: EVALUATES, COLLECTS, RETRIEVES, AND SYNTHESIZES INFORMATION FROM DIVERSE SOURCES

This chapter is about developing and assessing your knowledge, skills, abilities, and behaviors associated with section 5B of the RUSA "Professional Competencies," a section entitled "Evaluates, Collects, Retrieves, and Synthesizes Information from Diverse Sources." The identification, evaluation, and careful selection of the information sources and services that represent the best fit with the individual user or a targeted population group are essential for providing high-quality reference services to those users. This group of knowledge, skills, abilities, and behaviors requires careful consideration of the specific information needs of the individual or specific population group and the selection of a small set of those resources that will be most useful to them. Traditionally, special librarians who serve a more focused clientele have tended to practice these competencies each time service is provided to a client. However, with the increasing amount of information easily available on the Internet, the challenge is selecting from a continuously expanding universe of possibly useful information, and identifying the small set of information that best meets the needs of users. Thus, these competencies are becoming more important in all types of libraries and information organizations.

Competencies for Identifying and Presenting Highly Recommended Sources

The typical behavioral strategies suggested in the RUSA "Professional Competencies" that demonstrate competencies related to source selection are:

- Connects users to highly recommended, carefully selected sources in many formats
- Evaluates reference sources for quality, relevance, authenticity, authority, and inclusiveness
- Identifies any bias or point of view in an information resource
- Creates research guides, web pages, bibliographies, finding aids, and other appropriate tools in areas of expertise
- Compiles and maintains information about community resources
- Develops programming, displays, tutorials, and other specialized instructional materials reflective of the cultural diversity of the primary community

Development Methods for Identifying and Presenting Highly Recommended Sources

The success of readers' advisory interviews depends greatly on the librarian's ability to listen carefully to what the reader indicates are his or her preferences, to analyze these preferences, and then to match these preferences with new reading materials. The text box below, "Pejtersen and Austin's Dimensions of Fiction," presents a list of factors that readers take into account when they look for a fiction book to read, including subject matter, frame or setting, the author's intention, and accessibility.

Pejtersen and Austin's Dimensions of Fiction

Dimension 1. Subject Matter

The subject of the novel, including events, the development of characters, and their social relations.

Dimension 2. Frame

The time and place of the story, including geography, society, and environment.

Dimension 3. Author's Intention

The information, ideas, and emotions that the author wishes to convey to the reader.

Dimension 4. Accessibility

The reading level of the work, including the language used, the length of sentences, and the use of grammar to communicate ideas.

Source: Annelise Mark Pejtersen and Jutta Austin. 1983. "Fiction Retrieval: Experimental Design and Evaluation of a Search System Based on Users' Value Criteria (Part 1)." *Journal of Documentation* 39, no. 4: 234.

Joyce Saricks (2005, 40–73) discusses in detail specific questions librarians can ask which will help determine what is appealing about a book in relation to pacing, characterization, story line, and frame. She articulates the vocabulary regarding these aspects that the librarian should use in writing annotations, and should watch for in patrons' descriptions of books they like. These words are listed in the text box, "The Vocabulary of Appeal."

Ross, Nilsen, and Radford (2009) provide sample statements from readers, given below in the text box "The Perfect Book"; these statements can allow reference staff to practice identifying the appealing factors in a book of fiction. Using the Dimensions of Fiction as a starting point, you should analyze these statements for factors that indicate readers' reading preferences. Alternatively, after reading the statements, you can assign vocabulary words indicating the appeal in each statement.

The Vocabulary of Appeal

Pacing
Breakneck, compelling, deliberate, densely written, easy, engrossing, fast-paced, leisurely paced, measured, relaxed, stately, unhurried.

Characterization
Detailed, distant, dramatic, eccentric, evocative, faithful, familiar, intriguing secondary (characters), introspective, lifelike, multiple points of view, quirky, realistic, recognizable, series (characters), vivid, well-developed, well-drawn.

Story Line
Action-oriented, character-centered, complex, domestic, episodic, explicit violence, family-centered, folksy, gentle, inspirational, issue-oriented, layered, literary reference, multiple plotlines, mystical, mythic, open-ended, plot-centered, plot twists, racy, resolved ending, rich and famous, romp, sexually explicit, steamy strong language, thought-provoking, tragic.

Frame and Tone
Bittersweet, bleak, contemporary, darker (tone), detailed setting, details of [insert an area of specialized knowledge or skill], edgy, evocative, exotic, foreboding, gritty, hard-edged, heart-warming, historical details, humorous, lush, magical, melodramatic, menacing, mystical, nightmare (tone), nostalgic, philosophical, political, psychological, romantic, rural, sensual, small town, stark, suspenseful, timeless, upbeat, urban.

Style
Austere, candid, classic, colorful, complex, concise, conversational, direct, dramatic, elaborate, elegant, extravagant, flamboyant, frank, graceful, homespun, jargon, metaphorical, natural, ornate, poetic, polished, prosaic, restrained, seemly, showy, simple, sophisticated, stark, thoughtful, unaffected, unembellished, unpretentious, unusual.

Source: Joyce G. Saricks. 2005. *Reader's Advisory Service in the Public Library*. 3rd ed. Chicago: American Library Association, p. 66.

The Perfect Book

The following seven statements are accounts provided by avid readers when they were asked to describe what they considered to be the "perfect book." For each of the statements:

1. Identify the appeal factors that the reader looks for in a book. (What do you think are the most important clues, in each case, to the reader's preferences?)
2. Use readers' advisory tools to come up with a list of five books that you would suggest to the reader that he or she might enjoy.
3. If you are doing this as a group exercise, compare your lists with those of others and discuss the reasons for your choices.
   a. Most of the books I read are British and written by women, for example, Fay Weldon, Barbara Pym, Miss Read. I like books that present family life, probably because I'm looking for security. I'm honestly interested in how people react under different conditions—how they get through life and face their problems. In fiction, you understand that things are tough for people, but they seem to be solved so easily. Things seem to work out. It doesn't work that way in real life. Maybe that's why I like reading about families, written from a woman's point of view. (female reader, age 31)
   b. For a book to somehow touch me, I have to feel that whoever wrote it is sincere. And to me, in a novel especially—but even in a work of biography or history—there has to be something in it that tells me that the author, if not loves, then at least appreciates and is somehow able to understand the people that he or she has chosen to write about. There has to be some kind of grounding in reality for me. Even if the book is a total fantasy, like the devil coming to Moscow [in *The Master and Margarita*], I have to feel that there is a strong element of reality and a strong feeling that the author understands what it means to be alive. That's what a book needs to have to hold my attention. You know, in *The Invisible Man*, Ralph Ellison talks about how he and his

(Cont.)

The Perfect Book (cont.)

little brother—this is a black writer in the South—learned how to fish by reading novels by Ernest Hemingway. I've always enjoyed that. They'd go page by page and figure it out step by step. (male reader, age 26)

c. I like books about the life of a family—good, clean fiction without all the four-letter words. And not filled with sex, which is not necessary. A book can be written so that you can imagine [sex] without putting it in plain words. I'm reading a good book right now that is really "high society," and it's all about all the fancy clothes they have to wear to their big parties. I also like those stories set in hospitals—doctor and nurse stories. (female reader, age 75)

d. It would be long. I like books that are long because they're good and meaty. You get your value for your money. It would be about 500 to 800 pages. It would have lots of adventure in it. It would be suspenseful. It would have some instructional material in it. It would be very descriptive of places and people. During the book, there would be descriptions of how the people used to do things or the way things are done now or the way things are made—that sort of thing. The Tom Clancy books are good because they combine science fiction and instructional material right in them. (male reader, age 51)

e. Why don't we look at a book that I really thought was great and maybe that will tell me what I like? Well, for instance, *The Far Pavilions*. I like books that can tell me details of cultures and religions that I'm not familiar with. I like lots of sort of nonfictional detail immersed in fiction. I'm very fond of that. I like to immerse myself in a different time space. Perhaps that's why I like the India stories so much, because it is so different. So I guess the perfect book for me takes me to a different time and space. But then there's another element too, when I think of *The Bridges of Madison County*, for instance. I just loved that book because it was about a real person, my age, and it was a beautifully crafted book in the literary sense. But it was about a person my age who had some feelings and so on, that she had to deal with. It also involved her family. So I guess I like to read about women I can identify with, in a historically based novel or real life. (female reader, age 46)

f. I would like to have a novel based on fact, that actually happened in the world. But put it into a novel form, so that there are fictitious characters in the book. I want to be able to relate the book to an actual country, a world, a situation that took place, an earthquake, or a fire, or a bombing, or an incident in a war that you know of or have heard of. *The Bridge on the River Kwai* is probably the movie that has stuck in my mind more than anything else. But, if you actually read the book [the movie is based on] *The Bridge over the River Kwai*, it's not the exact situation of the movie, although some things are the same. There was a railway built, it was built by slaves, it was built by prisoners of war that the Japanese had. That's the type of book that I like. (male reader, age 60)

g. It would have to have strong characters, both good and bad. There's no use having strong heroines and weak villains because it doesn't make for an interesting book. One of the neat things about the Sherlock Holmes mysteries is that Moriarty is such an opponent. He matches Holmes move-for-move and word-for-word. The characters would be the most important thing. And it would have to have a good plot, something that followed and made sense, with a bit of suspense, even if it wasn't necessarily a mystery book. Even in a romance, you don't want to know what's going to happen, where the relationship's going. Those would be the main things—and a few interesting subplots, because they usually spice the book up, but not so many that you get confused. (female reader, age 26)

SOURCE: Catherine Sheldrick Ross, Kirsti Nilsen, and Marie Radford. 2009. *Conducting the Reference Interview*. 2nd ed. New York: Neal-Schuman, pp. 247-48.

For the appeal factors of various subgenres of narrative nonfiction, you can consult the program handouts (Reference and User Services Association, 2005) developed by members of the RUSA Readers' Advisory Committee and the PLA Readers' Advisory Committee in conjunction with participants in the program "Taking the Guesswork Out of Non-Fiction Readers' Advisory," which was held at the ALA Annual Conference on June 26, 2005, in Chicago.

Saricks (2005, 166) suggests these basic skills for readers' advisors:

- How to build on and expand familiarity with fiction and nonfiction
- How to think about books
- How to talk about books
- How to use reference sources
- How to write about books

Saricks (p. 167) goes on to suggest ways that her book, *Reader's Advisory Service in the Public Library*, can be used for training for readers' advisory. Figure 2.1 is a checklist from that publication.

Assignment	Date	Discussed/Initials
Philosophy of service		
Read and discuss chapter 1	_____	_____
Assess reading background	_____	_____
Design reading plan and set discussion dates	_____	_____
Keep track of what is read	_____	_____
Appeal		
Read and discuss chapter 3	_____	_____
Description exercise	_____	_____
Book summaries	_____	_____
Readers' advisory interview		
Read and discuss chapter 4	_____	_____
Read and discuss Hanff and Morley	_____	_____
Reference sources and questions		
Read and discuss chapter 2	_____	_____
Peruse collection of department book lists and bookmarks	_____	_____
"BookNotes" form		
Read and discuss chapter 5	_____	_____
Unannotated bookmark		
Read and discuss chapter 6	_____	_____
Annotated book list	_____	_____
On-desk activities		
Keeping track of questions	_____	_____
Setting interview goals	_____	_____
Filling Good Books truck	_____	_____
Filling displays	_____	_____

SOURCE: Joyce G. Saricks. 2005. *Readers' Advisory Service in the Public Library*. 3rd ed. Chicago: American Library Association, p. 167.

FIGURE 2.1 *Checklist for* Readers' Advisory Service in the Public Library

Comparison and contrast is another useful analytic technique. It is especially useful in examining resources. Comparing two particular electronic sources for the same search topic, or the access points for the same resource in print and electronically, would be good examples of this approach. Academic librarians often use this technique in introductory research classes to help students learn the differences between articles in the popular literature and those in the scholarly press. For example, the UC-Berkeley Library guides (http://guides.lib.berkeley.edu/evaluating-resources) compare the differences between popular and scholarly literature and between primary and secondary sources. Comparisons of search conventions between databases are also common. Farmer (2015) has developed a learning exercise for students to generate research questions, locate the relevant documents on subscription online database aggregators, and then compare the databases in terms of process and results.

The annotated book list, or bookmark, is another service to highlight parts of the collection for patrons. Saricks covers succinctly the processing of creating an annotated book list (2005, 145–55). A sample book annotation format is presented in figure 2.2.

A number of websites provide suggestions on how to write annotations, including the following ones:

Cornell University Library. (2017). "How to Prepare an Annotated Bibliography."

Purdue Online Writing Lab. (2018a). "Annotated Bibliographies."

University of Wisconsin, Madison Writing Center. (2017). "Academic Writing: Annotated Bibliography."

Additional guides are available by searching on "annotated bibliography" in the LibGuides Community: http://community.libguides.com/.

The University of West Florida Library offers a series of short video tutorials (https://secure.uwf.edu/library/research_help/tutorials/#form) on many topics, including writing an annotated bibliography.

Author: _____

Title: _____

Publication Date: _____

Number of Pages: _____

Geographical Setting: _____

Time Period: _____

Series: _____

Plot Summary: _____

Subject Headings: _____

Appeal: _____

Similar Authors: _____

Name: _____

SOURCE: Joyce G. Saricks. 2005. *Readers' Advisory Service in the Public Library*. 3rd ed. Chicago: American Library Association, p. 109

FIGURE 2.2 *Book Annotation Format*

A quiz is also included to test your learning after watching the video.

For ideas on the content and design of resource guides, you can examine the guides on many subjects featured in the LibGuides Community (http://community.libguides.com/), including site and guide picks. Other sources provide advice and guidance on developing library guides for library instruction and for community information, for example: "How to Create a Community Resource Guide" by Ginny Mies (2015) and the health guides featured in WebJunction (2017).

As discussed earlier in this chapter, one of the important issues for libraries is access to services for people with a wide variety of disabilities. About

15 percent of people in the world have a disability— a physical, mental, or sensory impairment that significantly impacts their daily life. The LibGuides project at the University of Illinois addresses this significant population by presenting the best information on a wide range of disabilities (Pionke and Manson, 2018). These guides are a very important resource for librarians who need to create accessible guides for people with disabilities. The guides are aimed at any user, not just public or academic ones, and include scholarly information, clinically based tools, disability organizations and communities, and popular culture resources. The LibGuides platform used at the University of Illinois is Springshare (https://springshare.com/libguides/), which is widely used by other libraries and has many accessibility features already embedded in the system. More than twenty guides that have been created are available on the Web through a table of contents (Pionke, 2017). In addition, to presenting information on disabilities to users, Pionke and Manson note that in the process of creating the resource guides, they discovered the strengths and weaknesses of the literature on disability both within the university's collections and outside of the university. Thus, librarians can benefit by recognizing that creating a resource guide on any topic has the potential to reveal gaps in the collection that need to be filled.

For librarians, creating resource guides has another excellent benefit, which is self-development. To create resource guides the librarian must either have or acquire significant knowledge of the subject, including the sources already in the collection and relevant new resources. In surveys of librarians in 113 libraries across Queensland, New South Wales, and the Northern Territory of Australia, over half of the respondents found subject guides essential for improving their skills (Bagshaw and Yorke-Barber, 2018). Creating the guides was also an opportunity to share their subject knowledge with both peers and users. The knowledge and skills gained from creating resource guides are an excellent example of McCauley's (2006) "development in place," which involves taking on new tasks in the workplace or local community. In the community, public librarians can work closely with an important community agency—for example, a local health organization—and through the creation of a health resource guide, enhance the knowledge not only of librarians but of many community members accessing health services.

Assessing Developments Efforts for Identifying and Presenting Highly Recommended Sources

In addition to developing their skills, librarians should also *assess* their competencies and knowledge related to the process of information-seeking. This is done, for example, when evaluating the design of organized presentations of services to groups of users, in the form of subject guides and library websites with pages directed at teenagers or other population groups. Library websites have become the major method of presenting information on services to groups of users. Figure 2.3 allows librarians to self-assess the degree to which they have incorporated a process-oriented approach to information-seeking into their presentation of information on web pages. The form presented in this figure could easily be modified to assess printed guides as well.

You can assess your competency in the organization and presentation of information to users (tutorials, bibliographies, displays, and so on) by comparing your drafts of information presentations with similar products from other institutions. Go on a virtual field trip, visit the websites of libraries with similar presentations, and compare your draft with the other library's product for accuracy, clarity, currency, and selection of the most appropriate content for the intended audience. Focus groups of users, whom you expect to be the primary audience for the material, are also a good way to assess your competency in the organization and presentation of materials. For the basics on user research methods, including focus groups and observation, see Usability.gov (https://www.usability.gov/how-to-and-tools/methods/user-research/index.html). Sage publishes a series of research guides: for a detailed practical

---

Name of Web Page: _____

URL (Web Address): _____

Purpose: _____

Assess the degree to which users in each stage of the information-seeking process (ISP) will find the content on this page useful:

	USEFUL		
	Very	Somewhat	Not at All
Initiation (recognizing the need for information)	_____	_____	_____
Selection (seeking background on general area)	_____	_____	_____
Exploration (seeking information to become adequately informed)	_____	_____	_____
Formulation (forming focused perspective on topic)	_____	_____	_____
Collection (gathering most relevant information on focused topic)	_____	_____	_____
Presentation (completing search and assignment)	_____	_____	_____

Recommended design changes and/or additional pages that should be developed to address user information-seeking needs in other stages of the ISP:

_____
_____
_____

SOURCE: Based upon the concepts of Carol C. Kuhlthau: Carol C. Kuhlthau. 2004. *Seeking Meaning: A Process Approach to Library and Information Services*. Westport, CT: Greenwood Press.

FIGURE 2.3 *Information-Seeking Process Assessment for Web Pages or Other Information Presentations*

guide, consult Krueger and Casey's (2014) book *Focus Groups*.

The observation of people who are actually trying to use your information presentation to locate needed information will also provide insight into the strengths and weaknesses in your organization and presentation of information. Consult *Qualitative Research & Evaluation Methods* by Patton (2014) to learn how to actually conduct observational studies. You can also introduce the information presentation to a specific population, such as a college class, to use as part of an assignment; or to a workshop designed for seniors interested in improving their web skills, and ask the class or workshop participants to evaluate the information presentation.

RUSA's Reference Services Section lists the following methods for web-based tools (Reference and User Services Association, 2007b):

Formal Usability Testing—Observe as patrons use a site to perform given tasks or achieve a set of defined goals.

Inquiry—Use interviews, surveys, and focus groups to gather information about patron preferences and the use of a particular site.

Inspection—Use to evaluate a site against a checklist of heuristics and design principles or simulations of typical user tasks.

Other possibilities are asking experts to evaluate collaborative web work, instruction assignments, web library guides, and similar web tools. See figure 2.4 for the PRIMO criteria for evaluating online tutorials.

Before beginning your own foray into online learning, or having your library users start online tutorials, it is often suggested that an assessment be done to determine your (or their) readiness to undertake online learning.

A number of good online assessments exist:

- Illinois Online Network. (2018). "Self Evaluation for Potential Online Students."
- University of North Carolina at Chapel Hill. (2010). "Online Learning Readiness Questionnaire."
- California Community Colleges. (2016). "Online Student Readiness Tutorials."
- Texas Wesleyan Center for Excellence in Teaching & Learning. (2018). "For Students: Test of Online Learning Success (TOOLS)."

Members of the PRIMO Committee review and evaluate instructional materials submitted for inclusion into the PRIMO database according to the following criteria:

Criterion #1
The instructional design is pedagogically effective, i.e., it teaches well according to the scope and learning objectives stated by the submitter.

- The purpose and objectives are clearly stated.
- The resource's organization supports the objectives.
- The resource's content supports the objectives.
- The resource offers opportunities to utilize higher-order thinking skills (think, reflect, discuss, hypothesize, compare, classify, etc.)
- The resource allows for different learning styles, e.g., kinetic, visual, auditory.
- The resource uses assessment technique(s).

Criterion #2
The technology used to create the material enhances the learning experience, i.e., is appropriate and effective.

- The technology enhances and does not distract from the learning experience.
- The technology chosen is stable and able to operate as an effective mode of delivery.
- The technology is cross-browser/cross-platform compatible, or clear guidelines and instructions are provided.
- The required plug-ins or downloads are easily obtained and easy to install.

Criterion #3
This material provides instruction using technology in an innovative manner.

The technology used has not yet been extensively used to create instructional material, or has been implemented in an unusual and/or creative manner.

- Score 5: yes
- Score 3: no

Criterion #4
The content and language of the material are clear and effective.

- Instructions and explanations are easy to follow.
- Language is appropriate to the goal(s) of the project.
- Language is appropriate to the audience of the project.
- Content is appropriate to the goal(s) of the project.
- Content is appropriate to the audience of the project.

Criterion #5
All information included within the material is accurate.

- The site does not contain significant typographical errors.
- There are no apparent factual errors.
- The site provides indications of maintenance, e.g., information about when it was last updated.
- The site offers some type of contact information (e-mail, phone, or postal address) for author and webmaster if questions or technical problems arise.

Criterion #6
Organization of the material is clear and easy to use.

- There is an index, table of contents, or site map to facilitate navigation.
- Users can easily find their way back to the home page and/or to other sections.
- The material has a visible and logical sequence or structure.
- The text is easy to read and graphics are easy to understand.

(cont.)

FIGURE 2.4 *PRIMO Selection Criteria*

FIGURE 2.4 • *PRIMO Selection Criteria* (cont.)

Criterion #7

This material demonstrates unique or creative use of graphics, examples, interactive elements such as programmed feedback and flexible learning paths, and other supporting elements.

- The material incorporates design elements such as graphics, multimedia, flexible learning paths, and/or interactivity.
- The design elements show evidence of creativity; they are not tired copies of material from other learning objects. (A Venn diagram isn't creative, but a Venn diagram of singing grapes is unusual.)
- The design elements are appropriate to the target audience.
- The design elements contribute to the coherence of the material.
- The design elements are well-executed and professional (i.e., graphics don't look like scribbles, animations aren't jerky, sound and video have been edited to flow smoothly, text within graphics is visible and legible, spoken words are comprehensible, interactive elements are easy to use, flexible learning paths don't turn into mazes).

Criterion #8

This material is relevant to those outside of the developer's institution because it presents a model for other developers.

- It is possible for people outside of the developer's institution to gain access to the material. If access to some elements is restricted, this does not significantly detract from an outsider's opportunity to investigate the material.
- The structure of the material (e.g., chunking, sequencing, transitions, connections, reinforcement, assessment, feedback) can be adapted to teaching other skills, resources, or ideas.
- The method of presentation (e.g., use of text, sound, graphics, animation, video, language, layout, pacing, examples) can be adapted to teaching other skills, resources, or ideas.
- The technology used to develop the material is available outside of the developer's institution.
- Information about the system requirements for effective use of the material is readily available.
- The developer's approach to teaching or to the use of technology is thought-provoking; it stimulates ideas about ways to communicate with learners.

How submissions are evaluated

Reviewers assign each of the criteria statements an agreement value using the following scale:

5 = Meets all the components covered in the description.

4 = Meets all but one of the components covered in the description. The missing component does not affect the working of the resource.

3 = Meets many (missing more than one) of the components covered in the description. The missing components do *not* significantly affect the project overall on this criterion.

2 = Meets many (missing more than one) of the components covered in the description. The missing components *do* significantly affect the project overall on this criterion.

1 = Meets only one component for the criteria and is lacking enough components that the resource is affected.

0 = Does not satisfy any components described.

After scoring each of the eight criteria, the values are totaled. Review scores from all reviewers are averaged. Submissions receiving an average score of 32 or higher are added to the PRIMO database.

A note on the project scope . . .

For PRIMO, quality is a greater goal than is comprehensiveness. However, materials may be refused because the technology that they teach and the methodology that they use are already well-represented on the site.

A note on legal matters. . .

The IS PRIMO Committee does not make any claims or guarantees whatsoever as to the accuracy or currency of the data represented on this site.

Go to PRIMO Submission Form
Peer-Reviewed Instructional Materials Online (PRIMO) database

SOURCE: http://acrl.ala.org/IS/instruction-tools-resources-2/pedagogy/primo-peer-reviewed-instruction-materials-online/primo-selection-criteria/.

CHAPTER **three**

Collaboration

SECTION 5C: INTERACTS WITH COLLEAGUES AND OTHERS TO PROVIDE CONSULTATION, MEDIATION, AND GUIDANCE IN THE USE OF KNOWLEDGE AND INFORMATION

This chapter is about developing and assessing your knowledge, skills, abilities, and behaviors associated with section 5C of the RUSA "Professional Competencies," a section entitled "Interacts with Colleagues and Others to Provide Consultation, Mediation, and Guidance in the Use of Knowledge and Information." The topics covered are collaboration, teamwork and partnerships, which are becoming increasingly important, particularly in organizations with highly skilled professionals. The organizational challenges of the twenty-first century require new leadership in the form of both self-leadership and shared leadership, with less reliance on top-down leadership. Self-leadership requires managing one's behavior to meet and evaluate existing standards and involves practical strategies such as self-observation, self-goal setting, self-reward, rehearsal, self-job redesign, and the self-management of internal dialogues and mental imagery. Shared leadership occurs when all the members of a team are fully engaged in the leadership of the team (Pearce, Manz, and Sims, 2009). Much of twenty-first-century work involves knowledge work, which requires both contributions from individuals who work independently and contributions from teams, where the knowledge of several individuals is integrated.

The *New Oxford American Dictionary* (2015) defines *collaborate* as to "work jointly on an activity, especially to produce or create something." Although librarians have always worked together, collaboration has assumed new importance in a world that has witnessed a phenomenal growth in information, new knowledge, and sophisticated technology, all within a relatively short time frame. Because of the explosion of information and the increasing variety of ways to access it, librarians must work with colleagues, professional organizations, agencies, and other groups to ensure that users receive the information service they need at the time of need and in the most suitable format. Librarians need to recognize and respect the role played by the user in the information interaction. And in today's world, librarians must actively pursue collaborations that enhance services for their users.

The key partnerships and relationships that librarians must develop and assess for their effectiveness are (1) relationships with users, (2) relationships with colleagues, (3) relationships within the profession, and (4) relationships beyond the library and the profession. Each of these types of relationships is treated in detail in the sections that follow.

COLLABORATES AND PARTNERS WITH THE USER IN THE INFORMATION-SEEKING PROCESS

Competencies for Collaborating and Partnering with the User in the Information-Seeking Process

In direct interactions with users, collaboration involves respecting the knowledge and skills of users and facilitating your understanding of users' backgrounds and needs through effective reference interviews. Effective collaboration requires that librarians treat users as collaborators and partners in the information-seeking process. Collaboration is essential because both the librarian and the user bring unique knowledge to the interaction. The librarian has an in-depth knowledge of service strategies and procedures, print and web collection resources, and web and database search strategies, but only the user is aware of what he knows about the topic and what he wishes to learn from his inquiry.

Collaboration, in which the user and librarian are equal partners, is most difficult in transactions at the reference desk, which tend to be short in duration, allowing little time or perhaps incentive for the librarian to determine the user's knowledge, interest, time, and the availability of appropriate information because of the pressure of others waiting or potentially waiting for service. One solution that many libraries use is to have a service desk with a mix of staff employed to answer certain types of basic questions that don't require extensive knowledge. Establishing collaborative relationships with users is somewhat less challenging with in-depth consultations, which are generally scheduled by appointment and are off the reference desk, or perhaps take place virtually, and last for twenty minutes or more. Rogers and Carrier (2017) found that users valued establishing a research relationship with a librarian and indicated an intent to continue to working with that librarian on the project or future projects because of the librarian's perceived expertise and the benefit of receiving individualized attention.

The typical behavioral strategies suggested in the RUSA "Professional Competencies" that demonstrate competencies related to user relationships are:

- Engages the user in the process and in making decisions
- Determines the user's prior knowledge and expertise
- Consults appropriate internal and external resources

Development Methods for Collaborating and Partnering with the User in the Information-Seeking Process

Kuhlthau, Maniotes, and Caspari (2007) define the verb *collaborate* as to "work jointly with others." In their view, collaboration is an intervention strategy at a critical point in the inquiry process that enables people to try out ideas, raise questions, and hear other perspectives. Collaborative strategies, which are productive activities for learning through inquiry, include brainstorming, delegating, networking, and integrating. The best development strategies for collaborating with users are those that McCauley (2006) terms "development in place," which is development on the job through practical experiences. For collaborating or partnering with users, Valentine and Moss (2017) briefly describe selecting and discussing a few transactions from the LibAnswers website and discussing these with reference services staff in order to suggest alternate ways to approach and answer questions. Reference staff could also create and test a list of sample questions that are designed to encourage users to become full partners in the reference encounter. These sample questions would address the criteria that are important to users, which are their perspectives on time, task, interest, and the availability of resources (Kuhlthau, Maniotes, and Caspari, 2007, 138).

A staff development exercise that can be both enlightening and entertaining involves developing scenarios that are designed to illustrate good and poor reference interview practices and presenting the scenarios in front of an interactive audience of reference staff. A reference librarian or team of reference staff could take this on as a project, involving actual users in playing roles and presenting the scenarios in the form of live amateur theater with public services staff as the audience.

Finally, you can design and deliver a workshop on the successes and failures of librarian-user collaborations in the information-seeking process. You will be an expert on the topic by the time you do all the selection of appropriate content and design and then present the workshop.

Assessing Development Efforts for Collaborating and Partnering with the User in the Information-Seeking Process

To review and reflect upon your performance, videotaping and/or audiotaping your interactions with users is recommended. Or, if you are reviewing virtual reference transactions, you can save the transactions after deleting the identity of the participants. The "Self-Assessment Checklist for Listening/Inquiring" (figure 1.6) is very useful for systematically analyzing the level of your performance. When recording interactions, the permission of users needs to be obtained. (See the sample permission form in figure 3.1.)

Kuhlthau, Maniotes, and Caspari (2007) discuss choosing an intervention strategy that enables people to control their own information-seeking process. Questions related to the criteria of time, task, interest, and the availability of information are useful in assessing the degree to which librarians elicit

---

We are asking for your help in evaluating certain aspects of our service. Your participation is voluntary. However, we strongly encourage you to permit us to record your interaction with the library staff and assist us in improving our understanding of reference services.

The confidentiality of your responses is assured. The recording will only be viewed by staff for the purpose of evaluating the services. The recordings will be placed in a secure locked location and erased after the study has been completed. No information that can identify you will be included in any published study.

I agree to permit recording of the reference interaction.

_____
(Signature)   *(Date)*

I have fully informed the user of his or her rights.

_____
(Librarian Signature)   *(Date)*

FIGURE 3.1 *Sample Permission Form*

> **User Perspectives on Their Time, Task, Interest and the Availability of Information Resources**
>
> 1. How much time do I have?
> 2. What am I trying to accomplish?
> 3. What am I interested in?
> 4. What information is available?

the users' perspectives on time, task, interest, and the availability of information in the reference interview. Transcripts of questions can also be reviewed to determine if the reference transaction identified all of the users' perspectives on their time, tasks, interest, and the availability of resources.

COLLABORATES WITH COLLEAGUES TO PROVIDE SERVICES TO USERS

Competencies for Collaborating with Colleagues to Provide Service to Users

Providing high-quality service to individual users frequently involves consulting and working closely with colleagues. Your colleagues have expertise in a wide variety of disciplines. Combining their knowledge and expertise with yours is essential in responding fully to users' complex information needs. Frequently, collaboration can produce more successful solutions to service problems than single experts can. The collective work of many experts enables teams to achieve goals beyond the efforts of any individual member.

The skills that facilitate collaboration will be increasingly important in the future. In 2016, the World Economic Forum (2016) issued a report on the future of jobs. The report's "Executive Summary" notes:

> On average, by 2020, more than a third of the desired core skill sets of most occupations will be comprised of skills that are not yet considered crucial to the job today, according to our respondents. Overall, social skills—such as persuasion, emotional intelligence, and teaching others—will be in higher demand across industries than narrow technical skills, such as programming or equipment operation and control. In essence, technical skills will need to be supplemented with strong social and collaboration skills.

Many of the top skills identified for 2020 are key to successful collaboration; these skills are difficult to evaluate in job interviews, but are easily observed in teamwork settings. The top ten skills for 2020 identified in the World Economic Forum report are complex problem-solving, critical thinking, creativity, people management, coordinating with others, emotional intelligence, judgment and decision-making, service orientation, negotiation, and cognitive flexibility.

The typical behavioral strategies suggested in the RUSA "Professional Competencies" that demonstrate competencies related to collegial relationships are:

- Establishes shared goals and values for excellent user services
- Facilitates team development with colleagues to improve user services
- Shares knowledge and expertise with colleagues
- Recognizes the unique knowledge, skills, and strengths of colleagues that can assist in responding to inquiries
- Elicits assistance from colleagues when appropriate to enhance the user experience

Development Methods for Collaborating with Colleagues to Provide Service to Users

Organizations can implement practices such as peer coaching and mentoring that encourage employees to build their own development networks. People who are effective at building their own networks reach out by asking others for advice, feedback, information, and support. They form relationships with people in different functional areas in the organization and in the larger community. One of the techniques for developing your colleagues' networking skills is relational development dialogues. Four key questions should guide these employee dialogues (Chandler, Hall, and Kram, 2010, 52):

1. How well are developmental networks of individuals meeting their current career needs?
2. How can individuals better utilize their existing networks to be more responsive now?
3. Given the career goals of individuals, how well are their existing networks positioned to help them attain those goals?
4. What actions can individuals take to create networks that help meet their desired outcomes?

Peer coaching promotes shared communication, collaboration, and behavioral service values. The learning benefits from peer coaching arise because of the collegial peer-based relationship (Ladyshewsky, 2017). We feel safer with a peer coach than with a manager or supervisor when we're uncertain how to deal with a work issue. As long as a trusting and confidential relationship can be developed, peer coaching is an excellent strategy for engaging in workplace learning and problem-solving. Ladyshewsky presents the SCARF model, which identifies the essential elements for successful peer coaching:

- S = *Status*—equal partnership
- C = *Certainty*—trust and confidence
- A = *Autonomy*—control and self-determination
- R = *Relatedness*—the building of positive relations between parties
- F = *Fairness*—honest and fair feedback

Basic rules include getting to know each other, building trust, each party identifying their goals for areas in which they want to learn or improve, and training in asking nonevaluative questions. Nonevaluative questions start with the words "who, what, where, when, and how" and do not involve providing advice. Parker, Kram, and Hall (2014) also describe the necessary steps in applying peer coaching: building the relationship, creating success, and internalizing the skills.

Assessing Development Efforts for Collaborating with Colleagues to Provide Service to Users

Peer coaching has the potential to provide "development in place" for both people in the coaching relationship. For assessing development, several features are important: goal-setting, work activities that promote experimental practice and learning, and encouraging learning through practice at work. Jones, Woods, and Guillaume (2016) found that coaching by internal coaches had a stronger effect upon learning and performance than external coaches.

An additional technique that is useful for reflecting upon and building collaborative skills is interviewing group leaders who have an excellent reputation for effectiveness. (See figure 3.2.) After analyzing the content of interviews, taking the self-quiz on "How Collaborative Are You?" (figure 3.3) is useful for reflecting upon areas in which to strengthen your collaborative skills. A useful tool for self-assessment is based upon the collaboration competencies provided in the "Personal/Interpersonal" section of the "Competency Index for the Library Field" (Gutsche and Hough, 2014). Figure 3.4 provides a self-assessment rating scale.

---

1. What specific skills do you see as the most important for effective teamwork?
2. What would you consider your strengths in working with groups?
3. What would you consider your weaknesses?
4. Do you have ideas or plans on how to strengthen these areas?

FIGURE 3.2 *Questions for Interviewing Effective Group Leaders*

In their book *Joining Together,* Johnson and Johnson (2016) provide an exercise for self-diagnosis which involves rating your behavior as a member of a group (p. 3). Another suggestion is to keep a personal journal (p. 43) that contains summaries of your conversations and material relating to group dynamics, and which records how you behave in group situations, with regard to your goals clarification, communication, leadership, expertise and knowledge, decision-making, advocacy of views, conflict resolution, and use of power. *Joining Together* contains many other useful and interesting exercises for improving your group skills.

The University of Ottawa's Human Resources' (n.d.) "Key Competencies Development Activities Guide" is a professional development tool for evaluating competencies, which includes recommendations for assessing competencies on your own, with your peers (a team), and with your supervisor. The "Teamwork and Co-Operation" section of the guide suggests discussing with colleagues your participation level and offering positive feedback. Carefully selected group development assignments provide opportunities for the use of problem-solving techniques and learning from peers. Another suggestion from the guide is to solicit feedback on your team participation skills from your supervisor. The guide also includes activity-based learning strategies.

Work Style Preference
  Work with group   Work alone
  1   2   3   4   5
Participation in Meetings
  Involved   Uninvolved
  1   2   3   4   5
Active Listening to Others
  Courteous   Discourteous
  1   2   3   4   5
Encourage Others to Speak
  Encourage   Discourage
  1   2   3   4   5
Active Support of Group Members
  High   Low
  1   2   3   4   5
Acknowledgment and Respect of Contributions and Views of Others
  Acknowledge   Ignore
  1   2   3   4   5
Offer to Help Others with Group Projects
  Always   Never
  1   2   3   4   5
Focus on Understanding the Work of Others
  Always   Never
  1   2   3   4   5
Focus on Task
  High   Low
  1   2   3   4   5
Share Expertise
  Successful   Unsuccessful
  1   2   3   4   5
Understand Roles and Responsibilities
  Clear   Hazy
  1   2   3   4   5

NOTE: On each scale **1** = Very, **2** = Somewhat, **3** = Neutral, **4** = Somewhat, **5** = Very
For example, on *Work Style Preference*
  Work with group   Work alone
  1   2   3   4   5
1 = Very strong preference for work with group;
2 = Somewhat prefer to work with group;
3 = No preference;
4 = Somewhat prefer to work alone;
5 = Very strong preference for working alone.

FIGURE 3.3 • *How Collaborative Are You?*

DEVELOPS COLLABORATIVE RELATIONSHIPS WITHIN THE PROFESSION TO ENHANCE SERVICE TO USERS

Competencies for Developing Collaborative Relationships within the Profession to Enhance Service to Users

Collaborative relationships within the profession enhance service to users because professional colleagues are a rich resource for keeping up-to-date on current practices and innovative services.

RATING SCALE

1 – No Skill: not at all familiar with the knowledge or skills
2 – Minimal Skill: demonstrates lack of confidence in knowledge and task performance; needs more training
3 – Moderate Skill: demonstrates knowledge or performs tasks adequately but could use more training or mentoring in certain aspects
4 – Strong Skill: demonstrates knowledge or performs tasks confidently and needs no further training

Skill/Knowledge	1	2	3	4
Treats everyone with honesty, respect, and fairness to build an environment of trust				
Contributes to a collaborative, committed, and collegial work environment				
Pursues an understanding and embrace of individual and organizational diversity				
Acknowledges own strengths and contributions, and recognizes the complementary strengths and contributions of others				
Shares knowledge gained through professional discussions, conferences, formal courses, and informal channels with colleagues				
Gives and receives constructive feedback from coworkers, supervisors, and users				
Contributes constructively to the achievement of the team's goals and objectives				
Assumes shared responsibility for collaborative work, and values the individual contributions made by each team member				
Contributes to a problem-solving environment and works toward mutually acceptable solutions, regardless of position or level				
Participates actively in information-gathering and decision-making in order to promote the best interests of the team				
Manages own and others' time effectively to deliver work on time				
Finds opportunities to help others to develop new ideas and achieve their full potential				
Gives or receives coaching or mentoring from team members as appropriate				
Understands that organizations are inherently political (including libraries) and develops strategies to become an effective player				
Understands a variety of difficult behavior patterns and develops responses appropriate to each				
Routinely examines own behavior, accepts accountability for own actions and adjusts appropriately				
Understands and applies strategies for conflict resolution				

SOURCE: Competency statements from: Betha Gutsche and Brenda Hough, eds. 2014. "Competency Index for the Library Field." webjunction.org/explore-topics/competencies.html.

FIGURE 3.4 *Self-Assessment Rating Scale for Collaboration*

The typical behavioral strategies suggested in the RUSA "Professional Competencies" that demonstrate competencies related to professional relationships are:

- Develops personal networks by actively participating in appropriate local, regional, state, national, and international organizations
- Identifies and seeks out possible partners in order to expand services
- Contributes to collaborative efforts that will benefit local users

Development Methods for Developing Collaborative Relationships within the Profession to Enhance Service to Users

Networking is a key reason for your involvement in organizations. By actively participating in organizations through committees, task forces, boards, and special interest groups, you can develop lasting relationships with people who have common interests and similar concerns. These informal relationships can be a source of guidance and useful insight and can serve as a support network when you need advice on a challenging situation in your workplace. You and your contacts can support one another in reaching your professional goals. Your network may also be useful in finding a new position.

Professional organizations also provide many opportunities to keep current in your profession and learn best practices as well as new ideas through conferences, seminars, workshops, courses, publications, and an increasing number of online resources. Committee work provides opportunities to develop, practice, and refine your skills at communication, negotiating, collaboration, leadership, and problem-solving. Organizations provide opportunities not only for development but for you to gain recognition in your field. For example, you can contribute articles to a newsletter, or speak on a topic of interest at a gathering.

Participating in professional organizations is the key to developing collaborative relationships within the profession outside of your workplace. Attendance at programs is important, but discussion groups and other less formal options, such as interest groups, are also ideal forums for information-sharing. Actively participating in the American Library Association or some other professional association has numerous benefits, including networking and getting to know colleagues with similar interests. Although the development benefits of doing this are very significant, time and money are important factors that you need to take into consideration. You also need to review your development and career goals in order to determine which organizations will be the best fit for you.

If your interests and career goals are broad, you may want to explore opportunities for participating in the ALA or one of its many divisions and affiliates, chapters, or related groups and organizations (www.ala.org/aboutala/). For new ALA members who are just beginning to explore participation in professional organizations, the New Members Round Table (www.ala.org/rt/nmrt/) provides a good introduction to the many possibilities for greater involvement in the ALA. As the organization that created the competencies that are the subject of this book, we certainly want to point out that the Reference and User Services Association (www.ala.org/rusa/about) is the organization within the ALA that focuses on reference services in all kinds of libraries.

Internationally, the International Federation of Library Associations and Institutions (IFLA, www.ifla.org) provides opportunities for individuals from around the world to share their expertise and network with each other. IFLA's Reference and Information Services Section (www.ifla.org/reference-and-information-services) promotes discussions on the role of reference work and the quality of that work in all types of libraries around the world, and hosts conferences and creates publications. *Wikipedia* (https://en.wikipedia.org/) under the "List of Library Associations" provides a good list of major library associations in Africa, Asia, the Caribbean, Europe, Latin America, North America, and Oceania. The ALA also provides a list of "Library Associations around the World" on its website (www.ala.org/aboutala/offices/iro/intlassocorgconf/libraryassociations).

Librarians interested in specialized subject areas may find a good home in one of the scholarly societies, in addition to professional library organizations. The American Council of Learned Societies Members (www.acls.org/societies/) is a good source to begin reviewing the possibilities for specialized subjects. The Society of American Archivists (https://www2.archivists.org/assoc-orgs) provides lists of archival organizations in the United States and Canada, international archival organizations, and allied professional organizations.

If your time and money are very limited, initially you may wish to focus on organizations that have a strong local presence. Certainly, associations for libraries at the state level tend to be more accessible to many individuals than national organizations because of the less arduous requirements for travel, and the opportunities to develop camaraderie within a regional group. For state library chapters, see the list at www.ala.org/groups/affiliates/chapters/state/stateregional. *Wikipedia* also provides a "List of U.S. State Library Associations." Some specific-area state organizations are particularly well-organized and offer training opportunities nationally. The North Carolina Library Association's (2018) Government Resources Section offers an excellent series of webinars entitled "Help! I'm an Accidental Government Information Librarian Webinars." Not only do these webinars provide learning opportunities for individuals no matter where they are located, but they also provide presentation opportunities, since the presenters in these webinars are from all over the world.

Sometimes joining an association is not enough. You should seek out other promising organizations that fit with your development and career goals. You

---

Chair sets a clear agenda and circulates it to members prior to each meeting.
1. Yes, very clear
2. Somewhat clear
3. No agenda prior to meeting

Chair identifies goals for the meeting and summarizes progress on the agenda's action items at end of meeting.
1. Yes, goals and progress evaluation
2. Very limited goal-setting and progress evaluation
3. No goal-setting or evaluation of progress

All members attend the meeting.
1. Yes, all present
2. Most present
3. Less than half present

Everyone appears to have reviewed the agenda and supporting information prior to the meeting.
1. Yes, all have
2. Only some have
3. No one has

Draft minutes of the last meeting were available shortly after the meeting.
1. Yes, promptly
2. Yes, but with delay of more than a few days
3. Not available until present meeting or later

Everyone is given an opportunity to express views is without prejudice.
1. Yes, everyone
2. Most people
3. Very few

Members who attended assigned meetings related to meeting business are given the opportunity to report back and share information acquired.
1. Yes, all
2. Yes, most
3. Yes, a few
4. None

If you could change one thing about the meeting process, what would it be?

SOURCE: Concepts adapted from Nicholas Spillios, Sally G. Reed, Donna McDonald, and Alan Smith. 2008. "A Library Board's Practical Guide to Board Self-Evaluation." United for Libraries: Association of Library Trustees, Advocates, Friends and Foundations. http://www.ala.org/united/sites/ala.org.united/files/content/training/trustee_academy/board-self-evaluation.pdf.

FIGURE 3.5 *How Effective Are Your Meetings?*

can become active through committees or similar groups, and explore a variety of opportunities until you find a good fit with your goals and interests.

Assessing Development Efforts for Developing Collaborative Relationships within the Profession to Enhance Service to Users

Identifying desirable professional networks plays a key role in building and enhancing your expertise. A first step is to explore and establish the areas in which you have or wish to develop professional expertise. After you have participated in promising groups, you can reflect upon and assess the value of each of these networks through a simple group assessment of the process after each formal or informal meeting of the group (figure 3.5). Professional networks are also important in helping you to provide the most successful service in your library. The "Self-Assessment Checklist for Follow-up" (figure 1.2) is a useful tool for determining how effectively the professional expertise of other colleagues is used in providing patrons with the highest-quality answers. The "Checklist for Follow-up" is also a useful tool for peer coaching when follow-up is an agreed-upon performance area for evaluation.

DEVELOPS AND MAINTAINS PARTNERSHIPS BEYOND THE LIBRARY PROFESSION TO STRENGTHEN SERVICES TO USERS

Competencies for Developing and Maintaining Partnerships beyond the Library Profession to Strengthen Services to Users

Developing and maintaining partnerships beyond the library and the profession play a vital role in strengthening services to users. Community relationships and partnerships are an important vehicle for updating information on your community's evolving information-seeking needs and its perceptions of the quality and effectiveness of your library's existing services. Moreover, partnerships are extremely useful for launching collaboratively designed, innovative services.

The typical behavioral strategies suggested in the RUSA "Professional Competencies" that demonstrate competencies related to general community relationships are:

- Identifies partners who are able to contribute relevant knowledge and expertise
- Communicates effectively with partners to ensure mutual understanding of goals, objectives, and values
- Forms partnerships to improve existing systems and to develop new products and services

Development Methods for Developing and Maintaining Partnerships beyond the Library Profession to Strengthen Services to Users

Collaboration is one of the six qualities that the global design firm IDEO measures as essential to innovation; these six qualities are purpose, looking out, experimentation, collaboration, empowerment, and refinement. IDEO defines collaboration as "working together across business functions to approach opportunities and challenges from all angles." Collaboration is also "the degree to which employees of different roles and within different departments work together to bring new ideas forward. Organizations with a high collaboration score tend to create multi-disciplined teams where members with different skills respect and value each other's craft" (IDEO, n.d.). The IDEO concept of collaboration can also be applied to working together across community organizations in order "to approach opportunities and challenges from all angles."

Starting close to home, you can explore the options for getting involved in local (nonlibrary) professional organizations. Galston, Huber, Johnson, and Long (2012) suggest that by becoming active in local organizations, librarians can embed themselves in those organizations and thereby extend the outreach of the library. Additionally, involvement in leadership roles in local organizations may offer more opportunities to develop your leadership skills than seeking them through national-level organizations. Other organizations offer development opportunities with local support and guidance, such as Toastmasters International (www.toastmasters.org), a nonprofit educational organization that teaches public speaking and leadership skills through a worldwide network of meeting locations.

If one is in a large enough area to have enough folks with the same interests, one can become active in a local group, such as Rails (https://www.railslibraries.info/about), which provides continuing education and networking in northern and west-central Illinois.

Your local city and county website will list boards, commissions, and community partner organizations such as Friends, foundations, environmental organizations, community nonprofits, youth organizations, business and professional organizations, and service organizations. Compatible library partners have been identified in a TechSoup for Libraries (2012) Cookbook as:

- business/chambers of commerce
- community services organizations/associations/clubs
- cultural groups
- economic development organizations
- educational organizations
- ethnic organizations
- family service organizations
- financial representatives
- government/political representatives
- health organizations
- legal organizations
- library representatives
- media representatives
- organizations of/for people with disabilities
- professional groups
- religious groups and organizations
- senior centers/service organizations
- technology experts
- women's centers/service organizations
- youth service organizations

A good initial development project is to become actively involved in an organization that appears to have potential as a partner. Join the organization, and get to know the goals and interests of its active members. Another approach is to become active in the local government of the community. The Aspen Institute Dialogue on Public Libraries (www.libraryvision.org/) provides an action guide for reenvisioning public libraries, community stories, and other relevant materials. The document "Local Libraries Advancing Community Goals, 2016" (International City/County Management Association, 2017) identifies five top community priorities in which local governments see libraries playing an important role:

- access to high-speed Internet service
- digital literacy
- early childhood education
- primary and secondary school attainment
- online learning/virtual learning

Community partnerships between school library media specialists and academic librarians in the area of information literacy instruction also may benefit the top priorities of the local community. Godbey (2013) notes that collaboration between school library media specialists and academic librarians requires:

- clearly defined practical goals
- clearly defined leadership structure and participant roles
- equality
- genuine personal commitment from all parties
- administrative support
- evaluation
- communication

The Pacific Library Partnership (2018) provides several examples of successful school-library partnerships throughout the United States. In an example overseas, collaboration between public librarians and secondary school teachers in Finland was not only rewarding, especially in joint teaching situations, but also resulted in a model for integrating information literacy with problem-based learning (Pietikainen, Kortelainen, and Siklander, 2017). Another source of current public library collaborations with community partners is the Urban Libraries Council (https://www.urbanlibraries.org). Information on partnerships in this website is available under several pages: "Innovations," "Initiatives," and "Publications," including a "Leadership Brief: Partners Achieving Community Outcomes" (Urban Libraries Council, 2016), which gives opportunities and examples of libraries supporting community leadership priorities.

Building healthy communities by improving access to credible health information is an area with great potential for collaboration. For example, public libraries have collaborated with the National Library of Medicine, the Queen's Health Network (Cabello and Butler, 2017), and the Washington University School of Medicine (Engeszer et al., 2016).

Within the academic community, the most important collaborations are partnerships between librarians and teaching faculty that enhance student learning. Two recent articles develop models that go far beyond the librarian's traditional "one-shot" lecture for a class: Kenedy and Monty (2011) and Diaz and Mandernach (2017). In these extended collaborations, librarians must not only teach a class but also be involved in curriculum and syllabus development, post-class instruction, and mentoring students. Developing relationships that lead to partnerships with faculty requires patience, expertise, follow-through, and responsiveness. The Association of College and Research Libraries' program Assessment in Action, which involved over 200 campus teams led by librarians, built librarians' competencies in initiating partnerships with individuals and departments across campuses, leading team-based activities, managing the process and practice of assessment, and communicating the library's contributions toward fulfilling the institution's goals for student success (Malenfant and Brown, 2017).

Assessing Development Efforts for Developing and Maintaining Partnerships beyond the Library Profession to Strengthen Services to Users

In this assessment scenario, you should first establish your goals and a plan for making contacts in the community whose potential knowledge and expertise are of value to the library. Then you should maintain a log of contacts and an accompanying reflective journal that will assist you in evaluating your skill and knowledge in building relationships within the community (figure 3.6).

A brief but useful assessment tool for evaluating collaboration potential is the "Evaluating Potential Partners" worksheet (figure 3.7). The Cornell University "Partnership Evaluation Rubric" (figure 3.8), with some modification for the type of partnership,

---

Date: _____ Time: _____

Name, Address, E-mail, Phone of Community Contact

Goal for Community Contact

Degree to Which Contact Was Successful in Meeting Goal

Reflection on Skills and Knowledge Contributing to Success, including

- Assessment of effectiveness in establishing mutual understanding of goals, objectives, and values,
- Assessment of success in identifying partnership possibilities for enhancing or developing new products and services.

Future Plans

FIGURE 3.6 *Reflection on General Community Relationships*

can serve as a useful tool to assess collaboration potential in crucial areas: mutual benefits and common areas of interest, governance, decision-making, resources, and software development process.

The Wilder Foundation's "Collaboration Factors Inventory" (Mattessich, Murray-Close, and Monsey, 2001) provides a detailed measure for evaluating the potential of organizations for collaboration. The factors assessed are the group's history of collaboration/cooperation in the community; group seen as legitimate leader in the community; favorable political and social climate; mutual respect, understanding, and trust; appropriate cross-section of members; members see collaboration as in their self-interest; ability to compromise; members share a stake in both the process and outcome; multiple layers of participation; flexibility; development of clear roles and policy guidelines; adaptability; appropriate pace of development; open and frequent communication; established informal relationships and communication links; concrete attainable goals and objectives; shared vision; unique purpose; sufficient funds, staff materials and time; and skilled leadership.

There are many items to consider when strategically choosing partners in order to ensure that the potential partner will assist in supporting and advancing your mission. This worksheet asks questions to guide your thinking process when assessing potential partners.

Recommended data collection, analyses, and interpretation: this "Evaluating Potential Partners" (EPP) worksheet is a qualitative measure of the perceived value and benefits of establishing and maintaining partnerships that should be addressed as part of a discussion of key members of your organization who have responsibility for establishing and maintaining relationships with your program's partners. The items are designed to be an organizational self-assessment of perceived willingness and capacity to engage in a partnering relationship. For each item members are to consider, you should discuss and come to an agreement as to the individual's, group's, or organization's partnership potential specific to: a) type; b) audience targeted; c) compatibility of values; d) benefit and challenges; e) mutual goals and aims; f) purpose [intended outcomes]; g) quality; and h) resources. Members are to take time and engage in a discussion that allow for agreements and disagreements on each item to be aired. Your team members' answers (second column) should reflect a consensus (mutual agreement) for each item that would lead to an overall decision about the viability of a potential partner(s).

Questions	Your Answers
Think about what type of organization would be most beneficial to pursue. Is it a nonprofit? Is it religious in nature? Is it large or small? Describe the organization *(Organization Type)*	
What audiences are you trying to reach and who would be most helpful in reaching that audience? *(Target Audience)*	
What benefits would this organization provide? What are the drawbacks?*(Benefits and Challenges)*	
Is this organization or individual well-regarded in the community? Connecting yourself with an organization that has a bad reputation may hurt your position in the community. *(Benefits and Challenges)*	

FIGURE 3.7 *Evaluating Potential Partners*

FIGURE 3.7 • *Evaluating Potential Partners* (cont.)

Questions	Your Answers
What does each organization want to accomplish by working together? *(Goals, Aims, and Objectives)*	
Is there sufficient trust and commitment to support these kinds of relationships? *(Quality)*	
Are there resources available for this kind of organizational relationship, such as time, skills, client understanding, financial resources, community support, commitment, and health and human resources? If not, can those resources be accessed? *(Resources)*	
How do the organization's values fit with yours? You will find managing a partnership much more difficult if your mission and goals do not align with	each other. List your organization's values and your potential partner's values and see where they align: *(Compatibility of Values)*

Your organization's values	Your potential partner's values

SOURCE: U.S. Department of Health and Human Services, Office of Adolescent Health. 2017. "Evaluating Potential Partners." https://www.hhs.gov/ash/oah/sites/default/files/1-4_evaluating_potential_partners_0.pdf.

To distinguish partnerships from simple transactional relationships, we define partnerships as having the following characteristics. A partnership

- requires seed funding from one or more partners, or an external source, and/or dedicated staff time;
- provides mutual benefits to all partners;
- requires shared risks and responsibilities for all partners; and
- results in measurable outcomes.

Partnership evaluation questions

1. Provide a brief, high-level description of the partnership (context for the questions that follow).
2. General questions
   a. Why do we wish to engage with this particular partner (or why is this a good potential partner)?
   b. What type of organization is the partner organization (e.g., nonprofit, for-profit)? Is it mission-driven?
   c. Describe the partner's history, track record, and standing in its community.
   d. How does the partnership advance arXiv's priorities?
   e. What are the potential opportunity costs?
   f. Why does the partner want to engage with us?
   g. Does the partner share a vision, and if it does, what is it?
   h. What evidence is there of the partner's commitment to the success of this partnership?
   i. What are the potential benefits to arXiv and to the partner?
   j. What are the potential risks to arXiv and to the partner?
   k. What is the partner's tolerance for risk?
   l. Is there a reasonable exit strategy (explain)?
   m. Note any other considerations/concerns.
3. Governance, decision-making
   a. How will governance be handled?
   b. How will priorities be set?
   c. How will decisions be made?
   d. How will IP be managed between the partners?
   e. What considerations or requirements might constrain or impact our ability to collaborate on grant proposals? What will the role of the partner be?
   f. Note any other considerations/concerns.
4. Resources
   a. What arXiv and partner resources are required to start and sustain the partnership?
   b. What is the partner willing to contribute?
   c. What costs will be incurred and how will they be distributed between the partners?
   d. Note any other considerations/concerns.
5. Software development process
   a. How will the work get done? Co-development, parallel, etc.
   b. What development practices will be employed?
   c. Note any other considerations/concerns.

NOTE: Adapted from Koltay et al. 2016. "Partnerships: Assessing When to Start, When to Hold, and When to Fold." *College & Research Libraries News* 77, no. 2. http://crln.acrl.org/content/77/2/62.full.

SOURCE: Gail Steinhart, Scholarly Communication Librarian at Digital Scholarship & Preservation Services, Cornell University Library. (2017). arXiv Partnership Evaluation Rubric. Retrieved from https://confluence.cornell.edu/plugins/servlet/mobile#content/view/343200050

FIGURE 3.8 *arXiv Partnership Evaluation Rubric*

CHAPTER **four**

Information Literacy

SECTION 5D: DEVELOPS APPROPRIATE EXPERTISE IN INFORMATION LITERACY AND INSTRUCTION SKILLS AND ABILITIES, INCLUDING TEXTUAL, DIGITAL, VISUAL, NUMERICAL, AND SPATIAL LITERACIES

Give a man to fish, and feed him for a day.
Teach a man to fish, and feed him for a lifetime.
—Ancient Chinese proverb

This chapter is about developing and assessing your knowledge, skills, abilities, and behaviors associated with section 5D of the RUSA "Professional Competencies," a section entitled "Develops Appropriate Expertise in Information Literacy and Instruction Skills and Abilities, including Textual, Digital, Visual, Numerical, and Spatial Literacies." The topics covered are information literacy and integrating literacy concepts into the full range of services, learning and engagement strategies, and learner-centered teaching environments. According to the ALA, libraries promote the "creation, maintenance, and enhancement of a learning society, encouraging its members to work with educators, government officials, and organizations in coalitions to initiate and support comprehensive efforts to ensure that school, public, academic, and special libraries in every community cooperate to provide lifelong learning services to all" (American Library Association, 2010). Given that libraries not only connect users with information, but also teach users how to find information for themselves, RUSA encourages reference staff to develop their competencies in a variety of information literacy skills, and to develop the skills employed in helping users to learn and become information-literate.

Just what is information literacy? A wide variety of definitions abound. The American Library Association (1989) defines information literacy as a set of abilities requiring individuals to "recognize when information is needed and have the ability to locate, evaluate, and effectively use the needed information." Another definition suggests that "skepticism, judgment, free thinking, questioning, and understanding" should be considered essential if one is to become information-literate (Gillmor, 2010). UNESCO (2017) suggests that media literacy and information literacy work together to "empower citizens to understand the functions of media and other information providers, to critically evaluate their content, and to make informed decisions as users and producers of information and media content."

Many other definitions of information literacy have been advanced. *Wikipedia* (2018a) includes a summary of the term focused on U.S. perspectives, and the Chartered Institute of Library Information Professionals' Information Literacy Group (2018) provides an interesting gathering of definitions by the library associations in the United Kingdom and beyond, as well as related literacies.

To explore people's views of information literacy, Christine Bruce used phenomenography, a research method that investigates the qualitatively different ways in which people experience or think about something. Bruce (2014) found that people think of information literacy in seven unique ways: as information technology, as information sources, as information process, as information control, as knowledge construction, as knowledge extension, or as wisdom or combining this information use with ethics. This research highlights how people approach information literacy with different experiences, expectations, and understandings. Bruce went on to identify different ways that information literacy can be taught using these frames: content frame, competency frame, learning to learn frame, personal relevance frame, social impact frame, and relational frame (Bruce, Edwards, and Lupton, 2006).

The American Association of School Librarians' (2018b) recent standards for student learning are anchored by six foundations—inquire, include, collaborate, curate, explore, and engage—which are also shared with their standards for school librarians and school libraries. This approach grew out of the "Big6 skills" research process developed by Mike Eisenberg and Bob Berkowitz (2017), which identified the process as task definition, information-seeking strategies, location and access, use of information, synthesis, and evaluation.

The Association of College and Research Libraries (2016), in an attempt to be less prescriptive and include other notions of literacies, created a "Framework for Information Literacy for Higher Education" which offers the following set of core ideas: authority is constructed and contextual, information creation as a process, information has value, research as inquiry, scholarship as conversation, and searching as strategic exploration.

While some public libraries may not see a clear role for themselves in teaching information literacy to their constituents, others do see a clear role in improving people's web and media literacy skills and thus indirectly increasing their participation in the democratic process, without venturing into political advocacy. "Civic engagement is neither pro-right nor pro-left on the political spectrum; it is pro-democracy" (Coward, McClay, and Garrido, 2018, 20).

It may be necessary, depending on the responsibilities of the reference librarian, to develop expertise in other literacies as well. The title itself of section 5D of the RUSA "Professional Competencies" mentions a few: textual, digital, visual, numerical, and spatial literacies. Textual literacy for most of us means being able to read, understand, analyze, evaluate, and write text documents, whether print or online. Digital literacy is the ability to locate, evaluate, interpret, and communicate information in digital environments. "Digital literacy is the ability to use information and communication technologies to find, evaluate, create, and communicate information, requiring both cognitive and technical skills," according to the American Library Association (2013). Visual literacy is the ability to critically read, interpret, and create visual images. Numerical literacy, of course, relates to numbers and mastering the basic symbols and processes of arithmetic. Spatial literacy relates to the use of space, and specifically the ability to use maps, mapping, and geographical and spatial data. More and more librarians are being asked to develop expertise in data literacy, which is the ability to read, understand, create, and communicate data as meaningful information. Another literacy that particularly pertains to reference workers is that of multicultural literacy, an awareness that culture impacts our behavior and beliefs, and impacts how we interact with others. For further discussions of the variety of literacies, see the article "Literacy" in *Wikipedia* (2018c) and The Current's blogs on literacy (http://thecurrent.educatorinnovator.org/post/key word/literacy). The Current is an open publishing site of the Educator Innovator online hub, which shares resources and stories about what educators are observing, doing, and reflecting upon with regard to learning and teaching.

DEFINES INFORMATION LITERACY

Competencies for Defining Information Literacy

The typical behavioral strategies suggested in the RUSA "Professional Competencies" that demonstrate competencies related to defining information literacy are:

- Creates a personal definition of information literacy
- Develops a shared understanding with colleagues
- Collaborates with users and colleagues to help the institution or organization develop its own definition of information literacy

Development Methods for Defining Information Literacy

Given the wide variety of definitions and conceptual frameworks for information literacy, creating your own personal definition of information literacy is a critical first step to understanding the topic. Reading the literature mentioned in the opening section of this chapter is a good first step. Reading blogs is a good way to keep up with changes in thinking in the field of information literacy. There are also many opportunities to discuss information literacy with

---

Information Literacy Blogs and Discussion Lists

Blogs

Information Literacy Weblog (international focus), http://information-literacy.blogspot.com/

Information Wants to Be Free, by Meridith Farkas, https://meredith.wolfwater.com/wordpress/

ACRLog, https://acrlog.org/

In the Library with the Lead Pipe, http://inthelibrarywiththeleadpipe.org/

Top School Library Blogs, https://www.teacher certificationdegrees.com/top-blogs/school-library/

Discussion Lists

- ili-1, @lists.ala.org http://lists.ala.org/sympa/info/ili-1
- lirt-1 @lists.ala.org http://lists.ala.org/sympa/info/lirt-1
- infolit–Information Literacy Discussion List (K-20 Collaboration)\ infolit@lists.ala.org http://lists.ala.org/sympa/info/infolit

colleagues. Look for online forums, and discussion groups at state and regional association meetings, as well as at national meetings. If you are in a larger metropolitan area, you may have a local group as well.

In addition to taking courses in teaching or learning about information literacy at a local college, one could consider attending workshops that are specifically designed for librarians who teach the subject. State and regional associations typically offer some type of workshop on information literacy on a regular basis. Other alternatives would be to attend an institute that focuses on digital learning, while a more time-intensive approach would be to take a course on information literacy at a school of library and information science, some of which are offered online rather than in-person.

Working within your organization to develop a sense of information literacy can be a long-term endeavor. On college campuses, working with faculty to develop a curriculum that includes information literacy, or getting involved in teaching improvement workshops, can help place librarians at the table when these issues are discussed. Some academic environments have shifted the teaching of information literacy skills from librarians to teaching faculty (Smith, 2006). Esther Grassian (2009) maintains web pages that have exercises and resources to assist teachers in improving students' information literacy skills. A recent study by Demasson, Partridge, and Bruce (2017) found that public librarians in Queensland, Australia, defined information literacy in four ways: as intellectual process, technical skills, navigating the social world, and gaining the desired result, which should be useful in designing and delivering public library information literacy programs.

Jane Harding (2008) identifies a number of strengths for public libraries as providers of information literacy instruction: public libraries have a recognized role as a place of learning; and they have information literacy expertise, a broad client base, lifelong contact with members of the community, opportunities for teachable moments, partnerships; and they are key access points to resources. So

---

Courses for Enhancing Teaching and Learning Skills

Institutes
- ACRL Information Literacy Immersion Program, a weeklong intensive training that is typically offered each summer, www.ala.org/acrl/conferences/immersion
- Librarians Active Learning Institute at Dartmouth, https://www.dartmouth.edu/~library/home/about/lali/

Library and Information Studies Courses
- ACRL, "Library Instruction Courses Offered by Accredited Master's Programs in Library and Information Studies," https://acrl.ala.org/IS/instruction-tools-resources-2/professional-development/library-instruction-courses-offered-by-accredited-masters-programs-in-library-and-information-studies
- The ACRL Instruction Section maintained a list of courses at schools of library and information until the summer of 2014, which can still serve as a guideline for schools and courses to explore. This list can be updated by consulting the websites of the ALA Accredited Programs: www.ala.org/educationcareers/accreditedprograms.

WebJunction
- "Design for Learning: 21st Century Online Teaching and Learning Skills for Library Workers," https://www.webjunction.org/news/webjunction/design-for-learning-course.html
- "Online Training Resources," https://www.webjunction.org/explore-topics/create-deliver-training/online-training-resources.html

American Library Association Courses
- ALA, "eLearning/Online Learning," covers webinars, courses, workshops, e-forums, and more, www.ala.org/educationcareers/elearning
- Brooklyn Public Library, "Teacher Lab," https://bklynlibrary.teachable.com/p/teacherlab. The Teacher Lab is an information literacy and research skills course for K-12 educators (teachers and school librarians). The course is designed to help educators feel more confident in finding a variety of texts and media for their classrooms.

public libraries are perfectly poised to reach out to their community to explore their literacy needs; for example, by supporting community organizations' workshops on information literacy skills in a digital environment. Libraries that hesitate to venture into this arena should be sure to check the many online sites that cover this kind of content. An example is Mozilla's "Web Literacy" web pages (https://learning.mozilla.org/en-US/web-literacy), which discuss twenty-first-century skills such as problem-solving, communication, creativity, and collaboration in a framework for entry-level skills; a concept map is provided for writing, reading, and participating. Participants can explore the map by selecting an area, and then reading further to see definitions, activities, and tutorials.

Assessing Development Efforts for Defining Information Literacy

Can you articulate your definition of information literacy? If you were riding up the elevator with the provost of your university or standing in line to get coffee with the president of your library board, a simple assessment is whether you can articulate and share your definition of the term in two minutes or less. Most of us have a sense of what we mean by information literacy, but have not taken the time to articulate it clearly enough to convey that sense to others. If you have had discussions in your department about information literacy, you should be able to come up with a shared definition.

One way of knowing if the conversations you're having in your broader organization have been fruitful is if the term *information literacy* has been worked into your organization's documents. At a university, for example, the term *information literacy* should be showing up in curriculum documents in individual departments, as well as in general education requirements as a part of critical thinking skills. In a municipal environment, *information literacy* might be a term that the city would be thinking about in terms of training municipal employees, or in terms of its goals for its citizenry.

INTEGRATES INFORMATION LITERACY CONCEPTS INTO THE FULL RANGE OF LIBRARY SERVICES, FROM CLASSROOM INSTRUCTION TO COMMUNITY PROGRAMS TO ONE-ON-ONE REFERENCE AND INSTRUCTION

Competencies for Integrating Information Literacy Concepts into the Full Range of Library Services, from Classroom Instruction to Community Programs to One-on-One Reference and Instruction

The typical behavioral strategies suggested in the RUSA "Professional Competencies" that demonstrate competencies related to integrating information literacy concepts are:

- Helps individuals to assess their own information needs, to differentiate among sources of information, and to develop skills to effectively identify, locate, and evaluate sources
- Adjusts communication style and methods according to learner needs and context
- Leads or facilitates discussion of controversial or unexpected issues in a skillful, nonjudgmental manner that helps individuals to learn
- Designs interactive presentations and exploratory activities
- Incorporates communication technologies to provide assistance to learners in and outside the classroom
- Requests feedback from users and peers on instruction-related communication skills and uses feedback to improve individual skills
- Develops and implements assessments that encompass the various aspects of learning in order to improve instruction

Development Methods for Integrating Information Literacy Concepts into the Full Range of Library Services, from Classroom Instruction to Community Programs to One-on-One Reference and Instruction

According to James Elmborg (2002), "perhaps the hardest part of learning to teach is learning to ask questions rather than supply answers." He goes on to hypothesize that as librarians, we are taught that our job is to answer questions, so we have "to unlearn that definition of our job in order to teach at the reference desk. Instead, we must see our job as helping students to answer their own questions" (p. 459).

Questions. The use of questions, in both a group and a one-on-one setting, is a great technique for helping individuals to assess their own information needs and participate in the differentiation of sources, as well as find and evaluate sources. According to Tofade, Elsner, and Haines (2013), teachers predominantly ask lower-level cognitive questions that do not effectively stimulate critical thinking. They suggest that instructors should use three types of questions to be effective: exploratory, spontaneous, and focused ones:

- *Exploratory questions* are used to find out how much individuals know about a particular issue. Five types of exploratory questions have been identified by Butler Scientifics (2017): role, characterization, prediction, differentiation, and thresholds.
- *Spontaneous questions* are used to probe an individual's thoughts in an effort to get him to explore his beliefs and assumptions. Susan Avery and David Ward (2010) share some sample exploratory questions, such as "User is asked what aspects of his or her topic he would like to expand on," or "User is asked to identify key concepts and terminology associated with his or her topic."
- *Focused questions* narrow the content down to specific issues, and force individuals to reflect on their perspectives. An example of a focused question: "User is asked what searches he or she has tried already, and about the results retrieved" (Avery and Ward, 2010).

Are you curious about developing "essential questions"? Check out *Essential Questions* by Jay McTighe and Grant Wiggins (2013). Although this book is geared toward essential questions to help promote deeper understanding on the part of students, it also includes valuable insights for educators who are working with educators. Vogt, Brown, and Isaacs (2003) suggest that "powerful questions" stimulate reflective thinking, challenge assumptions, are thought-provoking, generate energy and a vector to explore, channel inquiry, promise insight, are broad and enduring, touch a deeper meaning, and evoke more questions.

Avery and Ward (2010) suggest that the "overall search strategy is communicated to the user, including which resources will be searched, which search terms will be used, and what types of information are contained in the selected sources" (p. 51). This last example is a good illustration of modeling for the user what strategies should be used. Ross, Nilsen, and Radford (2009) suggest that the reference librarian should "be a role model for the skills of finding information in libraries. Provide a running commentary as you go through the information search process with a child or teenager . . . describe aloud each step—a form of inclusion" (p. 147).

Feedback and Assessments. The use of student learning assessments is critical to know whether or not the instruction is successful, if the students have learned, and how to improve the design of the instruction. Donald Kirkpatrick presented four different levels of evaluation for a training program, which can apply to other learning environments as well (*Wikipedia*, 2017). In the first level (Reaction), instructors determine the students' reaction to learning; that is, what they thought and felt about the instruction. But because some of these measures merely ask about the students' satisfaction and their reaction to environmental factors, they are of limited use in determining if learning occurred. In the second level (Learning), the instructor tries to determine if there is a resulting increase in knowledge and/or skills, and if there are changes in attitudes. Often this evaluation occurs in the form of a knowledge demonstration or test. In the third level (Behavior), the students' behavior is examined to see if there has been a transfer of knowledge, skills, and/or attitudes to them. Often this evaluation is done through observation on the job after several months, and so it is a difficult one for classroom instructors and librarians to implement. The final level (Results) is the results that occurred because of attendance and participation in the training or instruction program. Since this often cannot be determined until a student has graduated and is out in the workforce, it is much more difficult to administer.

A number of classroom assessment techniques (CATs) have been developed, though, that can help instructors get to the second level of assessment, learning. In general, CATs are simple, nongraded, anonymous, in-class activities that are designed to give you and your students useful feedback on the teaching-learning process as it is happening. Classic CATs techniques that are still relevant and widely used today are treated below.

Brookfield (2017) suggests four "lenses" or perspectives that will assist teachers in critically reflecting on the value of their teaching:

> *Students' eyes*—knowing how your students experience learning by checking in with them.
> *Colleagues' perceptions*—critical friends who can help you check your assumptions and open up new perspectives.
> *Personal experience*—reflecting upon your teaching experience in order to improve your practice.
> *Theory*—the scholarly literature provides an opportunity to review your teaching from different perspectives.

The University of Sydney's Faculty of Arts and Social Sciences (2017) has applied Brookfield's four lenses in the evaluation of teaching. Its "Four Lenses: Evaluation Resources" web pages provide many useful examples of methods of evaluating teaching from each of the four perspectives.

Barkley and Major (2016) develop assessment techniques further and provide fifty easy-to-implement active learning techniques using Fink's (2005) "Taxonomy of Significant Learning" as an organizational framework, embedding assessment within active learning activities. Bowles-Terry and Kvenild (2015) adapt twenty-four proven assessment tools and apply them in library-specific situations,

---

Classic Classroom Assessment Techniques

- *The background knowledge probe* is a short, simple questionnaire given to students at the start of a course, or before the introduction of a new unit, lesson, or topic. It is designed to uncover students' preconceptions.
- The *minute paper* tests how students are gaining knowledge, or not. The instructor ends class by asking students to write a brief response to the following questions: "What was the most important thing you learned during this class?" and "What important question remains unanswered?"
- The *muddiest point* is one of the simplest CATs to help assess where students are having difficulties. The technique consists of asking students to jot down a quick response to one question: "What was the muddiest point in [the lecture, discussion, homework assignment, film, etc.]?" The term "muddiest" means "most unclear" or "most confusing."
- The *what's the principle?* CAT is useful in courses requiring problem-solving. After students figure out what type of problem they are dealing with, they often must decide what principle(s) to apply in order to solve the problem. This CAT provides students with a few problems and asks them to state the principle that best applies to each problem.

Source: Thomas Angelo and Patricia Cross. 1993. *Classroom Assessment Techniques*. 2nd ed. San Francisco: Jossey-Bass.

grouping them by goal. For example, for assessing prior knowledge and understanding, they present the tools of the background knowledge check, preconception check, focused listing, minute paper, and muddiest point, along with multiple examples of the context in which each could be used.

Assessing Development Efforts for Integrating Information Literacy Concepts into the Full Range of Library Services, from Classroom Instruction to Community Programs to One-on-One Reference and Instruction

In order to assess one's integration of information literacy instruction into reference services, Pierce College has developed an end-of-shift checklist (figure 4.1) which not only asks questions relating to the RUSA "Guidelines for Behavioral Performance" on approachability, the use of reference interview techniques, and self-evaluation of one's knowledge of reference sources, but also whether or not the reference staff member has assessed the student's learning.

Another technique to assess your development efforts is to use the Brookfield (2017) lenses of self, students, colleagues, and the literature.

Self lens: Teachers may focus on their experiences as a teacher in order to reveal aspects of their pedagogy that may need adjustment or strengthening.
- Keep documentation of ways in which you've improved your teaching
- Reflect after each session what you would like to try next time
- Create a teaching philosophy statement
- Create a teaching portfolio

Student lens: Engaging with students' views of the learning environment can lead to more responsive teaching. The following are evaluations and assessments that can provide cues to improve teaching and learning.
- Student tests and quizzes
- Classroom assessment techniques
- Surveys

Rank the following from 5 to 1: **5** = All the time, **3** = Sometimes, **1** = Not at all, **NA** = Not Applicable

____ Was I *approachable and accessible* to students using all areas of the library?
- Make eye contact?
- Acknowledge those waiting?
- Give my full attention?
- Walk around/roving reference?

____ Did I use effective *reference interview* skills?
- Ask open and closed questions?
- Restate users' questions/needs?
- Get parameters of assignment?
- What have they already tried?

____ Did I adequately demonstrate how to use a *variety of relevant resources and strategies*?
- Catalogs (ours and others)? Specialized databases? Indexes? Internet?
- Subject headings vs. keywords?
- Boolean searching?
- Reference and circulating?
- Call numbers and organization?

____ *Did I know* our print and electronic resources well enough to be able to effectively help the students on the topics they were inquiring about?

____ Did I *follow up* with those students who proceeded to work independently?

____ If a student's need went partially or fully unmet, *did I offer alternatives*?
- ILL?
- Other libraries?
- "Reference Info Request" form?

____ Did I attempt to **assess** the student's learning?
- Asked an assessment question to obtain evidence of student learning
- Witness any "lightbulb" moments?
- Student's parting expressions? (Confident, satisfied, excited, confused, bored, anxious, overwhelmed, frustrated, exhausted)

Were there *extenuating circumstances* today? (Students having crummy day, I had a crummy day, etc.)

What did I do well during this reference shift or learn about the way I work with students?

What will I try to *do differently* next time to enhance or improve student experience?

SOURCE: Pierce College, Lakewood and Puyallup, Washington

FIGURE 4.1 *Reference Desk: End-of-Shift Checklist*

- Focus groups
- Interviews
- Minute papers
- Journals

Peer lens: Your peers can highlight hidden habits in your teaching practice, and also provide innovative solutions to teaching problems. Furthermore, colleagues can be inspirational and provide you with support and solidarity.

- Peer observation of a teaching session
- Peer observation of a micro-teaching session. Micro-teaching is a teaching exercise undertaken in a short period of time (e.g., under ten minutes) with a small number of colleagues. After the exercise, participants provide you with feedback on your teaching. Micro-teaching can be used to test out teaching methods that you haven't tried before and to test the extent to which the teaching exercises/activities that you already use are aligned with class/unit outcomes. See Ben Miller's (2010) "Planning a Micro-Teaching Activity."

Literature lens: Teaching theory provides the vocabulary for teaching practice, and offers different ways to view and understand your teaching. You can utilize scholarly literature in your teaching and critical reflection.

An interesting approach to seeing how information literacy has been integrated into reference services is to use the list of instructional methods used in all types of libraries (figure 4.2) identified by Esther Grassian, and systematically identify which methods your particular library uses, and into which ones information literacy efforts have been incorporated.

Instructional Methods	Currently in Use in My Library	Evidence of Information Literacy Instruction Integration
Reference Desk		
Chat Reference		
Credit Courses		
Exhibits		
Flyers or Posters		
LibGuides or Websites		
One-Shots for Credit Courses		
One-Time Classes or Workshops		
Online Tutorials		
Online Checklists		
Printed Handouts or Guides		
Social Media Posts		
Videos		

SOURCE: Instructional Methods identified in Grassian, Esther (2018). Trustworthiness: What are we teaching? *Reference & User Services Quarterly* 57 (3) 165.

FIGURE 4.2 *Types of Instruction in All Types of Libraries*

DESIGNS AND IMPLEMENTS PRESENTATION AND COMMUNICATION STRATEGIES TO FOSTER LEARNING AND ENGAGEMENT

Competencies for Designing and Implementing Presentation and Communication Strategies to Foster Learning and Engagement

The typical behavioral strategies suggested in the RUSA "Professional Competencies" that demonstrate competencies related to designing and implementing presentation and communication strategies to foster learning and engagement are:

- Makes the best possible use of voice, eye contact, gestures, and active learning methods in order to keep face-to-face instruction lively and learners engaged
- Seeks to clarify confusing terminology, avoid excessive jargon, and use vocabulary appropriate for level of learners
- Presents instructional content in diverse ways (written, oral, visual, online, or using presentation software) and selects appropriate delivery methods according to learners' needs
- Scales presentation content and learning activities to the users' needs and how people learn, adjusting to the time, space, and technology available
- Practices or refines instruction content as necessary in order to achieve familiarity and confidence with the planned presentation

Development Methods for Designing and Implementing Presentation and Communication Strategies to Foster Learning and Engagement

Entire books and extensive websites have been published on effective teaching and presentation techniques. Therefore, teaching and presentation skills cannot be completely addressed in this chapter. Those serious about improving their teaching and presentation skills should seek additional resources. While most of the resources identified (below) are from the academic library literature, their information can easily be applied in a public library setting when teaching seniors how to use the Internet, providing literacy instruction to second-language English learners, assisting parents in reading to their children, and so on.

The Association of College and Research Libraries' Instruction Section (2017) has written a comprehensive document detailing the roles and strengths of teaching librarians. We have turned this into a checklist (figure 4.3) that can easily be used as a mechanism for analyzing your training and development needs.

In teaching, not only are excellent presentation skills needed, but one also needs to develop an awareness of how the students are receiving the information, processing it, and learning. Active learning competencies, which are discussed at the end of this chapter, are critical in this setting.

Keeping students involved, motivated, and actively learning is challenging for all educators, yet there is good advice on how to accomplish this. *Student Engagement Techniques* (Barkley, 2010) is a comprehensive resource that offers college teachers a dynamic model for engaging students and includes over one hundred tips, strategies, and techniques that have been proven to help teachers from a wide variety of disciplines and institutions motivate and connect with their students. The book's ready-to-use format shows how to apply each of the techniques in the classroom and includes purpose, preparation, procedures, examples, online implementation, variations and extensions, observations and advice, and key resources. A summary of the contents of Barkley's book is provided in figure 4.4. Another useful resource is the "Community College Survey of Student Engagement" (University of Texas at Austin, 2018), which uses five benchmarks for effective educational practice in order to measure the level of student engagement in the teaching process. See figure 4.5 for the five practices and a list of useful techniques related to each practice.

ADVOCATE	Not Yet	Progressing	Proficient	Advanced
Advocates for professional development opportunities and other forms of career advancement for teaching librarians.				
Communicates the value of information literacy to campus library colleagues.				
Advocates for the library's role in student learning and development across the curriculum.				
Partners with faculty to encourage information literacy within courses and within the curriculum.				
Engages with representatives of campus programs and initiatives to integrate information literacy into co-curricular activities				
Promotes and advances information literacy to library leaders and campus administrators.				
Advocates for information literacy in relationship to student success in the context of institutional learning goals or learning outcomes.				

COORDINATOR	Not Yet	Progressing	Proficient	Advanced
Collaborates effectively and diplomatically, contributing to developing a welcoming culture of inclusive excellence in teaching, learning, and student success.				
Encourages, leads, and empowers other teaching librarians in their professional development and workload management.				
Uses emotional intelligence and political acumen with highly developed, inclusive communication skills to navigate complex and sensitive situations.				
Collaborates in the development of campuswide information literacy initiatives and goals and facilitates change while generating trust, support, and commitment from administration and faculty partners.				
Creates and cultivates an environment of assessment and value for the information literacy program.				
Maintains a consistent and effective information literacy program by leading amidst changes in administration, resources, and funding.				
Assumes responsibility for assessment results, project management, and best practices for instruction programs.				

FIGURE 4.3 *Roles for Instruction Librarians: A Checklist for Developing Proficiencies*

(cont.)

FIGURE 4.3 *Roles for Instruction Librarians: A Checklist for Developing Proficiencies* (cont.)

INSTRUCTIONAL DESIGNER	Not Yet	Progressing	Proficient	Advanced
Analyzes the instructional environment, and targets instruction delivery toward appropriate audiences.				
Identifies learning needs of students, and creatively addresses identified needs across multiple contexts drawing on a repertoire of tools, methods, and theories.				
Defines goals and outcomes for learning experiences.				
Creates innovative and appealing lessons with supporting instructional materials aligned with and supporting learning outcomes.				
Assesses the success and impact of learning experiences and makes appropriate adjustments to improve student engagement and learning.				
Stays current with trends and innovations in learning and instructional technologies.				

LIFELONG LEARNER	Not Yet	Progressing	Proficient	Advanced
Pursues professional opportunities to improve and refresh teaching skills.				
Maintains currency in both pedagogy and information literacy across disciplines.				
Actively participates in discussions on teaching and learning with colleagues online and in other forums.				
Demonstrates openness to implementing new ideas and new pedagogical practices and to exploring new instructional technologies.				
Participates in local, regional, or national professional associations.				

LEADER	Not Yet	Progressing	Proficient	Advanced
Works to model effective change management.				
Builds and models a personal record of excellent instructional practice, including modeling new pedagogies.				
Establishes credibility with other librarians in the workplace.				
Creates an environment of positive learning, trust, and reflection, addressing pedagogical or instruction-related conflicts and encouraging the development of confidence in teaching.				

LEADER *(cont.)*	Not Yet	Progressing	Proficient	Advanced
Advocates for financial and other resources for the instructional program to support human resources and professional development.				
Contributes valuable perspectives as a participant across campus communities.				
Navigates, communicates, and operationalizes information literacy within and among campus entities and structures.				
Builds organizational authority with regard to informational literacy regardless of place within the organizational hierarchy.				

TEACHER	Not Yet	Progressing	Proficient	Advanced
Analyzes the needs of each teaching/learning setting, environment, or group and employs appropriate pedagogical techniques to meet those needs.				
Articulates goals and learning outcomes for information literacy instruction.				
Selects from a repertoire of pedagogies and techniques for diverse learners and learning contexts and experiments with innovative instructional techniques and tools.				
Creates a positive and interactive learning environment which recognizes the importance of context.				
Engages in assessment to ensure that instruction is meeting the defined learning outcomes.				
Demonstrates enthusiasm for teaching and learning and a commitment to professional development, lifelong learning, and reflective practice.				
Adapts concepts from professional documents and guidelines such as the "Framework for Information Literacy for Higher Education" in the design and content of instructional situations.				

TEACHING PARTNER	Not Yet	Progressing	Proficient	Advanced
Seeks out and engages teaching partners, remaining open to various ways of collaborating.				
Builds mutual respect, trust, and understanding with collaborators.				
Models and encourages effective collaboration with other teaching partners.				
Articulates the benefits of collaborating with the teaching librarian.				

(cont.)

FIGURE 4.3 *Roles for Instruction Librarians: A Checklist for Developing Proficiencies (cont.)*

TEACHING PARTNER *(cont.)*	Not Yet	Progressing	Proficient	Advanced
With other teaching partners, develops shared vision and goals for the collaboration.				
Negotiates the librarian's responsibilities and expectations for the instructional setting with collaborators.				
Brings information literacy perspective and expertise to the partnership.				

ADAPTED FROM: Association of College and Research Libraries, Instruction Section. April 28, 2017. "Roles and Strengths of Teaching Librarians." http://www.ala.org/acrl/standards/teachinglibrarians.

Fifty student engagement techniques are presented in the following seven categories:

Knowledge, Skills, Recall, and Understanding (chap. 12)

1. Background knowledge probe
2. Artifacts
3. Focused reading notes
4. Quotes
5. Stations
6. Team jeopardy
7. Seminar

Analysis and Critical Thinking (chap. 13)

8. Classify
9. Frames
10. Believing and doubting
11. Academic controversy
12. Split-room debate
13. Analytic teams
14. Book club
15. Small group tutorials

Synthesis and Creative Thinking (chap. 14)

16. Team concept maps
17. Variations
18. Letters
19. Role-play
20. Poster sessions
21. Class book
22. WebQuests

Problem-Solving (chap. 15)

23. What's the problem?
24. Think again!
25. Think-aloud-pair-problem-solving (TAPPS)
26. Proclamations
27. Send-a-problem
28. Case studies

Application and Performance (chap. 16)

29. Contemporary issues journal
30. Hearing the subject
31. Directed paraphrase
32. Insights-resources-applications
33. Jigsaw
34. Field trips

Attitudes and Values (chap. 17)

35. Autobiographical reflections
36. Dyadic interviews
37. Circular response
38. Ethical dilemmas
39. Connected communities
40. Stand where you are

Self-Awareness as Learners (chap. 18)

41. Learning logs
42. Critical incident questionnaire
43. Go for the goal
44. Post-test analysis

Learning and Study Skills (chap. 19)

45. In-class portfolio
46. Resource scavenger hunt
47. Formative quiz
48. Crib cards
49. Student-generated rubrics
50. Triad listening

SOURCE: Elizabeth F. Barkley. 2010. *Student Engagement Techniques: A Handbook for College Faculty.* San Francisco: Jossey-Bass.

FIGURE 4.4 *Techniques for Engaging Students in Learning*

1. Active and Collaborative Learning

Ideas include:

Think, pair, share
Minute papers
Writing activities
Brainstorming
Games related to the subject; debates staged in class
Group work
Subject summaries
Research or independent study
Use technology
Case studies
Simulations, role-playing, or labs
Tutor or work with classmates
Spice up lectures with challenging questions
Provide red, yellow, and green cards to students to use in communicating with you during lecture
Wait up to a minute after a question has been posed or after asking "What are your questions?"
Incorporate service learning

2. Student Effort

Ideas include:

Ask students to complete a self-assessment about their learning habits
Require multiple drafts of a paper or an assignment
Award points for students who have answered questions
Require multiple sources as references for papers or projects
Provide a recommended reading list and assign bonus points for completing extra reading
Communicate expected amount of time students should spend preparing for class
Help students set challenging goals for their own learning
Expect students to complete their assignments promptly
Meet with students who fall behind to discuss their study habits, schedules, and questions
Appeal to students who need extrinsic motivation

3. Academic Challenge

Ideas include:

Ask students to analyze idea, experience, or theory as a small-group learning activity
Provide a case study assignment
Ask students to complete an assignment requiring judging the value or soundness of information
Choose textbook and readings that appropriately challenge students
Require written papers
Require oral presentations

4. Student-Faculty Interaction

Ideas include:

Provide first-day exercise in which students share their experiences and goals
Ice breakers to get to know each other
Interact with enthusiasm and energy
Treat students as human beings – Ask how they are doing
Communicate regularly through e-mail or other electronic media
Get to know students by name
Advise students about career and learning opportunities
Share experiences, values, and attitudes
Show an interest in students' activities and life
Prepare classroom exercises that provide immediate feedback on how well students are doing
Return examinations and papers within a week with written feedback on them
Use software that allows you to give feedback regularly
Handle student discipline in private
Foster good lines of communication with feedback in both directions
Call or send an e-mail to students who miss a class
Discuss the results of the final examination at the end of the course

5. Support for Learners

Ideas include:

Take students on a campus tour of relevant resources
Assign students to a group activity that encourages interaction
Encourage students to consult advisory services concerning their educational goals

SOURCE: Paradise Valley Community College, Health and Exercise Science Division. "Suggested Strategies for Student Engagement." https://www.paradisevalley.edu/sites/default/files/ie/ccsse/docs/SuggStratStuEng.pdf.

FIGURE 4.5 *Summary of Suggested Strategies for Student Engagement*

Teaching effectively requires active participation in the practice—teaching is not an activity one can learn only by reading about it. And improving one's teaching can only be done through self-examination, or as Brookfield (2017) calls it, "critical reflection." Options might include asking a trusted colleague to be a coach, or to give you some peer assessment; engaging in dialogue with other teachers; videotaping yourself so you can look for specific behaviors in the classroom; and keeping a reflective journal. Brookfield also suggests using direct student feedback, questionnaires, and group discussions with students to collect the data required for reflection. For engaging in dialogue with other teachers, Brookfield suggests some reflective prompts to get started and later to add more reflection to the conversations. Here are some simple starting exercises for prompting initial reflections (p. 120):

1. I know I have done good work when . . .
2. I know my students are learning when they . . .
3. The quality I most admire in a teaching colleague is when he or she . . .
4. Good teaching is all about . . .
5. If there's one piece of advice I'd give to someone starting to teach in my area, it's that . . .

Here are some useful reflective sentence completion prompts when familiarity and trust have developed (p. 121):

1. When my students talk about my class when they're out of my earshot, I'd most like them to say that . . .
2. In my teaching life the accomplishment that I'm most proud of is . . .

Additional Resources for Enhancing Teaching and Presentation Skills

American Library Association. 2013. "Presentation Skills." www.ala.org/tools/presentation-skills. These resources are designed to help people present better conference papers, and are helpful for many types of presentations.

The Library Instruction Roundtable (www.ala.org/ala/mgrps/rts/lirt/index.cfm) and the Instruction Section of the Association of College and Research Libraries (https://acrl.ala.org/IS/instruction-tools-resources-2/) both provide documents and learning opportunities through online and conference presentations that can be extremely useful.

LOEX (www.emich.edu/public/loex/loex.html), LOEX of the West (blogs.mtroyal.ca/lotw/), and WILU (Workshop for Instruction in Library Use) (https://ir.lib.uwo.ca/wilu/) all focus on teaching students about library use and information literacy skills.

The Institute for Information Literacy's Immersion Program (www.ala.org/acrl/immersionprogram) helps individuals develop as teachers. These intensive programs are held once a year, and there is a call for applications about nine months prior to each session.

The Australian Library and Information Association. "Standards of Professional Excellence for Teacher Librarians in Australia" (https://www.alia.org.au/about-alia/policies-standards-and-guidelines/standards-professional-excellence-teacher-librarians) notes that "this statement describes the professional knowledge, skills and commitment demonstrated by teacher librarians working at a level of excellence. It represents the goals to which all Australian teacher librarians should aspire and provides inspiration for quality teaching and ongoing professional practice."

Jeremey Donovan. 2014. *How to Deliver a TED Talk: Secrets of the World's Most Inspiring Presentations.* New York: McGraw-Hill Education. TED talks present a great idea in eighteen minutes or less and share ideas worth spreading. See https://www.ted.com/talks.

The Association for Talent Development (formerly the American Society of Training and Development) (https://www.td.org/) offers several current publications, such as:

3. If I could turn back the clock and talk to myself on my first day of teaching I'd say . . .
4. The mistake I've learned the most from is when . . .
5. The instructional problem I spend the most energy trying to solve is . . .

These reflective strategies should have evaluation techniques built in because student learning outcomes must be assessed as part of your teaching effectiveness. Choosing classroom assessment techniques that help instructors learn where students are in the learning process is critical. Observing students in the classroom as they grapple with assignments and discussions helps instructors get important, real-time information about the misconceptions and misunderstandings that students might have long before these show up in a written, formal test.

In an online as well as a classroom environment, dividing assignments into discrete parts provides opportunities for students and teachers to exchange information long before the final project is due. An example of a discrete assignment is provided below for use in a library and information science management class, but it could be adapted for projects in any discipline. This text box, "Classroom Assessment Techniques: A Sampler," provides many fine examples of techniques that can be used in the classroom to help improve the quality of learning.

There is no substitute for actually presenting to your colleagues. Many libraries use the divide-and-conquer approach to staff development by asking colleagues to take responsibility for learning particular resources or subject areas and teaching fellow staff members. As part of giving the presentation to your colleagues, you could ask for feedback on

- **Robert J. Rosania.** 2003. *Presentation Basics.* Association for Talent Development. This is a step-by-step trainer's guide for the planning, delivery, and follow-up for presentations.
- **Christee Gabour Atwood.** 2017. *Presentation Skills Training.* ATD Trainers Workshop. Association for Talent Development. This resource allows you to design presentation skills training for all levels and people in your organization and enables you to customize training programs that can be designed for one-hour, half-day, or one- or two-day events. There is also a step-by-step facilitator guide to ensure that your program stays on task.
- **Wayne Turmel.** 2011. *10 Steps to Successful Virtual Presentations.* ASTD 10 Steps Series. Association for Talent Development. This book is aimed at presentations in the virtual environment and helps you facilitate discussions, handle Voice over Internet Protocol (VoIP) issues, listen to and engage your audience, and multitask effectively.
- **Sivasailam Thiagarajan.** 2005. *Thiagi's Interactive Lectures: Power Up Your Training with Interactive Games and Exercises.* Association for Talent Development. The author helps your lectures become interactive using games and activities.

Lee Andrew Hilyer. 2007. *Presentations for Librarians: A Complete Guide to Creating Effective, Learner-Centred Presentations.* Oxford: Chandos. This book aims to provide novice and expert presenters alike with the tools they need to ensure an effective, learner-centered presentation.

Ron Hoff. 1996. *Say It in Six: How to Say Exactly What You Mean in Six Minutes or Less.* Kansas City, MO: Andrews and McMeel. Though designed more for presentations at meetings, this book nevertheless is helpful in cutting out unnecessary words and helping you get to your true message.

WebJunction. "Be Fearless: Public Speaking for Librarians." 2014. Webinar recording. https://www.webjunction.org/events/webjunction/be-fearless-public-speaking-for-librarians.html.

> **Classroom Assessment Techniques: A Sampler**
>
> **Assessing Course-Related Knowledge and Skills**
>
> *Background knowledge probe:* Ask students for general information about their prior learning in the area.
>
> *Focused listening:* Ask for learners to list several ideas that are closely related to the focus topic.
>
> *Empty outline:* Ask students to recall the relevant information or main points of the presentation.
>
> *Minute paper:* What was the most important thing you learned during this class?
>
> *Muddiest point:* What was the muddiest point in today's lecture?
>
> **Assessing Skills in Analysis and Critical Thinking**
>
> *Categorizing grid:* Students are provided with a grid of categories and sort terms, images, or equations.
>
> *Pro and con grid:* Ask learners to search for two sides to the issue and to weigh the value of competing claims.
>
> **Assessing Skills in Synthesis and Creative Thinking**
>
> *One-sentence summary:* Answer the question "Who does what to whom, when, where, how, and why?" about a given topic, and then synthesize those answers into a single, grammatical, and long summary sentence.
>
> *Word journal:* The student summarizes a short text in a single word, and then writes a paragraph or two explaining why he chose that particular word to summarize the text.
>
> *Concept maps:* These are drawings or diagrams showing the mental connections that students make between the concept being introduced and other concepts they have learned.
>
> **Assessing Skills in Problem-Solving**
>
> *Problem recognition tasks:* When presented with a few examples of common problem types, the student recognizes and identifies the particular type of problem each example represents.
>
> *What's the principle?* Students are supplied with problems and asked to state the principle that best applies to each problem.
>
> **Assessing Skills in Application and Performance**
>
> *Directed paraphrasing:* Students paraphrase part of a lesson for a specific audience and purpose, using their own words.
>
> *Application cards:* As principles, generalizations, theories, or procedures are introduced, students write down at least one possible, real-life application for what they've just learned.
>
> *Human tableau, or class modeling:* Groups of students create "living" scenes or model processes to show what they know.
>
> ---
>
> SOURCE: Thomas A. Angelo and Patricia K. Cross. 1993. *Classroom Assessment Techniques: A Handbook for College Teachers.* 2nd ed. San Francisco: Jossey-Bass

your presentation skills (see figure 4.6 for a useful checklist).

Another example of a way to share your expertise and practice presenting at the same time is the PHITE (Present Hypothesis in Team Environment) Club at Texas Tech University, which provides an opportunity to give a presentation to a group of peers, then answer questions and receive constructive criticism from them (Barba and Barba, 2011).

In creating presentations, you should make an effort to gain the interest of the participants. An important aspect to consider is how your audience connects to your topic. Pinola (2011) cites John Brubaker, who advocates that the topmost practice one should use is to answer the audience's question "W.I.I.F.M.–What's in it for me?" An example of this is giving real-life examples. The goal is to build a bridge between your message and the audience (and not waste their time).

Using slides and handouts in your presentations involves special considerations. Garton (2011) points out that, according to Richard Mayer's

	Not Yet	Progressing	Proficient	Advanced
9.1 Makes the best possible use of voice, eye contact, and gestures to keep class lively and students engaged.				
9.2. Presents instructional content in diverse ways (written, oral, visual, online, or using presentation software), and selects appropriate delivery methods according to class needs.				
9.3. Uses classroom instructional technologies and makes smooth transitions between technological tools.				
9.4. Seeks to clarify confusing terminology, avoids excessive jargon, and uses vocabulary that is appropriate for level of students.				
9.5. Practices or refines instruction content as necessary in order to achieve familiarity and confidence with planned presentation.				
The effective coordinator of instruction: **9.6**. Encourages librarians to experiment and take risks, to try new approaches and technologies, and to share experiences and materials.				
SOURCE: "Standards for Proficiencies for Instruction Librarians and Coordinators: Category 9.Presentation Skills," © 2008 ALA				

FIGURE 4.6 *Checklist for Presentation Skills Adapted from the "Proficiencies for Instruction Librarians"*

research, the design principles for such materials include the following:

- People learn better from words and pictures than from words alone.
- Exclude extraneous material.
- Corresponding words and pictures should be presented at the same time or next to each other on the screen.
- Animation and narration work well together, but not animation and text.
- Organize materials in clear outlines and headings.

Two examples of resources that you can use to reexamine your slide and handout designs are Nancy Duarte's (2009) "Glance Test" to ascertain if the audience can easily understand your slides (by just glancing at each of them for three seconds), and Garr Reynolds (2016) to learn more about design basics like unity, white space, and color.

In chapter 4 of *Active Training*, Silberman and Biech (2015) discuss how to prepare lectures that are "brain-friendly," or that maximize the participants' understanding and retention through participatory techniques. The chapter includes a worksheet listing techniques for interest-building strategies, understanding and maximizing retention, participant involvement, and lecture reinforcing, which can serve in designing well-organized presentations that promote learning. Examples of interest-building strategies include introductory exercises, preview of content, a leadoff story, visual interest, an initial case problem, or a test question (pp. 72–83).

Although self-reflection should be your primary development strategy, courses and workshops are useful for reinforcing your practice and self-reflection. You can participate in workshops at a university or college focused on teacher improvement, take a course in teaching at a local community college, take a course in information literacy at an iSchool,

> **Tips for Better Presentations**
>
> **Gain Interest**
>
> Real-life examples (what is in it for me?)
>
> Introductory exercise
>
> Leadoff story, or an interesting visual
>
> Problem, issue, or case study
>
> Test questions
>
> **Maximize Understanding and Retention**
>
> Give highlights or "coming attractions"
>
> Opening summary or advanced organizer
>
> Provide examples, particularly real-life illustrations
>
> Analogies, metaphors—create a comparison between new material and the knowledge or experience people already have
>
> Visual backup—use flip charts, transparencies, brief handouts, and desktop presentation tools
>
> Provide opportunities to use the information in an active way
>
> Structure information in a way that is more understandable, such as breaking down information into smaller, more manageable "chunks"
>
> Use spatial strategies that provide a visual display of substantial amounts of information, such as chain maps, spider maps, hierarchies, and frames. (A frame is a grid, matrix, or framework for representing knowledge.)
>
> **Involve the Participants**
>
> Assign responsibility for active listening
>
> Provide opportunities for guided note-taking
>
> Ask questions periodically to check for understanding
>
> Assign an illuminating exercise
>
> **Reinforce Learning**
>
> Have participants prepare questions
>
> Ask participants to review the content and memorize it, or give them a self-scoring review test
>
> Ask participants to reflect on the material's implications for them
>
> Pose a case problem for participants to solve based on the information given
>
> Design an activity that summarizes or illustrates the information given
>
> SOURCE: Melvin Silberman and Elaine Biech. 2015. *Active Training: A Handbook of Techniques, Designs, Case Examples, and Tips.* 4th ed. Hoboken, NJ: Wiley.

or explore the options for those courses and workshops that are held online, or are asynchronous.

Tailoring instruction to your learners implies that you know something about how they learn. Knowing something about the process of learning is important, so reading books such as *How People Learn* by the National Research Council (2000), or taking a class in educational psychology would be helpful.

Those working only with adults need to know something about "andragogy," or the study of adult learning theory. Malcolm Knowles suggested four principles that are applied to adult learning (Kearsley and Culatta, 2018b):

1. Adults need to be involved in the planning and evaluation of their instruction.
2. Experience (including mistakes) provides the basis for the learning activities.
3. Adults are most interested in learning subjects that have immediate relevance and impact to their job or personal life.
4. Adult learning is problem-centered rather than content-oriented.

Curtis (2017) notes that instruction for adults is an essential aspect of modern public library services because these services benefit the communities they serve; individual adults often will not venture into the unknown without the guidance provided by instructional services. Since professional trainers deal exclusively with adults, a lot of good, practical information comes from that arena. See the Association for Talent Development website (https://www.td.org/).

Similarly, those working with children need to know about developmental changes in children. All of us know that what works in teaching sixth-graders may not necessarily work with first-graders. The Child Development Institute (2018) has a website that summarizes childhood development, but there are many good resources on this topic available in most libraries. The National Association for the Education of Young Children (https://www.naeyc.org/) is a good resource for the principles of child development and learning. Again, this topic is far too extensive to cover in depth as only part of a chapter, and readers are encouraged to seek other sources.

Keeping up with changes in your community is important. Public librarians need to know about socioeconomic changes in their communities, as well as the demographics of their populations. To conduct an environmental scan of your campus and teaching environment, you can use the workbook for "Analyzing Your Instructional Environment" (Association of College and Research Libraries, Instruction Section, 2010).

Knowledge of a variety of teaching strategies is extremely valuable, and there are a number of resources for learning more about them. The ACRL Instruction Section's Teaching Methods Committee (2018) tracks the teaching methods used in academic libraries and highlights their uses by librarians. A particularly useful strategy is cooperative learning, which encourages small groups of students to work together for the achievement of a common goal. Understanding how to form groups, ensure positive interdependence, maintain individual accountability, resolve group conflict, develop appropriate assignments and grading criteria, and manage active learning environments is critical to the achievement of a successful cooperative learning experience. See resources like Common Sense's (n.d.) "Give Every Child a Stake in Group Work."

Project-based learning is a specific application of cooperative learning, based on the completion of a project, that allows participants to work together to solve a real-world problem and enhances critical thinking, problem-solving, teamwork, and self-management. See Educators of America (2018) for more resources and tips on how to integrate technology into project-based learning.

Additional Resources for Inquiry-Based Learning

Mindshift. 2015. "How Can Your Librarian Help Bolster Brain-Based Teaching Practices?" Retrieved from https://www.kqed.org/mindshift/38735/how-can-your-librarian-help-bolster-brain-based-teaching-practices. This work discusses how teachers and librarians can work together to create effective inquiry-based learning.

Jean Donham, Carol Kuhlthau, Diane Oberg, and Kay Bishop. 2001. *Inquiry-Based Learning: Lessons from Library Power*. Worthington, OH: Linworth. Based on real schools and the struggles of real library media specialists and teachers, this resource provides theory, principles, research, and concrete examples to illustrate how the Library Power initiative can move towards an inquiry-based approach to teaching, learning, and curriculum renewal.

Collette Cassinelli. 2018. *Inspiring Curiosity: The Librarian's Guide to Inquiry-Based Learning*. Portland, OR: International Society for Technology in Education. *Inspiring Curiosity* is a practical guide for secondary school librarians as they collaborate with teachers and students to develop inquiry-based research projects. The book provides strategies for using memorable events to activate students' natural curiosity, and activities to generate essential questions for exploration. It includes ideas and resources to help librarians be more effective in research and inquiry; tips for developing search strategies, locating and curating resources, evaluating sources, and celebrating students' inquiry beyond the traditional research paper; and lessons and assessment ideas to keep librarians current on information literacy topics.

Craig Gibson and Trudi E. Jacobson. 2018. "Habits of Mind in an Uncertain Information World." *Reference & User Services Quarterly* 57, no. 3: 183–92. This article discusses transformative learning through communities of inquiry, particularly those in which reflection is regularly practiced (pp. 187–88).

Digital Polarization Initiative. www.aascu.org/AcademicAffairs/ADP/DigiPo/. The Digital Polarization Initiative is a cross-institutional project that encourages college students to investigate and verify the information they find online. The articles on the site are student-produced.

PRESENTER: _____   OBSERVER: _____

Δ = Needs Improvement, √ = Adequate, + = Excellent, N/A = Not Applicable

Organization of Content	Δ	√	+	N/A	Comments
1. Stated Purpose of Presentation					
2. Structured Progression of Instruction					
3. Provided Closure for Session					

Clarity of Presentation	Δ	√	+	N/A	Comments
1. Defined New Terms / Concepts / Principles					
2. Chose Appropriate Vocabulary for Learners					
3. Presented Examples for Clarification					
4. Use of Transitions between Examples / Ideas					

Presentation Technique	Δ	√	+	N/A	Comments
1. Overall Voice / Body / Attitude					
2. Vocal Delivery (e.g., pitch and pace)					
3. Use of Speech Fillers (e.g., well, um, like, okay, ah, hmm)					
4. Movement and Gestures					
5. Learner Engagement (e.g., questioning, eye contact)					
6. Teaching Persona and Enthusiasm					

What about the presentation was particularly outstanding?

What about the presentation would you suggest the presenter consider changing?

FIGURE 4.7 *Presentation Feedback Form*

Similar to project-based learning, inquiry-based learning focuses on an initial question. The student approaches learning by asking questions, starting from problems or scenarios and involving exploration, discussion, questioning, and testing. This approach works well with real-world learning (*Wikipedia*, 2018b). School librarians are leading in this area, partnering with classroom teachers.

Assessing Development Efforts for Designing and Implementing Presentation and Communication Strategies to Foster Learning and Engagement

One of the best ways to assess your teaching efforts is to ask a trusted colleague to conduct a peer observation with you. A peer observation can be for assessment purposes, but it can also be used as collaborative professional development. In Flom's "Peer-to-Peer Observation: Five Questions for Making It Work," the five questions are: (1) What is the essential question being observed? (2) Are the essential questions for the observation created with a top-down or bottom-up approach? (3) What is the scope of the observation? (4) What is the purpose of the observation? and (5) What kind of time can be devoted to it? (Flom, 2014). For detailed step-by-step directions for peer observation, see the University of Illinois's version, which includes a five-step process, starting with a practice observation, and then having the following steps: (1) Identification; (2) Dialogue One; (3) Observation; (4) Dialogue Two; and (5) Post-Observation Write-Ups and Action Plans (University of Illinois at Urbana-Champaign, College of Agricultural, Consumer and Environmental Sciences, n.d.).

Another helpful way of obtaining feedback on your teaching is an "Observation Checklist" (Noonan, Gaumer Erickson, Brussow, and Langham, 2015), which helps to identify whether your presentations follow adult learning principles. This tool can also be used to provide ongoing feedback and coaching or as a guidance document when designing or revising professional development. The 22-item checklist addresses six domains present in high-quality professional development: preparation, introduction, demonstration, engagement, evaluation/reflection, and mastery.

Another helpful job aid for assessing your teaching is available online from the British Columbia Institute of Technology (2010). This resource helps you determine what aspects of your teaching you want to examine, suggests some ways to examine them, and tries to help you make sense of the results. In addition to examining your lesson plans for extraneous information, this job aid also suggests that you pay attention to clues in your classroom, suggests what to look for, and describes a technique called small group instructional feedback which utilizes a trained facilitator to talk to students in a more traditional classroom setting. A simple form that looks more at your use of voice and how you move your body is available in figure 4.7.

CREATES A LEARNER-CENTERED TEACHING ENVIRONMENT

Competencies for Creating a Learner-Centered Teaching Environment

The typical behavioral strategies suggested in the RUSA "Professional Competencies" that demonstrate competencies related to creating a learner-centered environment are:

- Designs group instruction sessions by defining expectations and desired learning outcomes in order to determine content, sequencing the lessons, and incorporating activities that facilitate learning
- Designs instruction to best meet the common learning characteristics of individuals, including their prior knowledge and experience, motivation to learn, cognitive abilities, and the circumstances under which they will be learning
- Implements active, collaborative, and other appropriate learning activities
- Modifies teaching methods and delivery to address different learning preferences,

language abilities, developmental skills, age groups, and the diverse needs of learners
- Integrates appropriate technology into instruction to support experiential and collaborative learning as well as to improve individual receptiveness, comprehension, and retention of information
- Designs effective assessments of individual learning and uses the data collected to guide personal teaching and professional development
- Reflects on practice in order to improve teaching skills and applies new knowledge of teaching methods and learning theories
- Shares teaching skills and knowledge with other instructional staff

Development Methods for Creating a Learner-Centered Teaching Environment

Creating a learner-centered teaching environment implies that you know something about how people learn, and that you keep this knowledge in mind when you design learning activities. Universal Design is a concept which recognizes that no one learns in the same way, so providing multiple means of representation, action and expression, and engagement will help the widest variety of learners. The National Center for Universal Design for Learning presents guidelines that will help instructors consider multiple means of expression (figure 4.8).

To further explain these guidelines, providing multiple means of perception means offering auditory as well as visual explanations, the ability to customize the display of information, and providing alternatives for visual information. With regard to language, you should clarify vocabulary and symbols as well as syntax and structure; support decoding text, mathematical notations, and symbols; promote understanding across languages; and illustrate through multiple media. To use Universal Design to aid comprehension, you should activate or supply background knowledge; highlight patterns, critical features, big ideas, and relationships; guide information processing, visualization, and manipulation; and maximize transfer and generalization.

Instructional Design. There are quite a few instructional design models that you can follow to improve your teaching. We will cover a few of the classics and some newer design models here: ADDIE, SAM, USER, and Backwards Design.

Almost all of these instructional design models start with determining the learning objectives. Patti Shank (n.d.) gives a helpful description of how to write learning objectives: "Learning objectives are not a list of what you are going to teach. Learning objectives are a list of what participants will be able to do on the job." Shauna Vaughan (2016) asks instructors to "consider where you really want your learners to be, cognitively, using the knowledge dimensions (factual, conceptual, procedural, or metacognitive), and then select the verb that best suits what you expect the learners to do. What will you be measuring or observing? How does the learning objective align with the assessment?"

ADDIE is a classic instructional design model, with the first letter in each keyword (see below) representing a step in the process. According to Kearsley and Culatta (2018a), ADDIE stands for:

Analyze—understand the core needs and characteristics of the product's users

Design—create a strategy that addresses the needs and characteristics of these users

Develop—construct and revise the product

Implement—deliver the product to the intended audience

Evaluate—conduct formative evaluation at all levels, with summative evaluation in the form of tests, as well as feedback from users

The analysis phase clarifies the instructional problems and objectives and identifies the learning environment and the learner's existing knowledge and skills. The process of asking these questions is often part of a needs analysis. The design phase deals with learning objectives, assessment instruments, exercises, content, subject matter analysis, lesson planning, and media selection. In the development

I. Provide Multiple Means of Engagement

Recruiting Interest
- Optimize individual choice and autonomy
- Optimize relevance, value, and authenticity
- Minimize threats and distractions

Sustaining Effort and Persistence
- Heighten salience of goals and objectives
- Vary demands and resources to optimize challenge
- Foster collaboration and community
- Increase mastery-oriented feedback

Self-Regulation
- Promote expectations and beliefs that optimize motivation
- Facilitate personal coping skills and strategies
- Develop self-assessment and reflection

II. Provide Multiple Means of Representation

Perception
- Offer ways of customizing the display of information
- Offer alternatives for auditory information
- Offer alternatives for visual information

Language and Symbols
- Clarify vocabulary and symbols
- Clarify syntax and structure
- Support decoding of text, mathematical notation, and symbols
- Promote understanding across languages
- Illustrate through multiple media

Comprehension
- Activate or supply background knowledge
- Highlight patterns, critical features, big ideas, and relationships
- Guide information processing and visualization
- Maximize transfer and generalization

III. Provide Multiple Means of Action and Expression

Physical Action
- Vary the methods for response and navigation
- Optimize access to tools and assistive technologies

Expression and Communication
- Use multiple methods for communication
- Use multiple tools for construction and composition
- Build fluencies for graduated levels of support for practice & performance

Executive Functions
- Guide appropriate goal-setting
- Support planning and strategy development
- Facilitate managing information and resources
- Enhance capacity for monitoring progress

SOURCE: CAST. 2018. "Universal Design for Learning Guidelines version 2.2." http://udlguidelines.cast.org.

FIGURE 4.8 *Universal Design for Learning Guidelines*

phase, instructional designers and developers create and assemble the content described in the design phase. The implementation phase develops procedures for training facilitators and learners and an evaluation of the design. The evaluation phase consists of two aspects: formative and summative. Formative evaluation is present in each stage of the ADDIE process, while summative evaluation is conducted on finished instructional programs or products. Donald Kirkpatrick's four levels of learning evaluation—reaction, learning, behavior, and results—are often utilized during this phase of the ADDIE process (Kirkpatrick Partners, 2018).

SAM, or the Successive Approximation Model, uses a similar approach, but it uses a quicker initial phase where individuals use prototypes to see if they are on the right track, and then go on to do more development. In all levels, the steps are to evaluate, design, and develop, but each of the three iterations goes deeper. In the first iteration, begin with a quick analysis of the situation, need, and goals; then design a quick, but thoughtful rough design for discussion; and then develop prototypes to gain a sense of the design idea in application. In the second iteration, each step goes a notch more in-depth, so you start with determining the success of the first iteration, developing the design by sketching new alternatives or refining previous ideas, and then further developing your prototypes so they are more thoroughly representative of the final product. The third iteration follows the same process, but focuses more on development than on design (Allen, 2012, 2015).

In the USER Model, Char Booth (2011) creates a design with the following steps:

Understand: identify the problem, analyze the learner, context, content, and educator

Structure: create targets, involve and extend

Engage: design the materials and deliver instruction

Reflect: assess impact, revise and reuse

Backward design is a method of designing educational curriculum by setting goals before choosing instructional methods and forms of assessment (McTighe and Wiggins, 2012). The backward design of a curriculum typically involves three stages and begins with planning with the end in mind by first clarifying the learning you seek—the learning results (Stage 1). Then, think about the assessment evidence needed to show that students have achieved that desired learning (Stage 2). Finally, plan the means to the end—the teaching and learning activities and resources to help them achieve the goals (Stage 3). The idea is that this helps people avoid being overly focused on activities or content coverage. A new publication by Heineke and McTighe (2018) adds a lens on language and culture to the widely used Understanding by Design framework.

Technology and Online Learning Environments. The appropriate use of technology is an important part of designing instruction, but its use is certainly constantly changing. Keeping up with the technology is difficult, and using it appropriately is even harder. Luckily, there are several sources that pull together online resources such as tutorials and provide peer reviews:

PRIMO (Association of College and Research Libraries, Instruction Section, 2018) promotes and shares peer-reviewed instructional materials created by librarians to teach people about discovering, accessing, evaluating, and ethically using information in networked environments.

The MERLOT system (California State University System, 2018) provides access to curated online learning and support materials and content creation tools, led by an international community of educators, learners, and researchers. With MERLOT you can access collections of digital learning materials, conduct peer reviews of those materials, and add student learning assignments.

The New York City School Library System (2018) has provided a similar kind of guide to resources from a number of educational institutions. These resources are related to topics around the research process, including proper citation and plagiarism, as well as website evaluation. The "Online Test and Tutorials" section of this website provides a number of interactive activities and presentations that educators can use when teaching information literacy classes.

The Public Library Association's (2018) digital literacy initiative, DigitalLearn.org, grew out of a Pew Research Center (2015) report which suggests that the public wants libraries to teach digital literacy, and that library efforts can help the most vulnerable groups of the population. According to the Pew report, 94 percent of respondents said libraries should "offer programs to teach people, including kids and senior citizens, how to use digital tools such as computers, smartphones and apps." A strong majority of all Americans—76 percent—say that libraries should "definitely" offer programs to teach people how to protect their privacy and security online. Pew research also shows the connection between library support of digital literacy skills and employment. Contributing to the economic health of the community, and to the economic success of individuals, are major reasons why teaching digital literacy skills is important. DigitalLearn.org includes a collection of self-directed tutorials for end-users to increase their digital literacy. Feedback from public library staff prompted the Public Library Association to develop courses on the most basic skills, such as using a computer, navigating a website, and searching. The course modules are video-based with narration, are 6 to 22 minutes long, are written at the fourth-grade reading level, and help learners practice skills like using a mouse and setting up passwords.

McCallum (2014) lists six important components of a successful online learning environment: curating and adding your own resources, supplementing text-heavy environments with other resources, encouraging and modeling participation, gradual releasing of responsibility, summarizing, and assessing. She also discusses the SAMR Model by Puentedura (2015), which highlights the continuum of the use of technology in teaching. In this model, the first level is substitution, where the technology acts as a direct tool substitute, with no functional change. The second level is augmentation, in which the technology acts as a direct tool substitution, with functional improvement. The third level is modification, in which the technology allows for significant task redesign. Finally, in redefinition, technology allows for the creation of new tasks that were not previously possible.

The Online Learning Consortium (2018) presents a "Quality Framework" for successful online education in five interrelated areas—learning effectiveness, access, scale (capacity enrollment achieved through cost-effectiveness and institutional commitment), faculty satisfaction, and student satisfaction. Each of these five pillars has identified effective practices that can support the pillar. For example, learning effectiveness suggests measures in the categories of course design, learning resources, faculty development, learner characteristics, pedagogy, interaction (with content, faculty, and other students), assessment, and learning outcomes, including student satisfaction, retention, achievement, performance, and so on. The Online Learning Consortium offers a variety of learning opportunities, including self-paced courses and workshops, as well as on-demand offerings. The pillars lend themselves well to developing a checklist for evaluation purposes.

The "Create and Deliver Training" and "Teaching Patrons" sections of the WebJunction (2018) "Course Catalog" offer webinars and self-paced courses, including "You Can Do It: A Recipe for Designing Web-Based Instruction" and "Digital Literacy Training Tutorials for Libraries." Another good way to prepare for creating online instruction is to personally participate in online instruction. Before participating, consider conducting a self-assessment listed in the "Assessment" section that follows (see below), or taking a tutorial such as the California Community Colleges' (2016) "Online Student Readiness Tutorials." Most academic campuses offer assistance in creating online learning environments, either through their educational technologies units or through their teaching improvement divisions. DigitalLearn.org also provides a twenty-minute tutorial on how to design digital learning content for their web environment.

Assessment of Student Learning. While the assessment of student learning was addressed earlier in this chapter, those sections mainly focused on assessing whether the students had learned only within the context of the particular instruction session, and on using formative assessment to improve the instruction. There is much yet to address about the assessment of student learning; in particular, trying to determine if the content learned in the session can actually be applied in coursework, or in the workplace. There are several standardized tests that should be considered in this regard. One of these is Project SAILS (Standardized Assessment of Information Literacy Skills), at https://www.projectsails.org/site/. This project originated at Kent State University, but since 2012 it has been managed by Carrick Enterprises. One can utilize individual test scores, a cohort of scores, or build your own test. A similar web-based, standardized test is the Information Literacy Test (ILT), at https://www.madisonassessment.com/assessment-testing/information-literacy-test/. The ILT was developed at James Madison

University, was designed for use across institutions, and is based on the now-defunct ACRL Standards (Cameron, Wise, and Lottridge, 2007).

In December 2016 the iSkills Assessment, formerly available via ETS (Educational Testing Service), was discontinued, but ETS provides other areas of testing that are related to literacy skills in the HEIghten Outcomes Assessment Suite (www.ets.org/heighten/). The areas in this suite include civic competency and engagement, critical thinking, intercultural competency and diversity, quantitative literacy, and written communication. There are also up to fifty locally authored, multiple-choice questions and nine demographic questions to meet specific program needs.

Lurleen B. Wallace Community College (2018) still maintains its Big 6 Grading Matrix, which was originally adapted from the Bay Area Community College's Information Competence Assessment Project. While the Bay Area project is no longer being maintained, the community college's website is, and it provides a Big 6 Research Worksheet that the student can fill out to be used with the Grading Matrix.

Allison Erlinger (2018) identifies three primary functions of information literacy instruction assessment that clearly emerge from the literature: providing feedback to learners, providing feedback to instructors, and demonstrating the value of programs to stakeholders and administrators. She further identified the following seven general assessment types: surveys, focus groups, objective tests (locally developed), classroom assessment techniques using (CATs)/performance measures, authentic assessment, rubrics, and standardized tests; and she went on to analyze their use. See figure 4.9 for details on the assessment types.

Megan Oakleaf (2009) has proposed the use of an Information Literacy Instruction Assessment Cycle (ILIAC), with seven stages to improve librarians' instructional abilities and improve students' information literacy skills. The ILIAC encourages librarians to articulate learning outcomes clearly, analyze them meaningfully, celebrate learning achievements, and diagnose problem areas. The seven stages are:

Stage 1: Review learning goals

Stage 2: Identify learning outcomes

Stage 3: Create learning activities

Stage 4: Enact learning activities

Stage 5: Gather data to check learning

Stage 6: Interpret data

Stage 7: Enact decisions

Method	Type	Kirkpatrick Level
Surveys	formative or summative	Level 1, reaction
Focus groups	summative	Level 1, reaction
Objective tests locally developed	summative	Level 2, learning
Classroom assessment techniques	formative	Level 2, learning
Authentic assessment	summative	Level 3, behavior
Standardized tests	summative	Level 2, learning

Erlinger notes that rubrics, as a flexible tool rather than an assessment method, cannot be assigned any specific type or level of assessment.

SOURCES: Allison Erlinger. 2018. "Outcomes Assessment in Undergraduate Information Literacy Instruction: A Systematic Review." *College and Research Libraries* 79, no. 4: 442–79; Donald L. Kirkpatrick and James D. Kirkpatrick. 2006. *Evaluating Training Programs: The Four Levels*. 3rd ed. San Francisco.: Barrett-Koehler Publishers.

FIGURE 4.9 *Erlinger's Seven General Assessment Types*

Oakleaf goes on to demonstrate the application of this process at North Carolina State University with an English 101 assignment where students were asked to evaluate websites for authority. In addition to demonstrating the cycle, this article also demonstrates the effective use of a rubric, and some discussion on how to create a rubric.

Active Learning. Michael Prince (2004) explains: "Active learning is generally defined as any instructional method that engages students in the learning process. In short, active learning requires students to do meaningful learning activities and think about what they are doing" (p. 223). So in active learning, students have to be engaged in activities that require them to do something and to think or reflect on these activities.

The University of Michigan's Center for Research on Teaching and Learning (2016) provides a list of active learning techniques, ranging from simple techniques like writing a one-minute paper (described earlier in this chapter) to more complex techniques such as role-playing or experiential learning. The University of Michigan's Active Learning materials include sections on implementation, examples and resources, and a worksheet (figure 4.10) for you to reflect on your current practice of using active learning, ranging from lower to higher complexity. The awareness gained from this reflection is the first step in intentionally incorporating more active learning into your teaching.

Reflective Practice. In "5 'Q.U.I.C.K' Steps of Reflective Practice," Eury, King, and Balls (n.d.) give the following suggestions: first, ask yourself questions about what happened today; second, understand how to get your objective—the "aha" moments; and third, ask others, such as the students or colleagues who witnessed your performance. Fourth, be honest in your personal assessment. And finally, keep a journal, since recording these thoughts provides an opportunity to reflect on your progress. Brookfield (2017) further explores reflective practice, using four lenses: self-reflection, student perceptions, peers, and the scholarly literature on instruction. He goes quite in-depth on how these can be more richly developed. In her article "DIY Skills: Upgrading for the Teacher Librarian," Ashley R. Lierman (2015) encourages librarians to plan out their improvement ideas for teaching by creating an action plan. She says: "As important as it is that you combine enrichment activities with actual classroom practice, it is equally important that you take the time to reflect and record your thoughts on both" (p. 89).

Parker Palmer's (2017) *The Courage to Teach* explores more fully the reflective practice of teachers, and posits that good teaching cannot be reduced

Additional Resources on Active Learning

Andrew Walsh and Padma Inala. 2010. *Active Learning Techniques for Librarians: Practical Examples.* Cambridge: Chandos. This book explains the theory of active learning, provides the reasons why librarians should use more active learning techniques in their sessions, and includes a large number of examples that can be used in teaching.

Persida Himmele and William Himmele. 2017. *Total Participation Techniques: Making Every Student an Active Learner.* 2nd ed. Alexandria, VA: Association for Supervision & Curriculum Development. Focused on K-12 students, this book provides 51 easy-to-use, classroom-tested alternatives to the traditional lecture format of teaching.

Theresa McDevitt. 2011. *Let the Games Begin: Engaging Students with Field-Tested Interactive Information Literacy Instruction.* New York: Neal-Schuman. In its provision of games for use in imparting information literacy, this book gives examples of card games, jeopardy games, individual games, and those requiring group work, the use of clickers, and students' use of whiteboards and chalkboards, as well as activities that require movement around the library.

John Kostek and Amanda Stewart. March 1, 2018. "No Attention Means No Learning." *TD Magazine.* https://www.td.org/magazines/td-magazine/no-attention-means-no-learning. This article gives a nice summary of active learning.

Active learning can also be implemented at varying levels of complexity. Use this worksheet to identify which techniques you may already be using, and the techniques you are open to incorporating into your practice.

Use the codes below to mark your selections in the columns for lecture ("Lec"), discussion/seminar ("Dis"), lab/studio ("Lab"), or online/blended ("O/B") courses, depending on your teaching context.

Y = I use this in my teaching
~ = I sort of use this in my teaching
N = I do not use this in my teaching
* = I would like to try this, though I may need more information or resources

Lec	Dis	Lab	O/B	
LOW COMPLEXITY				
☐	☐	☐	☐	Pause intentionally for 2–3 minutes during lecture and ask students to reflect on what they just learned, then ask if anything needs to be clarified
☐	☐	☐	☐	Have students participate in a brainstorming activity
☐	☐	☐	☐	Engage students in small writing tasks during class like the muddiest point or minute paper
☐	☐	☐	☐	Have students think individually and share ideas with a partner, followed by calling on a few of the groups to report out (think-pair-share)
☐	☐	☐	☐	Have students engage in in-class reading activities that are followed by a class discussion
☐	☐	☐	☐	Have students watch a short video or several video clips and discuss themes or issues in small or large groups

Lec	Dis	Lab	O/B	
MEDIUM COMPLEXITY				
☐	☐	☐	☐	Have students write one idea on a Post-it note about a question, then have the class sort the questions into categories, and discuss the categories
☐	☐	☐	☐	Have students peer-review a paper or assignment and give each other feedback
☐	☐	☐	☐	Engage students in a fishbowl activity (i.e., some students sitting in a circle ask questions, present opinions, and share information, while other students outside the circle listen carefully to the ideas presented and pay attention to the process. Then reverse the roles.)
☐	☐	☐	☐	Have students do paired annotations (e.g., students pair up to review/learn one article, chapter, or content area and exchange double-entry journals for reading and reflection)
☐	☐	☐	☐	Engage students in active review (e.g., discuss and review material or potential solutions to problems)
☐	☐	☐	☐	Engage students in guided, reciprocal, peer questioning activity (e.g., generate discussion among student groups about a specific topic or content area)
☐	☐	☐	☐	Have students take a short, ungraded quiz to check student comprehension of the material

FIGURE 4.10 *Reflecting on Your Practice of Active Learning*

MEDIUM COMPLEXITY *(cont.)*	
☐ ☐ ☐ ☐	Engage students in self-reflection individually or in small groups (e.g., use a self-assessment inventory)
☐ ☐ ☐ ☐	Have students work in pairs, triads, or small groups on class assignments
☐ ☐ ☐ ☐	Have students answer questions by using iClickers, or other technology tools, to check student understanding
Lec **Dis** **Lab** **O/B**	
HIGH COMPLEXITY	
☐ ☐ ☐ ☐	Have students in small groups work cooperatively on a task (e.g., do a jigsaw activity)
☐ ☐ ☐ ☐	Engage students in inquiry-based learning (i.e., distribute pertinent information and give students the flexibility to formulate their own problem, instead of merely asking students to replicate)
☐ ☐ ☐ ☐	Engage students in case-based learning (e.g., ask students to read and discuss complex, real-life scenarios that call on their analytical and decision-making skills)
☐ ☐ ☐ ☐	Engage students in problem-based learning (e.g., frame the problem as a long-term investigation permitting students to develop and enhance their investigative, procedural, and communicative skills)
☐ ☐ ☐ ☐	Have students engage in role-play exercises or simulations
☐ ☐ ☐ ☐	Engage students in real-world problems or situations (e.g., identify issues/problems on or off campus, proposing possible solutions. Then work with the community to improve the situations or solve the problems.)
☐ ☐ ☐ ☐	Engage students in reflective dialogue and activities using forum theater and similar methods

SOURCE: University of Michigan, Center for Research on Learning and Teaching. 2016. "Active Learning: Reflecting on Your Practice." http://crlt.umich.edu/active_learning_reflecting.
Some material adapted from Linse and Weinstein, Schreyer Institute for Teaching Excellence, Pennsylvania State University, 2015.

to technique, but is rooted in the identity and integrity of the teacher. Palmer says that all good teachers are deeply connected with their students and with their subject and are authentically present in the classroom, using techniques that reveal themselves as individuals rather than hiding them. The accompanying optional workbook, *The Courage to Teach Guide for Reflection and Renewal,* by Palmer and Scribner (2017), includes questions and exercises that can be used for individual or group study. Sample questions from the workbook are:

- As a teacher, are there moments when you have attempted to protect your identity and integrity from being violated? Are there other moments when you have allowed some sort of violation to occur? (p. 28)

- Share a story about one of your favorite teachers. What do you most vividly remember about that teacher? How did he or she make you feel? What was his or her relation to the subject taught? What was the ethos of his or her classroom? What does that scenario tell you about that teacher's identity and integrity? (p. 31)

- What are some of your fears in the classroom? In relation to colleagues? In relation to your professional career? How have you dealt with them? What have you learned about yourself and about fear as a result? (p. 36)

Sharing Our Practice. The notion of teaching as a solitary practice is one we have to work hard in the profession to counteract. Sharing teaching stories (including our failures), discussing shared concerns, exploring new teaching strategies, and opening up our classrooms for observation are all areas in which librarians as teachers can improve. Offering to serve as a coach or observer for someone else and suggesting team teaching approaches are also ways to share our teaching expertise. Often people only share what works well in the classroom. A more helpful conversation might ensue around what did *not* go well (Meyrink, 2015).

For someone to ask you to come watch them teach takes a lot of courage and confidence on their part. One alternative would be for you to offer to audio- and video-record their teaching, and then you could watch the recording together. In this instance, you might want to consider only asking questions that will help the teacher observe things for herself. "What do you notice about what you are doing here?" "What are the student's reactions when you did that?" You should also consider submitting your teaching story so that colleagues can read about them. The ALA journal *LIRT News* (www.ala.org/rt/lirt/lirt-news) is one example of a resource that takes this kind of submission regularly.

Assessing Development Efforts for Creating a Learner-Centered Teaching Environment

Assessing how well you're doing in creating a learner-centered teaching environment means delving into the evidence of your practice, interacting with students, assessing their learning, planning significant learning activities, reading the literature, and interacting with colleagues to both improve your practice and to help others. Figure 4.11 provides a useful guide for collecting and reflecting upon the evidence of your development in these areas.

You also need to evaluate the evidence of your use of active learning techniques. Figures 4.10 and 4.12 are forms that you can use to examine your active learning practice. Figure 4.10, from the University of Michigan, is a worksheet that can help you identify which techniques you may already be

---

Evidence of self-reflection, diary, journal, changes to instruction
- Do you keep a log or journal of teaching sessions, including objectives, activities, and your notes on student responses?
- Do you regularly review this log before teaching?

Evidence of interactions with students' opinions and views on course/class
- Do you ask students' opinions informally?
- Do you survey students?
- Do you have a formal teaching evaluation for a single session or course?
- What have you changed as a result of those evaluations?

Evidence of learning assessments
- What classroom assessments do you engage in?
- What kinds of authentic assessments do you use?
- How did you use the data gathered to improve your teaching?
- How did you use the data gathered to guide your professional development?

Evidence of interaction with colleagues, discussion, or peer observations
- Have you asked someone else to come into your classroom to observe?
- Have you engaged recently in a discussion of teaching techniques with colleagues?
- Have you discussed your teaching failures with others?
- Is there a group of individuals locally, whether librarians from other organizations, or people who teach different subjects, with whom you could discuss teaching?

Evidence of reading literature
- What journals are you regularly scanning?
- What blogs do you read on a regular basis?
- How do you keep track of the ideas you've gotten from these resources?
- How do you document what ideas you have tried in the classroom?

Evidence of use of instructional design process
- Do you use a specific instructional design practice?
- Do you start your planning for a class with what the students should get out of the experience?

FIGURE 4.11 *Using Evidence to Assess Your Development Efforts*

> - Do you incorporate assessment of student learning into that design?
>
> *Evidence of sharing teaching skills and knowledge with other instructional staff*
> - Do you have regular conversations with instructional staff at your institution about teaching?
> - Do you have conversations with instructional people outside of your unit or institution?
> - Have you team-taught?
> - Have you offered to team-teach with a new colleague?
> - Have you participated in micro-teaching sessions with others?
> - Have you coached someone else's teaching?
> - If you have coached someone else, have you asked someone to evaluate your coaching skills?
>
> NOTE: Use something like Research Collaboration's "Coaching Observation Checklist" (http://www.researchcollaboration.org/page/coaching-observation-checklist) or the Kansas Technical Assistance System Network's "Co-Teaching Guide" (https://ksdetasn.s3.amazonaws.com/uploads/resource/upload/1228/coaches_guide_nov_2016.pdf).

using, and which techniques you might want to consider using. Additionally, figure 4.12, "Time Allocation in a Class Session," which was created by Beth Woodard and used for many years in the ACRL's Immersion Teacher Program, focuses your attention on what the students are actually doing in the classroom, and helps you think about whether that is the right mix of activities for what you are trying to do.

Obviously, developing competencies for teaching information literacy in a wide variety of situations is outside the scope of this chapter; therefore, all you will find here are beginning suggestions for how to develop these competencies. Educators have formal programs in which they learn theory and have guidance in putting this theory into practice in real-world situations, and then they spend years perfecting this practice. Unfortunately, there are relatively few opportunities for librarians to replicate that experience, outside of school librarian preparation programs, and we often have to be proactive in our own learning process.

> What percentage of instructional time in a typical classroom period do you spend on the following activities?
>
> | | Percent |
> |---|---|
> | 1. You talking | _____ |
> | 2. You demonstrating and talking | _____ |
> | 3. You demonstrating | _____ |
> | 4. You watching students work | _____ |
> | 5. You asking questions of students | _____ |
> | 6. You listening to students talking to you | _____ |
> | 7. You listening to students talking to each other | _____ |
> | Total | _____ |
>
> Include all the time spent on instructional activities, but exclude activities such as passing out handouts, taking roll, and so on. Do not total above 100 percent. Even though students are probably thinking and writing while you talk, count only the times when they are thinking or writing with no other activity going on.
>
> What are students doing, and what percentage of the time are they doing it?
>
> | | Percent |
> |---|---|
> | 1. Students listening to you | _____ |
> | 2. Students talking to you | _____ |
> | 3. Students talking/listening to each other | _____ |
> | 4. Students writing | _____ |
> | 5. Students thinking | _____ |
> | 6. Students on computers individually | _____ |
> | 7. Students on computers in groups | _____ |
> | Total | _____ |
>
> ADAPTED AND USED WITH PERMISSION: Trish Ridgeway, Director, Handley Regional Library, Winchester, VA, books2u@shentel.net.
>
> SOURCE: ACRL Institute for Information Literacy. 2015. Beth Woodard.

FIGURE 4.12 *Time Allocation in a Class Session*

CHAPTER **five**

Marketing and Advocacy

SECTION 5E: PROMOTES AND DEMONSTRATES THE VALUE OF LIBRARY SERVICES THROUGH MARKETING AND ADVOCACY

This chapter is about developing and assessing your knowledge, skills, abilities, and behaviors associated with section 5E of the RUSA "Professional Competencies," a section entitled "Promotes and Demonstrates the Value of Library Services through Marketing and Advocacy." The topics covered are marketing theory and practices, marketing plans, and advocating the value of library services. "Marketing is the activity, set of institutions, and processes for creating, communicating, delivering, and exchanging offerings that have value for customers, clients, partners, and society at large" (American Marketing Association, 2013). "In the transformation of libraries, marketing will be the key to our success or failure" (Soules, 2001, 349). Almost two decades later, Soules's prediction appears to be on target. If the word *marketing* brings to mind advertising, selling, or perhaps consumer manipulation, these views indicate the lack of a customer-oriented mindset. Some of the benefits of programs with a customer-oriented mindset are increased revenues, increased utilization of services, more purchases of products, better compliance with laws, improved public health and safety, increased citizen protection of the environment, decreased costs of service delivery, improved customer satisfaction, and increased citizen support (Kotler and Lee, 2007b). Thus, marketing involves not only the promotion of libraries and their services, but customer focus, relationship management, collaboration, proactive engagement, and real partnerships in which customers and librarians are equal partners, with each possessing valued expertise.

This chapter focuses on developing and assessing the skills that are essential for identifying and promoting the library services that users value. The main competency goals are applying marketing theory and practices; developing, implementing, and evaluating a marketing plan for reference/public services; and advocating the value of the library's services to the community. Developing competencies related to marketing theory and practices ensures that librarians are able to determine the best reference/public services to provide for appropriate user groups. Competencies in developing, implementing, and evaluating an ongoing marketing plan will enable librarians to determine how best to serve the community within the constraints of existing resources. Competencies in advocating the value of library services will allow librarians to effectively

Key Resources for Marketing

ALA Connect. "Libraries Foster Community Engagement."
http://connect.ala.org/node/64933.

Association of College and Research Libraries. "Marketing for the Beginner."
https://crln.acrl.org/ index.php/crlnews/article/viewFile/16839/18438.

Association of College and Research Libraries. "Marketing the Academic Library."
www.ala.org/acrl/issues/marketing.

Dempsey, Kathy. 2006–. *The "M" Word—Marketing Libraries: Marketing News, Tips, and Trends for Libraries.*
http://themwordblog.blogspot.com/.

Institute of Museum and Library Services. "Community."
https://www.imls.gov/issues/national-issues/community.

Library Journal. "Library Marketer of the Year Award."
https://lj.libraryjournal.com/awards-info/library-marketer-of-the-year-award-nomination-guidelines/#_.
https://lj.libraryjournal.com/2017/ 10/marketing/sharing-story-lj-2017-marketer-year-award/.
https://lj.libraryjournal.com/2016/09/marketing/maximizing-the-message-lj-2016-marketer-of-the-year-award/.

Library Leadership and Management Association. "Marketing and Communications Community of Practice."
www.ala.org/llama/communities/marketing.

Library Video Network. "Marketing Your Library."
https://www.kanopy.com/product/marketing-your-library.

Public Library Association. "Community Engagement and Outreach."
www.ala.org/pla/resources/tools/community-engagement-outreach.

Public Library Association. "Marketing Strategies."
www.ala.org/pla/resources/tools/public-relations-marketing/marketing-strategies.

Reference and User Services Association. "Online Learning with RUSA (Marketing)."
www.ala.org/rusa/onlinece.

Reference and User Services Association. "Virtual Reference Companion—Marketing."
www.ala.org/rusa/vrc/marketing.

Urban Libraries Council. "Civic and Community Engagement."
https://www.urbanlibraries.org/civic-and-community-engagement-pages-685.php.

WebJunction. "Marketing."
https://www.webjunction.org/explore-topics/marketing-outreach.html.

communicate the nature and value of the reference and information services to the community.

UNDERSTANDS AND APPLIES MARKETING THEORY AND PRACTICES

Competencies for Understanding and Applying Marketing Theory and Practices

Marketing theory and practices originated in commercial organizations. Until about 1970, marketing theory and language focused on how goods and services were priced, promoted, and distributed by for-profit firms. But in the late 1960s, some scholars began to realize that noncommercial organizations might benefit by using marketing concepts in pursuit of their goals. Philip Kotler (2005) describes this broadening movement and the order in which several other fields began to adopt marketing language and concepts. Based on his own extensive list of publications, Kotler identifies the order as social marketing, educational marketing, health marketing, celebrity marketing, cultural marketing (museums and performing arts), church marketing, and place marketing.

Kotler notes that as marketing language and concepts entered each of these domains, serious opposition emerged from the old guard. Today, "the general consensus is that broadening marketing has been good for marketing and good for the areas that marketing has invaded" (p. 115). However, despite this consensus, when Singh (2017) reviewed the marketing curricula in LIS schools in the United States and Canada, he found that more than half of the LIS programs did not offer any separate marketing course. He concludes that many information professionals prefer using terms such as *advocacy*, *outreach*, and *public relations* rather than *marketing*; these misperceptions and conceptual barriers could be resolved by providing marketing courses on a regular basis in order to equip future information professionals with useful marketing skills. Because LIS educational programs have often not provided a good foundation in this field's theory, enhancing your understanding of marketing theory and best practices by reading professional literature, attending courses, and other forms of continuing education is vital. WebJunction's marketing pages (https://www.webjunction.org/explore-topics/marketing-outreach.html) are highly recommended for keeping up with current marketing news, and exploring the available documents, webinars, and self-paced courses related to marketing topics.

The typical behavioral strategies in the RUSA "Professional Competencies" that demonstrate competencies related to understanding and applying marketing theory and practices are:

- Practices the basic principles of marketing and applies them to library services
- Conducts research to assess the marketing landscape and to determine the current position among similar and/or competing businesses and organizations
- Identifies the strengths, weaknesses, opportunities, and challenges of library services to enhance marketing strategy
- Identifies, analyzes, and prioritizes target markets and audiences to determine how best to promote library services that can effectively serve them
- Determines community relationships and develops partnering models of services with groups within the community
- Conducts periodic reviews of the community for opportunities to align their needs with library services

Development Methods for Understanding and Applying Marketing Theory and Practices

As noted above, marketing concepts were first developed for product-based profit-making organizations. Traditionally, the important concepts in developing a marketing plan are the marketing mix factors known as the 4Ps: product, price, promotion, and place. *A Dictionary of Marketing* (Doyle, 2016) says that *marketing mix* was

> a term first used by Neil Borden of Harvard Business School in 1964 to describe the key ingredients, tools, and programme variables that marketers use to control the market. The image was one of a recipe to make a cake that was better than the individual ingredients themselves. The idea of a "marketing mix" was introduced in the belief that a company ought to coordinate and integrate its various marketing programmes in order to maximize their impact and effectiveness. Different mixes are required for different objectives. There are multiple marketing mix models, each with different ingredients. The most famous and popular mix of all has become known as the 4Ps model, the key ingredients being product, price, promotion, and place (or distribution), which was developed by E. Jerome McCarthy . . . The 4Ps model is now regarded as too simplistic for current marketing conditions, as well as being too focused on traditional consumer product marketing.

Understanding and Applying Basic Marketing Principles. In the for-profit world, the success of the marketing plan is judged by the bottom line—success in the marketplace. In the nonprofit world, the strategic plan is still an essential tool and the marketing mix concepts are very useful, but the effectiveness of the plan is more likely to be judged by an organization's success in changing users' behavior for the benefit of individuals, groups, or the whole society. Lee and Kotler (2016, 20) define nonprofit/NGO marketing as marketing efforts that most often focus on supporting the utilization of the organization's programs or services, advocacy efforts, and fund-raising. Many library marketing efforts fit best into the nonprofit/NGO marketing framework.

Although the 4Ps are the classic marketing mix model for profit-making organizations, which are primarily engaged in selling products, when dealing with services and customer-focused perspectives, additional Ps have been added to the marketing mix. When contrasted with products, services have five unique characteristics that influence marketing plans: lack of ownership, intangibility, inseparability, perishability, and heterogeneity/variability. The "service marketing mix," or the 7Ps, includes the traditional 4Ps—product, price, promotion, and place—along with three additional concepts: people, process, and physical evidence (LearnMarketing.net, 2018). In service marketing, these 3Ps are crucial additions because of their importance:

> *People:* Consumers make judgments and deliver perceptions of the service based on their interactions with employees.
>
> *Process:* Efficient service fosters consumer loyalty and confidence in the organization.
>
> *Physical Evidence:* Where is the service delivered? Is the environment, clean, friendly, comfortable, and easy to navigate?

Based on the marketing theory of the 7Ps, Potter (2012) outlines seven key concepts for marketing libraries:

1. Everyone is trying to get from A to B. We have to show them how we'll help get them there quickly and more successfully.
2. Market the service, not the product; market the benefits, not the features.
3. Market what *they* value, but continue to do what *we* value.
4. Market personally.
5. Never, ever market something you can't deliver.
6. Create and market different value propositions for different groups.
7. Understand the cost curve, and how it applies to libraries. (The cost curve is the value your users get from using a service versus the cost of their effort.)

Alternatively, instead of increasing the number of Ps, the original definitions of the 4Ps can be adapted for public sector organizations (Kotler and Lee, 2007a):

> *Product*—anything that can be offered to a market to satisfy a need

Price—whatever users "give up" in the exchange process

Promotion—persuasive communications to the target audience

Place—where, when, and how users access services and programs

Another nonprofit-based marketing perspective is social marketing. Morgan (2017) provides a good definition: "Social Marketing seeks to develop and integrate marketing concepts with other approaches to influence behaviours that benefit individuals and communities for the greater social good." Social marketing, according to Lee and Kotler (2016), uses marketing principles and techniques to change target audience behaviors that will benefit society as well as the individual. Information literacy, early childhood literacy, English as a second language, and other similar library programs are aimed at changing behaviors and thus may be considered social marketing. Lee and Kotler (2016) note that the commercial and social marketing models have several similarities:

- Customer orientation is crucial.
- Exchange theory is fundamental (the target audience views benefits as equal to perceived costs).
- Marketing research is used throughout the process.
- Audiences are segmented.
- All 4Ps are considered.
- Results are measured and used for improvement.

Coming from a social marketing perspective, Dev and Schultz (2005b) propose an alternate set of 4Ps, called SIVA (figure 5.1), that creates a more customer-focused approach to the marketplace. They note that as implemented, the 4Ps often have become internally focused rather than customer-focused, and the traditional concepts need to be updated for the twenty-first century (Dev and

Traditional Four P's Marketing Mix	SIVA Marketing Mix	SIVA Focus	Four P's Focus
Product	Solutions: How can I solve my problem?	Understand customer problem and develop products/services to address customer problem	Persuade customers to use already developed products/services to meet their needs
Promotion	Information: Where can I learn more about it?	Supply information to be used by customer when wanted and needed through chat rooms, social networking sites	Direct marketing, mass mailing, advertising in mass media
Price	Value: What is my total sacrifice to get this solution?	Customer time and effort as well as monetary costs	Primarily monetary cost of products/services
Place	Access: Where can I find it?	Type of distribution system that customer prefers to access	Physical store or building where customer goes to obtain products/services

SOURCE: Based on the concepts in: Chekitan S. Dev and Don E. Schultz. 2005. "A Customer-Focused Approach Can Bring the Current Marketing Mix into the 21st Century." *Marketing Management* 14, no. 1: 16–22.

FIGURE 5.1 *SIVA: The Marketing Mix*

Schultz, 2005a, 2005b). In social marketing, the marketing concepts, theories, and techniques are used to achieve social ends, not commercial ones. For example, instead of "product," these authors suggest "solutions" as a more appropriate concept.

Conducting Research and Assessing the Marketing Landscape. Research is important to determine the specific user groups to target and to answer questions such as: why specific groups should care about your service offering; how the service fits into the lives of users; and how the service supports the larger mission of the library. Potter (2012, 14) notes that "libraries don't always understand the lifecycle of their users—what they're doing in their lives." As Almquist (2014) observes, marketing is about identifying needs, and identifying and meeting users' needs help libraries create services that do not have to be sold.

Moreover, the marketing landscape must be surveyed in order to understand other channels through which users might obtain services that are similar to those you propose to offer. Examples of organizations that might offer similar services to the library are Google, Amazon, local bookstores, and publishers that sell directly to people. These competitors offer various information services. Therefore, reviewing the cost (time, effort, and money) to the user of the various "competitors" versus library services is one type of research. These organizations are not always competitors; sometimes partnerships work well with these groups, but if using these alternate services rather than library services saves the user much time and effort, the organizations and the library are indeed competing for the same customers.

Public services were once viewed as products to be designed and produced by professionals and consumed fairly passively by customers. Today, we see many public services as being coproduced by the provider and the user. Thus, visualizing the role and relationship of the user within the service process, called "service blueprinting," is a very useful research method. The service blueprint provides a detailed map of the service process, showing the actions of the provider and user, and the points of interaction within the process that support service delivery (Radnor, Osborne, Kinder, and Mutton, 2014). This approach allows the service to be viewed from the perspective of the user and identifies where failure points in the process impact quality and performance and fail to meet users' expectations or needs. Secret shoppers, real-time users' video diaries, and focus groups and surveys are also useful in capturing these user service experiences. Service blueprinting has been successfully used to evaluate shortcomings in library services and identify enhancement opportunities. Pretlow and Sobel (2015) provide a detailed study of computer services for library users that can serve as a good guide for librarians interested in applying service blueprinting to provide user-centered services. Another good resource is Marcia Johnston's (2016) discussion of how to map out your customer journeys.

Solomon (2016) suggests several research methods to determine the interests of current users:

- Reviewing keyword searches and related search terms used
- Looking at blogs and social media created and used by library patrons
- Customer interviews and surveys
- Web analytics assessment
- Creating marketing personas

A market persona is a profile of a particular group of users, which helps to determine what types of marketing communications are appropriate for a certain group (Solomon, 2016). Personas are a way to categorize users or potential users by goals and behaviors that represent a certain type of user. For current library users, personas might be developed based on the characteristics of groups with different library behaviors. Often 3–5 personas are employed to represent core audiences and these tend to cover the following characteristics, which include but go beyond basic demographic data:

- Age range
- Educational level
- Social interest
- Job status

- Work experience
- Sources most commonly used to get information
- Self-description, using three key adjectives
- Gender
- Location
- Comfort with different kinds of technology

Additional categories that are sometimes used are psychographics (lifestyles, hobbies, personality, attitudes, opinions, voting behavior); generation cohort; geography; and benefits sought.

Conducting research is essential for understanding who your audience is, what they want to find, where they want to find it, and how to deliver the most effective message to them. The "Quick Guide for Content Marketing Research" (Relevance, 2015) suggests that four key research assessments are essential:

1. *Audience* (who?)
   Recommended techniques are keyword research, user-generated content analysis, customer interviews and surveys, expert interviews, and web analytics assessment. Recommended tools are Google Analytics, BuzzSumo, and LinkedIn.
2. *Trends* (what?)
   Recommended assessments techniques are response analysis, angle identification, topic identification, compelling questions identification, resources cited, and quoted experts identification. Recommended tools are Google Trends and BuzzSumo.
3. *Media* (where?)
   Recommended assessment techniques are industry publication analysis, industry social influencers and experts, analytics, and social engagement analysis. Recommended tools are Share Tally, Followerwonk, Cison, GroupHigh, BuzzSumo, and Anewstip.
4. *Competition* (how?)
   Recommended assessment techniques are content inventory, sentiment analysis, keyword gap analysis, site architecture and navigation audit, and local SEO (search engine optimization) evaluation. Recommended tools are Screaming Frog, SEMrush, and Google Keyword Planner.

Analyzing Strengths, Weaknesses, Opportunities, and Threats (Challenges). Librarians must engage in assessment to obtain an in-depth understanding of the needs, expectations, preferences, and perceptions of primary user groups. In order to conduct assessment before writing a marketing plan, the external environment must be analyzed. Often, a SWOT (Strengths, Weaknesses, Opportunities, and Threats) analysis is conducted after collecting information from the environment. Key strategies for collecting information are conducting surveys and focus groups, networking with other libraries, and interviewing community leaders. Analyzing the data permits you to identify the unique primary user groups and their needs. *Marketing and Social Media* by Koontz and Mon (2014) includes a chapter on SWOT with exercises in the form of discussion questions (p. 51). This chapter provides an in-depth understanding of SWOT and tells you how to bring together the most important information for understanding the best opportunities and most important limitations and challenges in developing initiatives.

Identifying, Analyzing, and Prioritizing Target Markets. Segmenting and targeting markets conflict with the idealistic desire of librarians who wish to serve as many people as possible and all people equally. However, we may actually serve more people better by not serving everyone equally. Market segmentation helps us identify groups of people with the most pressing needs. Segmentation allows libraries to apply their scarce time and resources where they are most likely to produce lasting benefits. To expand your services to underserved groups, you should consider groups with characteristics that might benefit from library services; for example, undergraduates with library assignments, children with school assignments, and segments of the population who need spaces to get work done (quiet spaces, study rooms, and computer and printer access). For libraries, serving a select group well allows a library to build goodwill, promote referrals, and perhaps even increase funding (Heinze, 2017).

Successful marketing programs require agreement on which segments of our market should be the focus of our efforts, the purpose of those efforts, and how we will determine success (Heinze, 2017). Segments should drive marketing planning because not everyone perceives the same value in library services—it is the difference that matters in user values, rather than the similarities (Potter, 2012, 14). In marketing, the user is the center of all organizational actions. Marketing plans aim to establish stronger connections with unique communities of users. The unique communities of users that are a library's priority constituencies must be identified. The unique groups could be population segments that are identified, for example, by age (e.g., children, teens), disability (e.g., deaf, blind), school level (e.g., preschool, K–3, college), racial or ethnic groups (e.g., Hispanic, Chinese, African American), type of job (e.g., engineer, entrepreneur, lawyer), societal role (e.g., parent helping child with homework), or lifestyle (e.g., world traveler). After the unique priority user groups have been established and their needs, expectations, perceptions, and preferences have been analyzed, a written marketing plan can be developed with goals and strategies for each of the primary user groups.

Developing Community Relationships. A great way to demonstrate value to the community is to develop partnerships or collaboration around a community problem or issue; for example, child safety, family literacy, or employment skills and opportunities. Initiating community partnerships requires using a marketing approach, which involves exploring what community constituents want, segmenting the population based on market research, and using focus groups, surveys, and interviews of community leaders to ascertain their needs and views (Blake, Martin, and Du, 2011). Outreach programs are generally designed to connect, educate, and serve nontraditional or underserved community populations.

The book *Successful Community Outreach* by Blake, Martin, and Du (2011) provides many useful worksheets for planning outreach programs, and forms for developing a community outreach plan. Librarians interested in initiating and deepening their community relationships will find this community outreach manual to be an excellent resource for developing competencies in this area. Although it was primarily developed for public librarians, the authors note that with some adaptation the manual can be used in other settings. In our book, chapter 4, "Collaboration," includes many suggestions and ideas for developing competencies related to community partnerships and collaboration.

Assessing Development Efforts for Understanding and Applying Marketing Theory and Practices

The "Library Marketing and Advocacy Toolkit" by Law and Kovacs (2016) provides at least fifteen hours of workshop-style training in library marketing. The toolkit covers practices like engaging participants in group learning activities, reflecting on your prior experiences with marketing and advocacy activities, and becoming competent in developing, implementing, and assessing your marketing and advocacy activities. Through your library or a local library organization, engaging a facilitator and presenting a workshop are an excellent method of learning all of the concepts; and through reflection and participation in the toolkit's learning activities, you can test your understanding of marketing theory and practices. Finally, you should select and carry out a small marketing project in reference and user services to test your ability to apply your knowledge in practice. Moreover, reviewing the excellent and very practical case studies in *The Library Marketing Toolkit* by Potter (2012) will assist you in making the link between marketing theory and applying marketing plans in libraries.

We recommend reading books by Philip Kotler—Kotler has written over sixty marketing books, covering not only traditional marketing concepts and practices in profit-based firms, but also social marketing and marketing in public sector organizations.

The most highly recommended one is *Marketing in the Public Sector* (Kotler and Lee, 2007a), in part because many library examples are included throughout the discussion of the marketing mix (i.e., the 4Ps). Then, after reading the book, test yourself for each of the 4Ps: are you able to identify specific examples of the 4Ps in the reference and user services in your organization? Are you able to write a marketing plan for a specific reference or user service in your organization?

If you wish to develop skills in marketing library programs that are aimed at changing the behaviors of a target audience, such as information literacy or early childhood literacy, you should select the social program you wish to market and then use the text by Lee and Kotler (2016) to develop and implement a marketing plan. To assist you, Lee and Kotler (pp. 51–52) provide an outline of all the essential steps:

1. Describe the social issue, background, purpose, and focus.
2. Conduct a situation analysis (research and SWOT).
3. Select the target audience (segment it, and identify the primary and secondary targets).
4. Set the behavioral objectives and target goals.
5. Identify the target audience, analyze and understand perceived barriers, desired benefits, potential motivations, competition and influence of others for time and attention.
6. Develop a positioning statement (describe the desired behavior).
7. Develop the marketing mix strategies (4Ps).
8. Develop a plan for monitoring and evaluation.
9. Establish the budget and find funding sources.
10. Complete an implementation plan.

The appendixes in Lee and Kotler (2016) include worksheets for each step of the process. These worksheets can be used to structure your planning process. Included are sample social marketing plans and resources, for example: blogs, books, conferences, electronic media, journals and magazines, listservs and email digests, twitter feeds, websites, academic courses and the International Social Marketing Association's Academic Competencies.

DEVELOPS, IMPLEMENTS, AND EVALUATES AN ONGOING MARKETING PLAN FOR LIBRARY SERVICES

Competencies for Developing, Implementing, and Evaluating an Ongoing Marketing Plan for Library Services

Promoting everything to everyone is not marketing. The most important aspect of marketing is creating value for users, in contrast to the simplistic view of marketing as promotion or advertising (Heinze, 2017). While promotion is the most visible output, Heinze notes that if promotion is the most important part of marketing, then creating value for users will be neglected.

In his practical and action-oriented toolkit, Potter (2012) outlines the steps in the marketing cycle:

1. Decide on your goals
2. Research your market
3. Segment your market
4. Set objectives
5. Promotional activities
6. Measurement
7. Evaluation
8. Modification

The typical behavioral strategies suggested in the RUSA "Professional Competencies" that demonstrate competencies related to developing, implementing, and evaluating an ongoing marketing plan are:

- Sets measurable market goals and objectives, including brand strategy
- Develops consistent promotion and distribution strategies to meet goals and objectives based on the analysis of target audiences
- Participates in marketing training
- Implements marketing efforts, while maintaining records and clear communication with the staff and stakeholders
- Evaluates the effectiveness and impact of the strategies and revises as necessary

Development Methods for Developing, Implementing, and Evaluating an Ongoing Marketing Plan for Library Services

In the introduction to the marketing and public relations section in WebJunction's "Competency Index for the Library Field," Gutsche and Hough (2014) observe that "marketing efforts do not come from a single department; they need to be organization-wide." We will focus on marketing the library's reference and user services; however, coordination and collaboration with all areas of the library are vital even when the focus is primarily on these services. Collaboration within the library is enhanced through teams that coordinate marketing efforts. Almquist (2014) provides an example of the Steely Library's implementation of two library-wide permanent work teams on marketing and assessment. Each team has a liaison to the other team and a membership that is representative of the entire library. This structure not only provides coordination library-wide, but also provides excellent development opportunities for library staff. The University of Tennessee Libraries also established a dedicated marketing team in order to benefit from a more strategic approach to marketing (Bedenbaugh, 2016). Wilkes and Ward (2016) stress the benefits of marketing team projects in expanding staff abilities and increasing collaboration, thereby enabling the staff to develop their knowledge and recognize their strengths.

Library-wide marketing and assessment work teams can also monitor services to ensure that marketing promotions are supported by library service realities. Service standards and quality must be in alignment with marketing and advocacy messages (Law and Kovacs, 2016). Satisfied users become part of your marketing strategy. The fifth of Potter's (2012, 6) seven key marketing concepts is: "Never ever market something you can't deliver." Kotler and Lee (2007a) list practices that support customer satisfaction:

1. Support employees to deliver great service.
2. Ensure that infrastructure and systems help, not hinder service delivery.
3. Consider or enhance customer relationship management systems.
4. Discover the benefits of total quality management.
5. Monitor and track customer satisfaction levels.

Internal marketing is very important in the development, implementation, and evaluation of marketing plans even if they are focused primarily on reference and user services. Potter (2012) provides a good definition of internal marketing: promoting the value of the library to the wider organization in which the library exists. For public libraries, the wider organization includes city or county governing boards, library trustees, Friends groups, and agencies within the primary community that have significant relationships with the library. For academic libraries, the wider organization includes the college or university administration, the academic senate, library advisory boards, and other groups that have significant relationships with the library. Special libraries are usually part of a larger business, museum, or nonprofit organization, which defines the scope of internal marketing. The wider organizational contexts in which the library resides also provide some collaborative opportunities. For academic libraries, marketing professors and their classes are useful resources for developing a marketing plan. For public libraries, some sources worth exploring for marketing advice and collaboration are members of the library board of trustees, city and county officials, the chamber of commerce, and the local college.

For planning effective internal marketing, Potter (2012) suggests the following steps:

1. Conduct an audit of internal stakeholders—who they are, how important they are, what their needs are, and how those needs will be met.
2. Decide on appropriate messages to those stakeholders.
3. Determine how to communicate the messages successfully.

The *Library Marketing Toolkit* by Potter also includes a case study with ten rules for success.

Kotler and Lee (2007a) observe that marketing is the best platform for a public agency to meet citizens' needs and deliver real value to them. They suggest adopting a marketing mindset, which consists of five principles:

1. Adopt a customer-centered focus.
2. Segment and target markets (i.e., unique groups of users).
3. Identify the competition (i.e., those organizations or activities that customers use to fulfill the same needs).
4. Utilize all 4Ps available in the marketing mix: product, price, place, and promotion.
5. Monitor efforts and make adjustments.

In considering customer-centered focus, every marketing activity should result in an intentional impact, which is to deliver services with meaning and value to people—the customer focus requires understanding why people care about a service and how the service fits into their lives (Heinze, 2017). Unlike products, services are consumed at the same moment they are created; because users are an integral part of the services we produce, there is no way to create a service "for" users; we can only create services "with" users. Thus, we should make opportunities to increase users' involvement in all of our services. Heinze observes that business does a better job than libraries in thinking about the total service relationship from both customer and organizational perspectives: Are the benefits the customer receives worth the customer's time, effort, and money? Are the benefits library users receive relative to the library's costs worth the costs of serving those users?

According to Solomon (2016), content marketing creates content that is not simply information but is truly useful and valuable to a particular target audience. We need to create engaging experiences for the communities we serve through effective content marketing that focuses upon solutions, access, value, and education (Singh, 2015). In content marketing, service providers try to understand the journey that customers make, starting with discovering they have a need, finding the service or product, consuming it, and reflecting upon their experience and level of satisfaction. Applying content marketing to the school library, Houghton (2016) suggests that we must engage and solidify our relationships with various target audiences: students, teachers, administrators, parents, and the community. For each segment, we must develop content that addresses the particular audience, and we must determine how they benefit from it, what success looks like, and what part the school library plays in meeting their needs.

Setting Measurable Goals and Objectives, including Brand Strategy. A planning process is essential in order to identify and promote service to users. A strategic plan of operations provides a framework for marketing goals and objectives. Alman and Swanson (2014, 2) provide a good example of basing a marketing plan goal (e.g., create a makerspace for the community) on a more general goal in a library's strategic plan (act as an agent of innovation for the community). A marketing plan is an aspect of strategic planning that is a promotional mechanism by which goals, objectives, and strategies can be measured in a quantitative manner. Issues that need to be addressed in developing the plan are: who is providing reference and user services, what services are being provided, and the effectiveness of the services. All planning efforts, including marketing plans, should be based on the library's mission statement, vision, core values, and organizational goals. A marketing plan involves the essential steps of assessment, communication and outreach, and evaluation.

Branding is a strategy that an organization can use to secure a desired position in a potential customer's mind. Enhanced awareness, understanding of features, personality, and recognition of a trusted image will make participation more likely (Kotler and Lee, 2007b). Kotler and Lee (2007a) discuss six major qualities that should guide the selection of a brand: it should be memorable, meaningful, likeable, transferable, adaptable, and protectable. They also outline general steps for establishing a brand identity:

1. Establish the brand's purpose.
2. Identify the target audiences for the brand.
3. Articulate your desired brand identity.
4. Craft the brand promise.

5. Determine the brand's position relative to the competition.
6. Select the brand's elements.

Potter (2012) builds upon Kotler and Lee's general outline with an excellent practical chapter on branding specifics for libraries: branding with case studies, and information on marketing online, in social media, and with new technologies. He also recommends the following steps for libraries to take in establishing their brands:

1. Do your homework: find out how people perceive the library.
2. Make the brand accessible.
3. Choose a color palette.
4. Invest in design.
5. Make language a priority.
6. Write a house style manual.

Peters and Kemp (2014) report on a very interesting library project that greatly increased reference questions by using branding strategies: the library established a "Blue Crew" brand with a tagline of "Ask Us Anything." Their case study illustrates many of Schmidt's (2012) observations about logos, which are part of branding: the logo should express the library's values, serve as a form of communication, provide a visual identity for the library, let users understand in an instant what the library is about, and make the library approachable. Marketing campaigns for new reference services cannot only create additional recognition through branding, but also promote more in-depth use of the service (Thorpe and Bowman, 2013).

Developing Promotion Strategies. In the marketing world, promotion is often called "marketing communications" and is used to inform, educate, and persuade targeted segments of the market (Kotler and Lee, 2007b). As part of developing communication strategies, a survey to determine the communication preferences of targeted market segments will assist in your making the most effective use of limited resources. At the College of Wooster, while students supported a broader range of communication channels than faculty or staff did, social media were generally unpopular across all three groups, with only Facebook achieving majority support and only among students. These results differed from student preferences at Western Oregon University, thus reinforcing the need for each library to survey its own users (Gustafson, Sharrow, and Short, 2017). For libraries, Alman and Swanson (2014) provide one chapter covering the creation of a media list of local sources, including newspapers, radio and television stations, websites, school newspapers, church bulletins, and community center newsletters. The chapter also discusses contacting people on your media list, creating press releases and public service announcements, and making a press kit and a calendar of events. A second chapter on social media covers Facebook, Flickr, Instagram, Pinterest, Snapchat, Tumblr, Twitter, WordPress, and YouTube, with advice on managing social media through social media policies, evaluating social media success, and identifying popular social networking sites. An appendix contains a sample marketing plan.

For developing promotional materials, Jennifer Burke (2017) has compiled a list of top marketing tools, including image-editing tools, stock media sources, video tools, social media tools, better writing tools, and projects/planning tools. Regarding the content of promotional materials, Mansfield (2015) reminds us of the importance of stories. She advises us to show our constituents what matters most by sharing human interest stories with them. A good story can promote both the collection and the role of the library by focusing on impacts. She observes that marketing is about building community—and using compelling stories will help us commit to what matters most. To support international goals for sustainable development, the International Federation of Library Associations (2018a) has just published a storytelling manual, which provides guidelines on telling effective stories and using stories to promote community engagement. IFLA (2018b) is publishing the stories on its "Library Map of the World" site.

Implementing the Marketing Plan. The most widely recommended method for developing skills in marketing is to actually develop and implement a marketing plan for a new or expanded organizational service; for example, virtual reference, reference for distance learning students, makerspaces, or information literacy services through a distance learning platform. Achieving the deep understanding that librarians need to succeed at marketing requires opportunities to consider and apply marketing principles as part of their daily work (Heinze, 2017).

Evaluating the Marketing Plan. Finally, evaluation competencies are the librarian's key to improving the effectiveness of marketing programs. Evaluation goals and strategies must be an integral part of the written plan at the time the marketing plan is first developed. You should make certain that your marketing plan goals and objectives are SMART (Specific, Measurable, Achievable, Relevant, and Timely) so that you can actually measure the extent to which your marketing plan has been successful. Ideally, you will want to know if the marketing plan was successful in changing users' knowledge, beliefs, attitudes, or behavior. Conducting focus groups, surveys, and observing changes in the current environment are important strategies to meet the goal of enhancing and improving the existing marketing plan for reference services.

Evaluation of the marketing plan should be ongoing, with the library continuously monitoring its efforts and making adjustments. Critical components in ongoing evaluation are a clear understanding of goals and objectives, the identification of tools to measure outcomes, the analysis of outcomes, and identifying steps for course corrections (Kotler and Lee, 2007a).

Assessing Development Efforts for Developing, Implementing, and Evaluating an Ongoing Marketing Plan for Library Services

The "Marketing Assessment Checklist" (figure 5.2) will assist individuals in determining their level of

Marketing Assessment Checklist	No experience	Little experience performing, but some knowledge	Experience performing, but infrequent practice	Perform and practice regularly	Practice regularly and able to teach skill to others
Conducts research to assess the marketing landscape and to determine current position among similar and/or competing businesses and organizations					
Identifies the strengths, weaknesses, opportunities, and threats (challenges) of library services to enhance marketing strategy					
Identifies, analyzes, and prioritizes target markets and audiences to determine how to best promote library services that can effectively serve them					
Determines community relationships and develops partnering models of services with groups within the community					
Conducts periodic reviews of the community for opportunities to align needs with library services					

FIGURE 5.2 *Marketing Assessment Checklist*

expertise in the various areas related to community assessment. Asking a marketing professor or member of the community who has experience in marketing products and services to evaluate a draft marketing plan for a reference service also provides valuable feedback on your level of understanding and skill in applying assessment concepts.

Your marketing planning and implementation competencies may be evaluated holistically by reflecting upon the answers to the following questions:

How valuable was the plan for:

1. Identifying the strengths and weaknesses of the specific reference service?
2. Identifying new methods of service and new service products?
3. Improving the reference service?

Suggested scale:

1 = little or no value; **2** = somewhat valuable; **3** = very valuable.

Another very useful assessment method is to present your marketing plan and implementation process as a case study. Once the case study is prepared, ask a marketing professional in the community or a marketing professor in a university to evaluate the strengths and weaknesses of the plan and its subsequent implementation.

Finally, the "Marketing Evaluation Checklist" (figure 5.3) provides a useful tool for evaluating your competencies in each task related to planning and implementing a marketing program for a specific reference or information service. This checklist is designed to be used to self-assess your competencies in each step once a marketing program has been planned and implemented.

To assess the effectiveness of your communication and outreach competencies, the bottom line is the community's response to the library's outreach efforts. After conducting the communication and outreach campaign for specific services intended to meet the needs of a specific community population, you can conduct phone or in-person interviews of randomly selected individuals from the specific community population. Analyzing users' responses to the open-ended questions below will provide excellent feedback on the effectiveness of outreach efforts.

Interview Questions

- Have you heard about "X" service?
  If respondents indicate yes, follow up with:
- How did you learn about the service?
- Have you used "X" service?

  If respondents indicate yes, follow up with:

  Where did you access the service?

  To what extent did the service fulfill your expectations?

  What would you suggest to make other people aware of "X" service?

  What do you think would motivate other people to use "X" service?

ADVOCATES THE VALUE OF LIBRARY SERVICES TO THE PRIMARY COMMUNITY

Competencies for Advocating the Value of Library Services to the Primary Community

The American Association of School Librarians (2007) defines advocacy as the "ongoing process of building partnerships so that others will act for and with you, turning passive support into educated action for the library program." Advocacy and marketing are closely related—they are both about the promotion of libraries and library services (Potter, 2012). "Advocacy is about changing attitudes toward the library; marketing is about increasing use of the library" (Law and Kovacs, 2016, 4). Libraries must adopt advocacy initiatives to reach community leaders, who often do not use library services; and they must adopt marketing initiatives to engage library users so that they will be able to benefit from all of the available library services. Because libraries benefit local communities,

	No Knowledge	Beginner	Intermediate	Advanced
Establish objectives based upon mission and goals				
Write clear goals and specific objectives				
State written objectives in measurable terms so that specific information can be gathered for evaluation				
Determine the measurement plan at the beginning of the marketing plan				
Determine the type of information needed to measure success				
Identify the sources of information				
Determine methods of collecting information, e.g., personal interview, telephone survey, focus group, mail questionnaire, observation				
Determine the types of questions				
Design questions to get essential information				
Sequence the questions				
Pilot test the questions				
Estimate the budget, resources required for evaluation process				
Prepare written guidelines and training for information collectors				
Determine the sampling method and size				
Analyze and interpret the information collected				
Compare the results of information analysis with stated objectives				
Identify gaps in performance				
Develop a plan to reduce performance gaps				
Establish plan for periodic performance evaluation				

FIGURE 5.3 *Marketing Evaluation Checklist*

the best hope for government funding is to concentrate their advocacy efforts at the local and state levels, coordinating efforts across all types of libraries. Libraries are inherently political institutions; they have become community centers for education, inclusion, employment, social services, public spaces, digital literacy, community development, and other community needs (Jaeger, Zerhusen, Gorham, Hill, and Taylor, 2017). Therefore, library and information schools need to provide students with the research, marketing, and advocacy skills necessary to contribute to advocating for our libraries. All members of the library staff—trustees, Friends, patrons, partners, community leaders, and educators—need to participate in advocacy.

For targeted user groups, communication and outreach competencies allow librarians to effectively increase the users' awareness of services that are designed to meet their particular needs. Communication and outreach strategies are employed to inform users about the new or existing programs and services that will best meet their needs. Leaders from each of these unique user communities are generally able to advise librarians regarding which strategies are the best investment of time and money for informing and raising user awareness in that particular community.

The typical behavioral strategies suggested in the RUSA "Professional Competencies" that demonstrate competencies related to advocating the value of library services are:

- Engages with target audiences, connecting via the most appropriate tools and sources
- Communicates with library users, potential users, and other stakeholders through multiple communication formats and channels
- Maintains current awareness of the communication tools and media sources used by target audiences
- Builds relationships with partners who can advocate on behalf of the library
- Develops and maintains relationships with diverse cultural groups

Development Methods for Advocating the Value of Library Services to the Primary Community

Three excellent resources to increase your advocacy knowledge and expertise are:

1. The WebJunction topic area devoted to "Advocacy" (https://www.webjunction.org/explore-topics/advocacy.html), which provides access to examples of advocacy in action, documents, news, and webinars. For example, you can learn how to organize an advocacy campaign in five phases: plan, create awareness, generate engagement, encourage action, and continue ongoing advocacy efforts.

2. The website of United for Libraries: The Association of Library Trustees, Advocates, Friends, and Foundations (www.ala.org/united/) supports Friends groups and library board trustees in their efforts to advocate, promote, and fund-raise on behalf of all types of libraries. The site provides access to webinars, success stories, videos, talking points, postcards, petitions, information sheets, flyers, brochures, bookmarks, and guides and resources, as well as tools for promoting your library's value. One United for Libraries web page provides selected resources for library supporters to advocate for libraries (www.ala.org/united/advocacy/advocacyala). United for Libraries also provides free online access to *A Power Guide for Successful Advocacy* (Reed, Nawalinski, and Kalonick, 2013), which provides not only a blueprint for action on passing a library referendum or bond issue, but also a guide for continuing promotion of the library in the community.

3. The ALA's Office for Library Advocacy website (www.ala.org/aboutala/offices/ola) provides access to popular resources and advocacy training events.

For schools, the American Association of School Librarians (2018a) has published the "AASL Advocacy Toolkit." The introduction in the "Advocacy Toolkit"

Marketing and Advocacy

Key Resources for Advocacy

American Association of School Librarians. "Advocacy." www.ala.org/aasl/advocacy.

American Library Association. "Advocacy, Legislation & Issues." www.ala.org/advocacy/.

American Library Association. "Advocacy University." www.ala.org/advocacy/advocacy-university.

American Library Association. "Public Awareness Tools and Resources." www.ala.org/advocacy/advleg/publicawareness/.

Association for Library Service to Children. "Everyday Advocacy." www.ala.org/everyday-advocacy/.

Association of College and Research Libraries. "Advocacy & Issues." www.ala.org/acrl/issues.

International Federation of Library Associations and Institutions. "The International Advocacy Programme (IAP)." https://www.ifla.org/ldp/iap.

Library and Information Technology Association. "Advocacy & Issues." www.ala.org/lita/advocacy.

Public Library Association. "Advocacy." www.ala.org/pla/resources/tools/public-relations-marketing/advocacy.

Public Library Association. "Leadership Development and Advocacy." www.ala.org/pla/leadership.

United for Libraries. "Citizens-Save-Libraries Power Guide." www.ala.org/united/powerguide.

WebJunction. "Advocacy." https://www.webjunction.org/explore-topics/advocacy.html.

Young Adult Library Services Association. "Advocacy." www.ala.org/yalsa/advocacy.

---

indicates that standards for school librarians include their advocacy and leadership skills: school librarians must be able to clearly explain to stakeholders the impact of library programs and resources upon student achievement and to build positive learning environments by designing and leading professional development opportunities for other educators. Stakeholders include teachers, administrators, learners, parent/guardians, and community members. Everyday advocacy includes library newsletters, brief talks at faculty and school board meetings, invitations to special events at the school library, the distribution of photos of events and student workers, publishing data and information via the school website and other appropriate media, staying current on local issues, and recognizing stakeholders who support the library. Many resources are included in the "Advocacy Toolkit," which certainly would also be useful to public and academic librarians who wish to develop advocacy skills.

For public libraries, Stephen Abram (2017), executive director of the Federation of Ontario Public Libraries, provides a case study and excellent advice on supporting public libraries through marketing, advocacy, research, and professional development:

- Build talking points that can start a real conversation—statistics and measurements are important but are not enough.
- Fight perceptions with emotion and fight data with facts—and the best approach is to combine the two.
- Be succinct and memorable.
- Build relationships with key community funders and opinion leaders.
- Tell a story, but tell it well—with a great ending that inspires people to action and insight based on emotional engagement and values alignment.
- Just do it—treat every interaction, event, and moment as an opportunity for influencing stakeholders.

As Abram indicates, data are not sufficient for library advocacy, but they are still very important. Measures That Matter, a joint project of the IMLS and the Chief Officers of State Library Agencies (2018), notes that without sound public library data that measure and track impact, public libraries may be at risk. The project is intended to streamline data-collection efforts and provide a foundation for telling the public library story, including the diverse communities served, tools and information for people, and the ways in which public libraries improve people's lives and their communities.

For academic libraries, a major advocacy initiative is Value of Academic Libraries. This project is focused on demonstrating the value of academic libraries to key stakeholders and funders in higher education. Significant reports and progress on the initiative are available on the Value of Academic Libraries website (www.ala.org/acrl/issues/value).

Assessing Development Efforts for Advocating the Value of Library Services to the Primary Community

The "Advocacy Assessment Checklist" (figure 5.4) will assist individuals in determining their level of expertise in the various areas related to advocating for the value of libraries. As you participate in more advocacy activities, your expertise will grow.

	No experience	Little experience performing, but some knowledge	Experience performing, but infrequent practice	Perform and practice regularly	Practice regularly and able to teach skill to others
Engages with target audiences, connecting via the most appropriate tools and sources					
Communicates with library users, potential users, and other stakeholders through multiple communication formats and channels					
Maintains current awareness of communication tools and media sources used by target audiences					
Builds relationships with partners who advocate on behalf of the library					
Develops and maintains relationships among diverse cultural groups					

FIGURE 5.4 *Advocacy Assessment Checklist*

CHAPTER **six**

Assessment

ASSESSMENT SECTION 5F: ASSESSES AND RESPONDS TO DIVERSITY IN USER NEEDS, USER COMMUNITIES, AND USER PREFERENCES

This chapter is about developing and assessing your knowledge, skills, abilities, and behaviors associated with section 5F of the RUSA "Professional Competencies," a section entitled "Assesses and Responds to Diversity in User Needs, User Communities, and User Preferences." The topics covered are user needs, information services, information resources, service delivery methods, user interfaces for information resources, and evaluating information providers. Libraries evaluate and assess both their users' needs and their own provision of information to meet those needs.

Historically, a culture of assessment has been slow to develop in libraries. In the twentieth century, competencies in assessing libraries' resources and services were not emphasized as an essential element of professional education either at the master's degree level or "on the job." Professional education grew out of a skills-based orientation toward developing technical knowledge, skills, and abilities in the various functions of libraries—acquisitions, cataloging, developing and maintaining collections, and providing reference and circulation services. Libraries also continued to emphasize performance related to conducting daily operations in functional areas.

But today, because of the increasing emphasis on accountability throughout our society, professional educators and library practitioners view assessment competencies for librarians as very important. Accountability, or being able to justify the allocation of scarce resources to funding agencies, has become increasingly important in these times of increasingly scarce resources. Libraries must be able to demonstrate the value of their services to the community and answer the key question: how do libraries add value to people's lives? Librarians who continue to focus primarily on effective daily operations (are we doing it right?) will have a difficult time developing the competencies required to ask the more difficult questions of community value (are we doing the right things?).

In the twenty-first century, many libraries have created assessment positions or assigned assessment responsibilities to librarians along with their other duties. As part of the increasing emphasis on accountability, the Association of College and Research Libraries (2017) recently approved the "Proficiencies for Assessment Librarians and Coordinators." In the public library field, the Institute of Museum and Library Services and COSLA (Chief Officers of State Library Agencies) have initiated a project with the goal of demonstrating the role, value, and impact of public libraries through data. This project, Measures That Matter (http://measuresthatmatter.net/), is focused on outcome-based assessments as opposed to counting outputs. The Institute of Museum and Library Services (2017) defines outcomes as benefits to people: specifically, achievements or changes in skill, knowledge, attitude, behavior, condition, or life status for program participants. Measures That Matter builds on three existing initiatives: Project Outcome, the Impact Survey, and the Edge Initiative (Koerber, 2017b). In the international arena, the International Federation of Library Associations publishes a bibliography on the "Impact and Outcome of Libraries" (Poll, 2016). Evaluation is an important component of the Bill & Melinda Gates Foundation's (2018) programs, including the Global Libraries program, which works to transform libraries as engines of development, and which has created an "Impact Planning and Assessment Guide" (Bill & Melinda Gates Foundation, 2015) for collecting information on how libraries contribute to key development areas, such as health, education, and economic opportunity.

After professional education, the most important way to keep up in the field is on-the-job learning. The process known as "action research" provides a framework to improve your practice through assessment activities that are situated in everyday experience. Action research is distinctive because practitioners research their own practices; in most traditional forms of research, a professional researcher does the research on, rather than with, the practitioners (McNiff, 2017). McNiff notes several reasons for conducting action research: (1) improve learning in order to improve practice; (2) advance knowledge and theory by identifying new ideas about how and why things can be done; and (3) explain how you are contributing new understandings for yourself and others.

Libraries and librarians must schedule time on the job to reflect upon the effectiveness of daily operations so that they're able to develop and maintain their essential competencies in assessment. For evaluation and assessment competencies, on-the-job learning is the most significant development method. In *The Library Assessment Cookbook* (Dobbs, 2017), 122 "chefs" have cooked up 80 assessment recipes. The recipes provide practical approaches to assessing library services and resources. Experimenting with these recipes on the job is an excellent strategy for developing your assessment competencies. In addition, all of the chefs are willing to answer e-mail inquiries about their recipes.

To develop their assessment competencies, librarians must incorporate basic problem-solving steps into their professional practice and routine work habits. A seven-step model, "Basic Problem-Solving and Decision-Making Skills" (figure 6.1), would, if adopted by libraries and actively used by

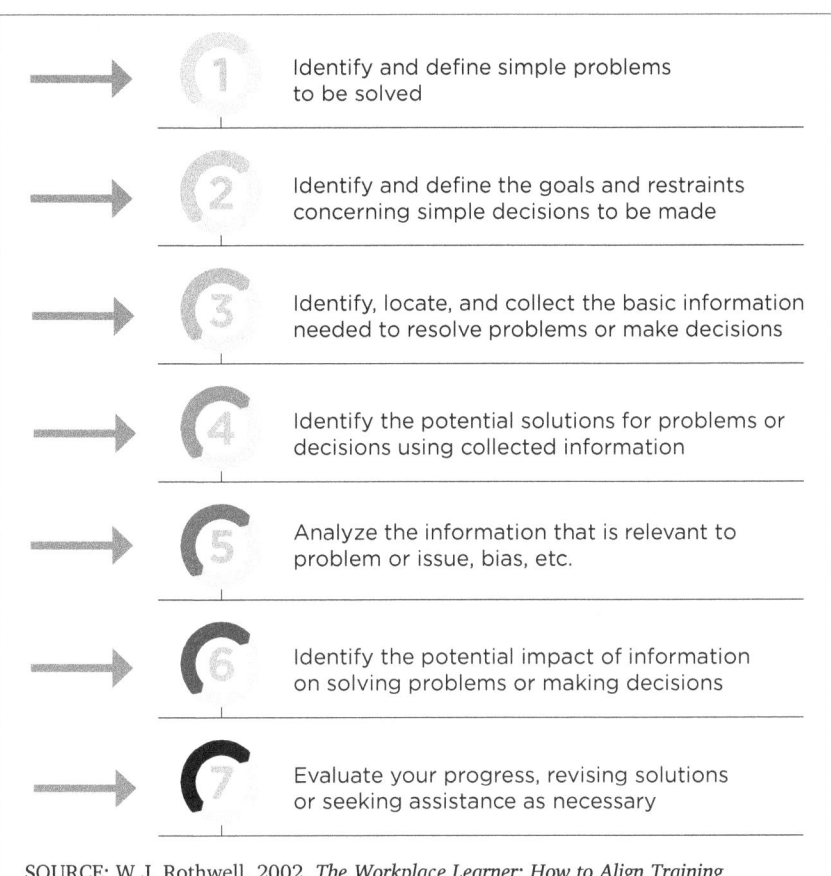

FIGURE 6.1 *Basic Problem-Solving and Decision-Making Skills*

1. Identify and define simple problems to be solved
2. Identify and define the goals and restraints concerning simple decisions to be made
3. Identify, locate, and collect the basic information needed to resolve problems or make decisions
4. Identify the potential solutions for problems or decisions using collected information
5. Analyze the information that is relevant to problem or issue, bias, etc.
6. Identify the potential impact of information on solving problems or making decisions
7. Evaluate your progress, revising solutions or seeking assistance as necessary

SOURCE: W.J. Rothwell. 2002. *The Workplace Learner: How to Align Training Initiatives with Individual Learning Competencies.* New York: American Management Association, p. 65.

librarians, support the development and maintenance of professional competence. Another useful model, the "Process for Seven Steps in Practitioner Research" (figure 6.2), can best be viewed as a continuous process which cycles back through the steps.

The consistent assessment of resources in the context of users' needs is essential to keep the library's information services vital and relevant. A parallel effort in assessing and evaluating the delivery of information services is equally important. A large and growing set of delivery channels provides a wide range of information services to users. There are print collections visited on site, print materials that are delivered to the user, electronic collections delivered over the Internet, and information services provided through in-person, telephone, fax, e-mail, and web-based virtual

SOURCE: Rebecca Watson-Boone. 2000. "Academic librarians as practitioner researchers." *Journal of Academic Librarianship* 26, no. 2: 85-93.

FIGURE 6.2 *Process for Seven Steps in Practitioner Research*

sessions. For all of these services, the goal is to make the resources of the library available to the user in a way and a format that meets the user's needs.

The most critical element in any information service is the staff providing it. Using evaluation measures for the performance of the staff is a challenge, however. Many aspects of the information service interaction are intangible and difficult to measure objectively. However, the goal of assessing and evaluating performance remains valid, if elusive.

Reference and user services librarians must have competencies in both formal and informal methods of evaluation and assessment. Assessment methods vary greatly and can include the effective use of closure questions in the reference interaction, a user feedback form on interlibrary loan documents, and structured surveys and studies that use unobtrusive observation. The use of these and other assessment and evaluation measures will vary across time and across institutions to fit particular needs, but the competencies required to conduct them will endure over time.

Individuals also benefit by enhancing their evaluation and assessment skills. In relationship to professional development for assessment, John Watts discusses the importance of perseverance:

> As with any long-term process in which most aspects are beyond your control, assessment will cause you to question your expertise, to reframe your thinking, and to doubt what you knew. But—if you persevere—it can also bring a new depth of understanding, breakthroughs in awareness, and a rejuvenation of your professional practice. (Hinchliffe, 2015, 852)

ASSESSES USER NEEDS

Competencies for Assessing User Needs

Evaluating user needs requires the effective use of tools and techniques to survey users and their information needs.

The typical behavioral strategies suggested in the RUSA "Professional Competencies" that demonstrate competencies related to evaluating user needs are:

- Identifies the user population and the potential user population
- Analyzes one's own cultural background and assumptions, and the racial, ethnic, cultural, and other diversities of the community
- Collects and analyzes information about users and user interactions with the library and its services, while respecting user privacy and confidentiality
- Plans and conducts regular assessments of the information needs of primary user groups, using various formal and informal methods
- Translates assessments of user needs into a plan for services that addresses the needs and preferences of diverse user groups

Development Methods for Assessing User Needs

On-the-job learning is the most effective development method. Engaging in a planning process that employs the seven-step model (see figure 6.1) and that involves working with consultants or staff members who have previously assessed user populations will result in a very rich learning experience for librarians who have not previously assessed user needs.

Another important method is scanning the research literature for articles of interest and studies that you might want to replicate in your library setting. The Research and Statistics (RSS) Committee of RUSA provides an excellent introduction to current research through its website (www.ala.org/ala/mgrps/divs/rusa/sections/rss/rsssection/rsscomm/rssresstat/researchstatistics.cfm). The RSS Committee also sponsors an annual Research Forum on reference at the annual conference of the American Library Association, and this is a very good investment of your time to meet active researchers in the field and stay abreast of the latest developments. The website of RUSA's Evaluation of Reference and User Services Committee (www.ala.org/ala/mgrps/

divs/rusa/sections/rss/rsssection/rsscomm/evalu ationofref/evaluationreference.cfm) also has valuable assessment information, including a guide to "Measuring and Assessing Reference Services and Resources." Regularly scanning the professional literature through subscriptions to key journals, for example, *Reference & User Services Quarterly*, the *Journal of Academic Librarianship, Library & Information Science Research*, the *Internet Reference Services Quarterly*, and the *Reference Services Review*, is another recommended method of keeping up with reference research.

Assessing Development Efforts for Assessing User Needs

An understanding of the marketing process is essential for developing competencies in evaluating user needs. The tools provided in chapter 5, such as the "Marketing Assessment Checklist" (figure 5.2), are very valuable in self-assessing your level of skills and competencies that need additional development. Because community relationships are also vital in determining user needs, the "Reflection on General Community Relationships" (figure 3.6) is also useful in determining the quality of your relationships with community leaders.

ASSESSES INFORMATION SERVICES

Competencies for Assessing Information Services

Assessing the effectiveness of the information services provided to users is essential for understanding the perspectives of users and understanding how your library's services might better serve users' needs.

The typical behavioral strategies suggested in the RUSA "Professional Competencies" that demonstrate competencies related to evaluating information services are:

- Develops and incorporates measures of evaluation into any new service
- Develops service standards for new and existing information services
- Creates an organizational climate of assessment
- Analyzes the resources available and distributes resources to service programs most effectively meeting the user needs of a designated community
- Analyzes demographic and other information about the community to develop a wide variety of services, which meet the needs and interests of diverse communities

Development Methods for Assessing Information Services

The four basic methods used in reference research are surveys, observation, focus groups, and transcript reviews (Saunders, 2016). An understanding of the strengths and weaknesses of these four methods of evaluating information services is best acquired through education, followed by actual field experience with the methods. Replicating previous studies in a library or information service is highly recommended for developing competence and an in-depth understanding of the various evaluation methods. An example that builds upon previous research is a study on specialized reference services (Lenkart and Yu, 2017), which utilizes the READ scale (http://readscale.org) that has been tested in a number of libraries. The READ (Reference Effort Assessment Data) scale records the librarian or staff effort, skills, and knowledge that are required during a reference interaction. A study that assessed the chat reference service offered by undergraduate students (Keyes and Dworak, 2017) utilized both the READ scale to rank transactions by the level of difficulty and the RUSA "Guidelines for Behavioral Performance" to identify observable behaviors. The authors conclude that well-trained undergraduate students staffing a chat reference service is a viable, and even desirable, option. Replicating these studies that use standard instruments is highly recommended for the development of competencies.

Again, on-the-job learning is the most effective development method. King and Lutz (2017) present a SERVE (Smile, Eye Contact, Recognize, Voice, Exceed) rubric that is adapted from the Four Seasons service philosophy. This rubric for observing and providing feedback to all public services staff addresses the sections on approachability, interest, and listening in the RUSA "Guidelines for Behavioral Performance." Engaging in a planning process using the suggested steps in the models in figures 6.1 and 6.2 (given earlier in this chapter) and working with consultants or staff members who have previously assessed the effectiveness of information services will result in a very rich learning experience for librarians who have not previously assessed information services.

An earlier section in this chapter, which discusses the "Development Methods for Assessing User Needs," covers strategies for keeping up with the latest developments in reference research. Attending the American Library Association's conferences and participating actively in its key committees, such as the Evaluation of Reference and User Services and the Research and Statistics committees, will provide you with outstanding development and networking opportunities.

Assessing Development Efforts for Assessing Information Services

The seven-step models (figures 6.1 and 6.2) include evaluating the problem-solving process. Developing an implementation plan for the introduction of new information services by following the process steps in these models will provide you with outstanding on-the-job learning opportunities. Because understanding and applying the common evaluation methods—surveys, observation, focus groups, and transcript reviews—is essential in developing competencies, a self-assessment checklist has been provided (figure 6.3).

ASSESSES INFORMATION RESOURCES

Competencies for Assessing Information Resources

Librarians must assess and evaluate resources in all formats both in terms of objective standards and how well resources meet the library's user needs.

The typical behavioral strategies suggested in the RUSA "Professional Competencies" that demonstrate competencies related to evaluating information resources are:

- Maintains the quality of collection resources by evaluating all formats for accuracy and currency
- Determines the authority of these resources
- Identifies any bias or point of view in an information resource
- Evaluates new information sources appropriate for the primary users
- Consults a wide variety of reviewing sources to identify those best meeting the needs of the primary community
- Writes and distributes reviews of new information resources to appropriate online and print media

Method	No Experience	Little Experience Performing, but Some Knowledge	Experience Performing, but Infrequent Practice	Perform and Practice Regularly	Practice Regularly and Able to Teach Skill to Others
Surveys					
Observation					
Interviews					
Focus Groups					

FIGURE 6.3 *Understanding and Applying Basic Information Service Evaluation Methods*

Development Methods for Assessing Information Resources

Reviewing reference materials in the librarian's subject areas develops her skills, knowledge, and understanding. A general guide to writing book reviews is available at the Purdue Online Writing Lab's (2017) website. Emerald Publishing (2018) has a series of useful guides for writing book reviews, including a checklist in part 4.

A first step in developing the skills to write book reviews is to read and analyze the reviews in sources such as *Choice, Library Journal, Booklist,* and other journals; at the same time, these journals are potential sources for publishing your own reviews, given your areas of reference expertise and subject knowledge. Often, formally serving as a reviewer comes about by invitation, as when one is asked to serve as a reviewer for a journal's editorial board. Other options for serving as a reviewer are by application:

- *Choice*—see the ALA's information on book reviewing (www.ala.org/acrl/choice/reviewers) and this journal's application form (http://choiceconnect.org/apply).
- *Library Journal*—see this journal's guidelines for reviews (http://reviews.libraryjournal.com/about/guidelines-for-library-journal-reviews/) and the application form (http://reviews.libraryjournal.com/about/review-for-library-journal/).
- *Booklist*—As a reviewer, you should try playing the role of the writer's intended audience, considering their level of knowledge, and think about how this audience would respond, so that you respond primarily to the substance and significance of the topics: see this journal's guidelines for reviews (https://www.booklistonline.com/writing-for-booklist).

Using a checklist each time you evaluate an information source is another very useful development method for improving your skills through practice in applying each criteria. Figure 6.4 will provide structure for the review process and ensure

Useful Questions for the Analysis of Published Reviews

Is the review's bibliographic description of the source (i.e., the book) accurate and complete?

Is the review's documentation—references or links to other sources—appropriate, current, and accurate?

Does the review:

contain information covering the source's purpose, scope, and nature of contents?

note the intended audience and discuss the appropriateness and adequacy of coverage of the source content for that audience?

discuss the creator of the source and the creator's qualifications?

note the degree to which up-to-date information appears in the source?

convey a sense of the source's style and biases?

note the source's arrangement and ease of use?

identify sources of similar scope and purpose?

evaluate the strengths and weaknesses of this source as compared to similar sources?

explain how the source can be used in everyday reference work?

include a summary of the source that contains a recommendation?

contain suggestions for improvement of the source?

that you practice applying all the criteria to an individual information source.

Analyzing published reviews develops your skills and understanding of the use of important criteria in evaluating information sources. However, another equally important development method employs summarizing user feedback in evaluating information sources. Figure 6.5 is an example of a brief questionnaire, which was employed at San Jose State University to assist librarians in understanding students' experiences with specialized databases that librarians had introduced in a class. This form is best used in conjunction with a class assignment so that the students are motivated to

NAME OF INFORMATION SOURCE: _____

Criteria	Fully Meets Requirement	Needs Improvement	Notes
Parentage and Provenance [creation/publisher]			
Authority [experience and qualifications]			
Audience [intended population group]			
Content [broad and deep enough for needs]			
Creation and Currency [date of creation and updating frequency]			
Design [aesthetic; appropriate appearance]			
Usability [ease of use; organization; arrangement]			
Medium [appropriate use of text, graphics, other media]			
SOURCE FOR CRITERIA: J. Rettig and C. LaGuardia. 1999. "Beyond 'Beyond Cool': Reviewing Web Resources." *Online* 23, no. 4 : 51–55.			

FIGURE 6.4 *Checklist for Evaluating Information Resources*

fill out and return the form to the librarian via the classroom instructor.

Assessing Development Efforts for Assessing Information Resources

After you have reviewed materials in a subject area, figure 6.6 provides a useful tool for self-assessing your progress in this practice. Generally, the more reviews you have published, which apply all of the criteria on the checklist, the greater will be your expertise.

ASSESSES SERVICE DELIVERY

Competencies for Assessing Service Delivery

New or existing services must be evaluated both in terms of users' capabilities and your service's technological requirements. Are typical users able to understand and use the service delivery system? Is the library's technology advanced enough to provide uninterrupted service to users?

The typical behavioral strategies suggested in the RUSA "Professional Competencies" that

Thank you for taking a few minutes to fill out this survey, providing us with feedback on our Web databases.

Database

Which database(s) were you using? Scroll down the list and select as many as you like using the <Ctrl> (on a Mac this may be the Command or Clover) key and your mouse to highlight more than one name.

[Place list of current databases in alphabetical order in box]

Location *(Check one)*
○ SJSU Computer Lab   ○ SJSU Housing-Dorms
○ SJSU Campus Office   ○ SJSU Library
○ Off Campus

User Category *(Check one)*
○ SJSU Undergraduate   ○ SJSU Graduate Student
○ SJSU Faculty   ○ SJSU Administrator
○ Other Status

How many times have you used this database? *(Check one)*
○ First time   ○ Two to Five times
○ Six to Ten times   ○ More than Ten times

Did you locate the information you need in the database? *(Check one)*
○ Yes, just what I wanted
○ Yes, with limitations
○ Yes, not what I needed, but other materials or information that will be helpful
○ Yes, but not really what I wanted
○ Only partly   ○ No, found nothing

Would you use this database again?
(Check one)
○ Yes, absolutely   ○ Probably
○ Maybe   ○ Never

How easy was it to find the information you needed? *(Check one)*
○ Very easy   ○ Easy
○ Neither easy nor difficult   ○ Difficult
○ Very difficult

What did you find in this database that was useful?

What had you hoped to find in this database that you didn't?

How would you change this database if you could?

For a response or assistance, let us know how to get in touch with you:

Name: _____

E-mail: _____

Phone: _____

FIGURE 6.5 *Reference Electronic Database Questionnaire*

demonstrate competencies related to evaluating service delivery are:

- Determines the appropriate mix of technologies and delivery channels to meet diverse user needs and preferences
- Experiments and evaluates changes in services to users
- Evaluates the allocation of human and fiscal resources to ensure they are supporting priority services and delivery methods

Development Methods for Assessing Service Delivery

Unobtrusive surveys are a good tool for assessing the degree to which the library's various service delivery channels are effective in meeting users' needs. The results of the surveys will enable librarians to evaluate the strengths and weaknesses of both the various technologies and the difficulties that staff experience in using the different technologies to provide reference assistance. Parallel, structured observation forms should be developed for each delivery channel, and the same basic questions should be asked using each of the service technologies. Proxies also need to be trained in asking questions. Figure 6.7 provides observation forms for in-person, telephone, and e-mail surveys. Administering these surveys and analyzing the results is an excellent way to develop your skill at evaluating service delivery channels. In addition, figure 6.8 is a useful tool for gaining experience in tracking and

Criteria	Familiar with concept	Employed in review analysis	Used in a few published reviews	Used in a large number of published reviews
Parentage and Provenance [creation/publisher]				
Authority [experience and qualifications]				
Audience [intended population group]				
Content [broad and deep enough for needs]				
Creation and Currency [date of creation and updating frequency]				
Design [aesthetic; appropriate appearance]				
Usability [ease of use; organization; arrangement]				
Medium [appropriate use of text, graphics, other media]				

SOURCE FOR CRITERIA: J. Rettig and C. LaGuardia. 1999. "Beyond 'Beyond Cool': Reviewing Web Resources." *Online* 23, no. 4: 51–55.

FIGURE 6.6 *Checklist for Assessment of Competencies in Evaluating Information Resources*

IN-PERSON OBSERVATION SHEET

Observation Start Time _____ AM PM *(circle one)*   Observation End Time _____ AM PM *(circle one)*
          (hour/minutes)   *(hour/minutes)*

Type of Library: _____ Academic _____ Public

Approachable/Accessible

3a. Was it easy to locate the in-person reference service within the library?

_____ Very easy   _____ Moderately easy   _____ Somewhat difficult   _____ Very difficult

3b. Check one of the following statements that best describes what you saw as you approached the library staff member for help. The staff member was:

_____ free to assist you   _____ assisting other patron(s) at the reference desk

_____ away from the reference desk   _____ on the telephone or talking with a staff member

_____ doing other work at the reference desk

3c. If the staff member was engaged in an activity when approached *(see question 3b)*, did (s)he acknowledge your presence?

_____ Yes   _____ No   _____ Not applicable

Reference Interview

4a. Did the staff member who assisted you conduct a reference interview by asking *(check all that apply)*:

_____ you to provide more information about your topic

_____ what types of information sources you need *(books, articles, web pages, etc.)*

_____ how much information you had already found

_____ how much information you need

_____ other (please describe): _____

_____ staff member did not conduct any reference interview

Follow-up

5a. At the end of the interaction, did the staff member use a follow-up question, i.e., some kind of question to let you know that s/he was interested in finding out whether you got what you needed?

_____ Yes   _____ No

Explain what (s)he said: _____
_____

Satisfaction/Value

6a. Describe the content of the information you received as a result of this interaction:
_____
_____

6b. List the sources that the library staff member consulted to answer your question:
_____
_____

6c. List the sources that the library staff member recommended you consult on your own:
_____
_____

(cont.)

FIGURE 6.7   *Observation Forms for In-Person, Telephone, and E-Mail Surveys*

FIGURE 6.7 • *Observation Forms for In-Person, Telephone, and E-Mail Surveys* *(cont.)*

6d. Rate the value of the information added in terms of completing your library guide/pathfinder assignment:
_____ No value   _____ Some value   _____ Considerable value

6e. Given the nature of the interaction, if you had the option, WOULD YOU RETURN to this staff member with another question?
_____ Yes _____ No _____ Not sure Other: _____

7a. Please provide any other information that you believe would be useful. Include information on any behaviors (verbal/written or nonverbal actions) that you believe contributed either negatively or positively to the success/failure of the interaction:
_____
_____

CHAT REFERENCE OBSERVATION SHEET

[Use questions for in-person observation sheet with the following substitutions]

Type:_____   Question Point: _____   Other (name): _____

3a. Was it easy to access the chat reference service?

_____ Very Easy   _____ Moderately Easy   _____ Somewhat Difficult   _____ Very Difficult

3b. Check one of the following statements that best describes what you experienced when you contacted the chat reference service. The staff member:
_____ was immediately available to assist you   _____ asked you to wait for an available library staff member
_____ no one appeared to assist you after _____ minutes

3c. If you had to wait, how long did you wait before someone became available?   _____ *(minutes)*

[If you checked "no one appeared to assist you after ___ minutes," please try another chat reference query, and include a second and new observation form for Chat Reference]

3d. Did the staff member indicate that (s)he was assisting other people at the same time (s)he was assisting you?
_____ Yes   _____ No   _____ Not sure
Comments:_____
_____

5b. Did the staff member suggest that you visit the library in person?   _____ Yes   _____ No
If yes, why did (s)he suggest an in-person visit (please explain): _____

TELEPHONE OBSERVATION SHEET

[Use questions for in-person observation sheet with the following substitutions]

3a. Was it easy to locate the telephone reference service from the telephone book or website?

_____ *(circle method used)*

_____ Very Easy   _____ Moderately Easy   _____ Somewhat Difficult   _____ Very Difficult

3b. Check one of the following statements that best describes what you experienced when you contacted the reference service by telephone. The staff member:
_____ was immediately available to assist you   _____ asked you to wait for an available library staff member
_____ no one answered the phone

3c. If you were asked to wait, how long did you wait before someone became available? _____ *(minutes)*

3d. If no one answered the phone, did you:
_____ receive a message to call back at another time
_____ receive no message at all (telephone just rang—up to 20 rings)

[If you checked "no one answered the phone" and you choose to try another telephone query, include a second and new observation form for Telephone]

5b. Did the staff member suggest that you visit the library in person? _____ Yes _____ No

If yes, why did (s)he suggest an in-person visit (please explain): _____

E-MAIL OBSERVATION SHEET

[Use questions for in-person observation sheet with the following substitutions]

Duration

1a. Write down the _____ _____ AM PM *(circle one)* when you sent your e-mail question.
　　　　　　　　　　(date) (time)

1b. When did you receive an initial response to your e-mail query? _____ _____ AM PM *(circle one)*
　　　　　　　　　　　　　　　　　　　　　　　　　　　　　　　　　　　　(date) (time)

3a. Was it easy to locate the e-mail reference service from the home page of the library's website?
_____ Very Easy _____ Moderately Easy _____ Somewhat Difficult _____ Very Difficult

3b. How soon did you receive an initial response to your e-mail query?
_____ within 24 hours _____ within 48 hours _____ over 48 hours _____ no response received after one week

[If you checked "no response received after one week" and you choose to try another e-mail query, include a second and new observation form for E-Mail]

3c. After the initial e-mail response, did you receive any more responses? _____ Yes _____ No
If yes, please explain: _____

4a. Did the e-mail question service provide a form for you to complete in order to ask your question?
_____ Yes _____ No   If yes, please explain: _____

4b. If yes, what information did the form ask for *(check all that apply)*:
_____ what types of information sources you need *(books, articles, web pages, etc.)*
_____ how much information you had already found _____ how much information you need
_____ other *(please describe)*: _____
_____ library did not provide a form

5a. At the end of the e-mail answer, did the staff member use a follow-up question, i.e., some kind of question to let you know that (s)he was interested in finding out whether you got what you needed?
_____ Yes _____ No
Explain what (s)he said: _____

5b. Did the staff member suggest that you visit the library in person? _____ Yes _____ No
If yes, why did (s)he suggest an in-person visit (please explain): _____

6e. Given the nature of the interaction, if you had the option, WOULD YOU E-MAIL this staff member with another question?
_____ Yes _____ No _____ Not sure

Question Category	8-9 AM	9-10 AM	10-11 AM	11 AM-12 Noon	12 Noon-1PM	1-2 PM	2-3 PM	3-4 PM	4-5 PM	5-6 PM	6-7 PM	7-8 PM
Non-resource Based												
Skill Based												
Strategy Based												
Consultation												
TOTAL												

Non-resource Based. Questions that do not require a resource to answer and might be answered by a sign or help sheet (e.g., geographic or policy questions). Usually answered at the *service* desk.

Skill Based. Questions that require a demonstration to answer (i.e., "how-to" questions that might be answered by a well-developed set of directions. Most often the library staff have to move to a location and demonstrate a skill. The same question should always get the same answer.

Strategy Based. Questions that require the formulation of a strategy to locate an answer and require selection of resources. May require individualized subject approaches.

Consultation. Usually longer encounters outside of regular desk duty. May be for the selection of curriculum materials. The librarian will often have to research recommendations or prepare reports for consultation work.

NOTE: See also the categories in the Reference Effort Assessment Data (READ) Scale: Gerlich, Bella Karr & Berard, G. Lynn. (2010). Qualitative statistics for academic reference services. *College & Research Libraries,* 71 (2), 116-137.

SOURCE: Categories are based on a new classification for reference statistics as described in: Warner, Debra G. (2001). A new classification for reference statistics. *Reference & User Services Quarterly* 41 (1): 51-55

FIGURE 6.8 *Reference Activity Counts*

analyzing the workload levels associated with the various delivery methods.

Assessing Development Efforts for Assessing Service Delivery

Conducting evaluations of the services offered through the various delivery channels is the most effective method of building your competencies in this area. Therefore, the assessment of your competencies is tied to your level of experience in evaluating various delivery service channels. Figure 6.9 is a useful tool for reflecting upon your level of expertise.

ASSESSES USER INTERFACES FOR INFORMATION RESOURCES

Competencies for Assessing User Interfaces for Information Resources

The format, access, and presentation aspects of resource interfaces are important facets to consider in the overall assessment of the value of tools.

The typical behavioral strategies suggested in the RUSA "Professional Competencies" that demonstrate competencies related to evaluating information interfaces are:

- Identifies factors that impede the use of the resource

Competency	No Analyses	Conducted Single Analysis	Conducted 2 to 3 Analyses	Conducted 3 or More Analyses
Determines the appropriate mix of technologies and delivery channels				
Assesses new technologies to see if they can meet service needs more effectively than current				
Experiments with and evaluates changes in services				
Assesses the distribution of human and fiscal resources				

FIGURE 6.9 *Assessment of Service Delivery Evaluation Competencies*

- Evaluates the format, access, and presentation aspects of resources
- Communicates with the information resource designers about usability and accessibility concerns
- Determines if there are alternative resources that have better user interfaces and resources

Development Methods for Assessing User Interfaces for Information Resources

For reference and information services staff, evaluating information interfaces requires an understanding of usability, which is the quality of the user's experience with the information source's interface. Schmidt (2013) suggests that three characteristics provide a great way to analyze the users' experience with library services and products:

1. *Useful*—Does the interface actually help people do something?
2. *Usable*—Is it easy enough for people to use?
3. *Desirable*—Does it meet expectations for convenience, and for social and emotional experience?

Jakob Nielsen (2012) believes that five quality components define usability:

1. *Learnability*—ease of learning basic tasks
2. *Efficiency*—speed of task performance
3. *Memorability*—ease of reestablishing task proficiency
4. *Errors*—ease of recovery from errors
5. *Satisfaction*—attractiveness, subjective enjoyment

The most basic and useful method for testing interface usability is user testing, which involves getting representative users to perform typical tasks using the interface, observing what users do, and recording their successes and failures. Cunningham, Mays, and Mercer (2017) discuss best practices for usability testing and website design, including asking users to accomplish specific tasks, observing their behavior using screen capture software, and

Behavior	Frequently	Sometimes	Seldom
Regularly conducts usability tests to identify barriers			
Scans information marketplace to identify alternatives to existing databases			
Meets regularly with vendor database designers to discuss usability issues			

FIGURE 6.10 *Assessment of Evaluation Behaviors for Information Interfaces in Area of Responsibility*

also asking users to explain their reasoning as they perform each task. These authors support Nielsen's belief that five users are generally enough, provided the users are representative of the population. Conducting user testing through the observation of user behavior is a very good way to develop your competencies in evaluating user interfaces. Observing user behavior will enable you to understand the strengths and weaknesses of an information interface from a user's perspective. Understanding user perspectives is essential for developing your competencies in evaluating information interfaces.

In assessing accessibility for users with disabilities, DeLancey (2017) recommends a number of tools, beginning with the WAVE Validator (http://wave.webaim.org). The WAVE Validator is a free community service that will quickly provide a list of potential accessibility issues with your web pages.

User surveys can complement and supplement studies of user behavior. The "Reference Electronic Database Questionnaire" (figure 6.5) can be used in conjunction with class assignments or community group projects to collect, analyze, and reflect upon users' reactions to an interface. Experimenting with new interfaces, meeting with vendors, and providing feedback on products in the early testing stages are additional useful methods for developing your competencies in this area.

Assessing Development Efforts for Assessing User Interfaces for Information Resources

Engaging in behaviors that develop and refine your knowledge of information interfaces is a recommended way to develop and maintain your evaluation competencies related to information interfaces. Figure 6.10 provides a self-assessment tool that is useful for reflecting upon the level of your competencies in this area.

ASSESSES ASSISTANCE TO USERS BY INFORMATION SERVICE PROVIDERS

Competencies for Assessing Assistance to Users by Information Service Providers

This section does not cover performance evaluation for all jobs that a librarian might perform, but focuses on measures that are directly related to providing reference and information services to users. High-quality staff form the core of library services. The development of quality staff requires a sophisticated understanding of how to assess that staff's performance. Librarians must be able to identify and employ the evaluation techniques that measure staff performance.

The typical behavioral strategies suggested in the RUSA "Professional Competencies" that demonstrate competencies related to evaluating information service providers are:

- Identifies and applies those performance measures that have been developed by the profession, for example, the RUSA "Guidelines for Behavioral Performance"
- Consults with information service staff to develop a consensus on service standards
- Develops measures that will be useful in assessing whether or not service standards are being met
- Promotes and encourages an esprit de corps that will work to evaluate and improve service behaviors

Development Methods for Assessing Assistance to Users by Information Providers

Beginning with the RUSA "Guidelines for Behavioral Performance," a team of librarians and reference staff can develop a set of standards for each type of reference service provided: in-person, telephone, e-mail, and chat. Once the reference unit has approved the service standards, the unit's members need to discuss and agree upon the measures, which will determine whether the standards are being met.

For measuring the service performance of the reference unit as a whole, unobtrusive measures and surveys, which collect data from both users and service providers, are recommended measures for determining the degree to which the standards are being met. The relevant research highlights the important role that unobtrusive reference surveys play in evaluating the degree to which staff meet the model reference behaviors. In developing skills to meet these behaviors, Gers and Bolin (2000) note the importance of training programs that provide four essential components:

1. Presenting the theory and rationale for the importance of using the skills
2. Modeling the reference behaviors so that participants can observe the application of skills
3. Practicing the skills and obtaining structured feedback in a nonthreatening manner
4. Peer coaching

Jim and Wendy Kirkpatrick (2015) have developed a training evaluation form that emphasizes many of the qualities emphasized by Gers and Bolin, including engagement during the program, activities and exercises, the opportunity to practice what participants were learning, and the ability to use learning immediately. The Kirkpatrick levels of evaluation are:

Reaction—participant satisfaction with the training event

Learning—degree to which participants acquire knowledge, skills, and attitudes

Behavior—degree to which participants apply on the job what they learned

Results—degree to which desired outcomes occur as a result of the training event

Training programs intended to enhance assistance to users by information providers should include all of these elements. Assessing behavioral changes and impact upon desired outcomes is necessary to determine the effectiveness of the training. The work by Gers and Bolin demonstrates that changes in behavior, which will result in enhanced service to users, must go far beyond classroom presentations and assessing the participants' satisfaction with the course content.

For developing competencies in evaluating individual providers, a valuable development method is coaching. Once service standards have been agreed upon, a checklist should be developed to use for peer observation. The peer observer monitors the use of skills for information provision and provides nonthreatening, tactful, but direct feedback on the service provider's strengths and weaknesses. Practice sessions using real user questions can be organized with librarians playing the roles of librarian, user, and observer. Thus, peers in the coaching process help each other apply new skills and in the process learn how to develop their evaluation competencies as well. Individual service providers can also self-assess their own performance by asking a feedback question during each interaction with a user. The follow-up section of the RUSA "Guidelines for Behavioral Performance" contains a number of very useful suggestions for appropriate feedback questions, such as:

5.1 Asks patrons if their questions have been completely answered.

5.2 Encourages the patrons to return if they have further questions by making a statement such as "If you don't find what you are looking for, please come back and we'll try something else."

Through self-assessment of their own skills, librarians can develop expertise in evaluating the competencies of service providers. Some of the figures provided in chapter 1, such as figure 1.2: "Self-Assessment Checklist for Follow-up," and figure 1.3: "Behavioral Observation Scale for Follow-up," are useful tools for developing expertise in evaluating your own skills and those of other individual service providers.

To develop competencies in evaluating reference librarians, an appraisal process needs to involve both parties and provide opportunities for interaction and the exchange of perspectives. The process described in the following paragraph provides such opportunities.

As part of the appraisal process, each reference librarian should complete an up-to-date profile on her qualifications, experience, and achievements and a self-assessment of the strengths and weaknesses in her past year's performance. The assessment should also include an analysis of any organizational barriers that inhibit her successful performance. In turn, the appraiser should do a separate assessment of the strengths and weaknesses of each individual's performance. The person being evaluated and the appraiser should agree upon a plan for achieving objectives, including training, learning, and job assignments. Both the appraiser and the person being evaluated should address the following topics in their assessments:

1. What are the librarian's performance strengths in providing information services?
2. What are the librarian's performance weaknesses in providing information services?
3. What has the librarian done particularly well?
4. What should the librarian do differently to improve performance?

Assessing Development Efforts for Assessing Assistance to Users by Information Service Providers

Generally, appraisals have more successfully evaluated librarians in areas such as publishing and committee service than in the quality of services provided to users. In fact, the evaluation of the quality of services provided to users is often the most neglected part of a reference librarian's performance evaluation. This section will focus on assessing the competencies of reference librarians in their provision of information services to users. The true test is the successful evaluation and application of service standards and measures as part of the performance appraisal process. Figure 6.11 permits individuals to reflect upon their experience in successfully practicing these evaluation competencies.

All assessment is best accomplished by using multiple methods. The appraisal process described in this chapter incorporates more than one source of information and incorporates behavioral standards as part of the process. However, an even more complete system for assessing information providers could incorporate all of the nine key components of a performance management system:

1. Model defining the competencies for all work activities
2. Leadership development program for managers
3. Goal-setting for both the organization and the individual
4. Explicit behavioral norms
5. Performance improvement process
6. Performance assessment, including a 360-degree feedback process
7. Coaching
8. Recognition system for both individual and team achievements
9. Assessment of team and group effectiveness

Figure 6.12 is designed to allow individuals to assess their competence in each of these nine components.

Competencies	Not Available	Incomplete	Fully Developed
Service standards for provision of information services			
Measures to determine success in meeting each standard			
Data collected to determine level of measures			
Application of measures in individual performance evaluations			

FIGURE 6.11 *Assessment of Competencies in Evaluating Information Service Providers*

Components	Not Available	Incomplete	Fully Developed
Model defining competencies for all work activities			
Leadership development program for managers			
Goal setting for both the organization and the individual			
Explicit behavioral norms			
Performance improvement process			
Performance assessment, including 360-degree feedback process			
Coaching			
Recognition system for both individual and team achievements			
Assessment of team and group effectiveness			

SOURCE OF COMPONENTS: R. D. Stueart and M. Sullivan. 2010. *Developing Library Leaders*. New York: Neal-Schuman.

FIGURE 6.12 *Assessment of Competencies in the Components of a Performance Management System*

CHAPTER seven
Future Services

> **SECTION 5G: INVESTIGATES, ANALYZES, AND PLANS IN ORDER TO DEVELOP FUTURE SERVICES**

This chapter is about developing and assessing your knowledge, skills, abilities, and behaviors associated with section 5G of the RUSA "Professional Competencies," a section entitled "Investigates, Analyzes, and Plans in Order to Develop Future Services." The topics covered are learning as a lifelong process, planning for future services and resources, and promoting innovations.

As part of a visionary and planning exercise, Thorpe (2017) discusses four key themes related to future trends and opportunities for reference services:

1. *Changing community expectations and user behavior.* Today's reference user often wants help with doing things rather than finding things. Public libraries have often become a help desk for the community and provide a range of services from job-searching to e-government services. Libraries play a vital role in supporting people to gain skills and access to technology.

2. *Defining and reshaping modern library and reference services.* Libraries are hosting services that contribute to personal well-being and creativity, such as makerspaces. Along with these services comes an increasing awareness of the need to measure their impact in the primary community, using measures related to literacy and lifelong learning, informed and connected citizens, digital inclusion, personal development and well-being, stronger and more creative communities, and economic workforce development.
3. *Offering flexibility in spaces and service delivery.* Library spaces need to be viewed as trusted, safe places that are locally connected to their communities' problem-solving needs in learning, work, recreation, creativity, and innovation. These spaces need to stimulate both collaboration and social interaction while also supporting quiet reflection and discovery functions, which can be difficult to balance. Thorpe notes that even in an ever-growing digital service environment, human-to-human interactions remain a significant community need.
4. *Reviewing the roles of library staff and future skills sets.* Staff expertise and commitment are what make a library's service so valued to users. The challenge is to put users at the center of services as we change and innovate. Librarians have a role in encouraging self-reflective behaviors, working alongside users to support their informal learning, decision-making, and research.

The book *The Future of Skills: Employment in 2030* (Bakhshi, Downing, Osborne, and Schneider, 2017) predicts a strong emphasis on interpersonal skills, including teaching, social perceptiveness, coordination; and higher-order cognitive skills, such as originality, fluency of ideas, and active learning. This broad-based knowledge will be needed in addition to more specialized skills for specific occupations. The key trends that are likely to determine the bigger picture of work are environmental sustainability, urbanization, increasing inequality, political uncertainty, technological change, globalization, and demographic change.

LEADS A LIFE AS A LEARNER

Competencies for Leading a Life as a Learner

Planning for the future requires continual learning using a variety of methods, such as communities of practice, environmental scanning, professional discussions and activities, and active learning. The *IFLA Guidelines for Continuing Professional Development* (Varlejs, 2016) outline the principles and best practices involved in professional development by role: the learner, the employer, professional associations, library/information science (LIS) degree-granting programs, and all providers. Learners are primarily responsible for pursuing ongoing learning that constantly improves their knowledge and skills (the principle), and professionals are in charge of their personal development (best practice). As part of best practices, an individual should:

1. Conduct regular self-assessments congruent with job responsibilities and aspirations
2. Participate in performance appraisals
3. Monitor developments that impact the profession, and seek out and use opportunities to close competency gaps and to advance knowledge and skills
4. Develop a personal learning plan that will lead to improvement in current performance and further career advancement; make judicious choices of formal and informal learning resources based on best available information
5. Seek learning needed for present responsibilities before preparing for a new position.

The typical behavioral strategies suggested in the RUSA "Professional Competencies" that demonstrate competence related to lifelong learning are:

- Devises and implements strategies to learn about emerging tools and techniques, and

connects with professional communities to seek and share best practices
- Identifies potential new services and programs through contact in the professional community, readings, and other exploration
- Seeks opportunities to be informed, gathering news and information about the local, national, and international environment
- Encourages discussion with colleagues that furthers reflection on services offered and on potential needs
- Practices self-reflection, including an awareness of personal strengths and limitations
- Maintains currency with developments in understanding how people learn and with the best ways of facilitating learning in both formal and informal settings

Development Methods for Leading a Life as a Learner

Communities of Practice. A "community of practice" is a group of people who share a craft, concern, or profession and who come together to learn from and share practices and ideas with each other. These groups are often self-created and occur across different organizations. Communities of practice are distinguished from other groups and communities by three elements: (1) an identity defined by a shared domain of interest; (2) community members who engage in joint activities, help each other, and share information; and (3) members who are practitioners. These groups develop shared resources, experiences, tools, and ways of addressing common problems (Wenger-Trayner and Wenger-Trayner, 2015). A community of practice is much more informal than a work group or task force. The members of these communities are not typically assigned, but join based on their interest in the domain and their ability to contribute to the practice. Together, the members of the community share their expertise and mutual understanding about the domain in order to develop greater knowledge and build the practice. Some members meet primarily face-to-face, while others communicate mostly virtually. Some communities of practice are embedded in one organization, while others belong to various organizations. Because members in the community are actively participating in the practice, they have the capability to put what they are learning directly into practice.

Most communities of practice do need some type of guidance—leaders, coordinators, stewards—to be effective and to provide value to their members. Traditionally, groups operated in a single organizational context and were created by a manager; however, today such groups may be self-created and operate across organizations. These groups may be small and temporary, with a changing membership over time, but they are still perceived as distinct entities (Hackman, 2012). Because communities of practice are a type of group, when forming such a community, Hackman's six conditions that foster group effectiveness will still apply in order to achieve success:

1. A social system with members who work together to achieve a common purpose
2. A compelling purpose that fully engages group talents
3. The right number and mix of members
4. Clear norms of conduct on behaviors that are acceptable and those that are not
5. A supportive context
6. Competent and well-timed coaching

Nonprofit organizations can benefit from communities of practice. For example, within the National Council of Nonprofits, the state association network serves as a community of practice, facilitating knowledge-sharing between the state associations (National Council of Nonprofits, 2018). To encourage learning through reflection on practice and offer peer-to-peer learning activities, the Library Leadership and Management Association (2018) has established communities of practice in several areas, including assessment. Another interesting project is the University of Oklahoma Health Sciences Center Library's partnership with public library staff to expand consumer health information outreach throughout the state. To engage public library staff in exploring the relationships between access and need, the Health Sciences Center Library is developing a community of practice that provides continuing education and networking opportunities for public library staff who are interested in consumer health resources and services (Clifton, Jo, Longo, and Malone, 2017).

Yon and Albert (2013) explore how a professional online community of practice, KMaya (www.kmaya.com.my), can be utilized for sharing knowledge, transferring best practices, and contributing to success for librarians. Interviews with its members revealed that the online environment helped them to be more open in sharing knowledge and created a convenient and fast avenue for interacting with each other. Grassroots librarian groups have also formed communities of practice to develop new initiatives. For example, librarians from British Columbia were interested in developing, advocating, and managing open educational resources (OERs). With their common interest in OERs, and through a community of practice, BC OpenEd Librarians (https://open.bccampus.ca/bcoer-librarians/) developed and shared activities, tools, and resources to advance their learning and promote the use of OERs. As a result, the librarians have provided an important service and broadened their own professional expertise. One of the important lessons is that a distributed leadership, some administrative support, and being open to new members and ideas are key to sustaining an active community of practice (Smith and Lee, 2016).

In an acknowledgment that unique knowledge can come from a lively group of peers interacting on a regular and often instantaneous basis to help solve problems, Elsevier hosts several communities, dubbed Innovation Explorers, including a librarian section that is capped at 150 members. This closed and moderated community allows librarians to meet virtually in a protected environment where they participate in discussions, initiate their own queries, and provide feedback via surveys, polls, and interviews on tools and topics that are pertinent to their profession. They are also able to gain insight into planned products and services long before these hit the general public and, more importantly, to help shape them into the very best tools to meet their needs (Zwaaf, 2012). This venue allows the international flavor that might be missing in other, more local opportunities.

For reference librarians, communities of practice also have the potential to develop and maintain their general and subject specific knowledge. A community of practice could enable reference librarians to apply their expertise and to construct knowledge by collaborating with their colleagues through in-house training, internal databases, blogs, wikis, and other tools (Miller, 2011). Communities of practice also have promoted collaboration between teaching faculty and librarians concerning student needs, instructional roles, and strategies

---

Resources for Communities of Practice

Michigan Library Association. "Communities of Practice."
www.milibraries.org/prof-development-networking/communities-of-practice-listserves/.

Educause. "Community of Practice Design Guide."
https://library.educause.edu/resources/2005/1/community-of-practice-design-guide-a-stepbystep-guide-for-designing-cultivating-communities-of-practice-in-higher-education.

Institute of Museum and Library Services.
"Communities of Practice for Librarians."
https://www.imls.gov/news-events/events/communities-practice-librarians.

Association of Research Libraries. "Assessment Community of Practice."
www.arl.org/focus-areas/arl-academy/communities-of-practice/assessment.

International Federation of Libraries.
"Continuing Professional Development and Workplace Learning." This section of the IFLA engages members in a community of practice.
https://www.ifla.org/about-cpdwl.

for learning. The communities of practice at IUPUI (Indiana University-Purdue University Indianapolis) focus on collaborative learning and problem-solving to investigate a wide range of issues, including the effective teaching of information literacy and critical thinking (Kissel et al., 2016).

Professional Discussions and Activities. There is a great deal of advice out there on discussing issues with colleagues. In general, the advice centers around being prepared, being open to listening to the other person's viewpoint, and trying to keep your own emotions in check. See the text box "Gallagher's Six Steps for Telling Anyone Anything" (below) for a checklist on how to prepare for such discussions.

Using an open question (one that requires more than a "yes or no" answer) will often help move the discussion forward. Open questions start with words like what, where, why, when, and how.

In a group discussion, it is important to make your own contributions to the topic. However, make sure that you:

- focus on the topic of the discussion—stick to the facts and avoid going off at a tangent
- present your points calmly—colleagues will not appreciate you shouting to make your point
- respect other people's contributions—colleagues will not appreciate you hogging the conversation or lecturing them with your thoughts
- acknowledge people's feelings—empathizing with other people's concerns will be appreciated by many colleagues

To prepare to take part in a group discussion with your team, think carefully about what you want to say about the topic so that you've got something to say early on in the discussion—before someone else makes your point. Make some notes about your main points on a card to remind you in case you get nervous. Check that your facts are correct and remember to think before you answer questions. Finally, once you and your colleagues have reached a mutually acceptable agreement, the conclusion should be documented and shared with all participants.

Gallagher's Six Steps for Telling Anyone Anything

Step 1: Compartmentalize

Present information in a manner that will not make an individual defensive, and use the content to create a neutral opening, such as asking the person how they are doing or how their work is going.

Step 2: Ask

Gather information about the person's views, using empathetic questions and paraphrasing the other person.

Step 3: Normalize

Recognize, validate, and identify with the other person's feelings.

Step 4: Discuss

Engage the other person by presenting a factual, nonemotional description of the issue, solicit her ideas for resolving the issue, and empathize with her responses.

Step 5: Incentivize

Stress the benefits to the other person in discussing the outcome based on the person's values, preferences, and desires.

Step 6: Disengage

Change the topic of conversation to regular work issues and/or common interests.

SOURCE: Based on concepts from Richard S. Gallagher. 2009. *How to Tell Anyone Anything: Breakthrough Techniques for Handling Difficult Conversations at Work.* New York: AMACOM, pp. 196-99, Appendix A.

Information that all colleagues share also establishes a common knowledge base, which is useful in discussing issues. One of the most difficult issues in reference service is internal communication among colleagues. But reference wikis, blogs, and Twitter and Facebook all provide excellent opportunities to quickly disseminate the same news and changes to all reference staff (Gottfried, DeLancey, and Hardin, 2015).

The classic work *Getting to Yes* (Fisher, Ury, and Patton, 2012) outlines principles that can be used to discuss issues with friends, colleagues, and opposing parties. At its core, the process involves an analysis of the issue, other people's interests and perceptions, and the existing options. The basic principles of *Getting to Yes* are:

1. Separate people from the issue. In other words, recognize and acknowledge your colleagues' perceptions and interests and the fact that people do interpret reality differently.
2. Focus on interests, not positions. Try to create value for both parties in a proposed solution.
3. Invent options for mutual gain. Satisfy the interests of all parties to the greatest extent possible.
4. Insist on objective criteria. Discuss and agree upon a fair outcome.

In the chapter on "Working with Groups" in their book *Communicating Professionally,* Ross and Nilsen (2013, 208–21) discuss five types of face-to-face communications—the book discussion, the problem-solving group, the focus group, the formal meeting, and the self-directed work group; and three types of virtual groups—virtual teams, virtual conferencing, and virtual discussion sites. Other types suggested in the literature are the internal unconference and communities of practice.

Ross and Nilsen note that a book discussion is successful when it "allows all members to share their responses to the book, compare their differing interpretations, and ask each other questions" (p. 208). They note that something has gone wrong if the discussion turns into a lecture with only one person expressing an opinion. They make a distinction between booktalks and book discussions, with a booktalk being a presentation that sells the book to a potential audience (pp. 285–88). See the text box "Booktalk Questions" (below) for tips on analyzing the audience before a booktalk.

Problem-solving groups need to use analytic and evaluative skills in a systematic, structured way. Ross and Nilsen (2013, 210–11) suggest that the following outline might be used to help a leader prepare for a meeting:

1. Describe the problem: What is its nature and extent?
    a. What background information is needed?
    b. What is the specific question to be decided?
    c. How serious is the problem?
    d. What factors should be considered in deciding on a solution?
2. What solutions are proposed?
    a. List the solutions without evaluating them.
    b. What are the advantages of each solution?
    c. What are the disadvantages of each solution?
    d. Which solutions can be discarded because no one considers them workable?
3. What is the group's initial reaction?
    a. On what points does the group substantially agree?
    b. What are the chief differences on matters of fact?

Booktalk Questions

Questions to ask about the audience when preparing a booktalk presentation:

- What is the nature of the group?
    - Grade nine English class?
    - Book club?
    - Group of retirees?
    - Naturalists club?
- What is the ratio of males to females?
- What is the group interested in?
- What are their reading tastes?
- What books have you presented to this group before?
- How long a presentation are they expecting to hear?

SOURCE: Catherine Sheldrick Ross and Kirsti Nilsen. 2013. *Communicating Professionally.* 3rd ed. A How-to-Do-It Manual for Librarians. Chicago: ALA Neal-Schuman, p. 286.

c. What are the chief differences on matters of opinion?
   d. How fundamental are these differences?
4. Which solution, or combination of solutions, seems best?
   a. Can a compromise be reached that will find general approval?
   b. If not, which solution, after debate, is favored by the majority?
5. How will the chosen solution be implemented and made effective?
   a. What can this group do?
   b. What can each member do?
   c. How will the implementation be evaluated?

Focus groups bring together a small number of people who represent a particular interest or characteristic for a group interview on a particular topic, with the goal of gathering information and options (Ross and Nilsen, 2013, 211). Because focus groups consist of participants who are carefully chosen, but who are often unfamiliar with each other, care needs to be taken to establish trust and develop ground rules so that the relatively short amount of time when the group meets can be maximized.

According to Eliot and Associates' "Guidelines for Conducting a Focus Group," focus group leaders should:

- listen attentively with sensitivity and empathy
- be able to listen and think at the same time
- believe that all group participants have something to offer no matter what their education, experience, or background
- have adequate knowledge of the topic
- keep their personal views and ego out of the facilitation
- be someone the group can relate to, but also possess authority (e.g., a male moderator is most appropriate for a group of men discussing sexual harassment in the workplace)
- appropriately manage challenging group dynamics

All librarians have experiences with formal meetings. Indeed, in some libraries, much of the work is conducted through committee structures. Formal meetings require establishing rules, a plan for the meeting, an individual to conduct or chair the meeting, a mechanism for keeping a record of the meeting, and establishing the roles that both the chair and the participants play.

For meetings in complex organizations, some sort of standard procedure needs to be followed, which usually means adopting a particular set of rules, such as a formal parliamentary procedure. Examples are given in the text box below. In more informal settings, the chair should have the group discuss ground rules that everyone can agree to.

The person conducting the meeting, the chair, usually creates an agenda with the order of business, and communicates this to the attendees. In some instances, a maximum time limit is allotted to the discussion of any item, and a decision must be made on whether or not to take action on the item. The other responsibilities of the chair are to make sure that the meeting starts and stops on time, that all who wish to speak can do so, that one or more individuals do not monopolize the conversation, that the discussion does not get bogged down unnecessarily, and that the meeting ends on time.

According to Tony Reiss (2013), the chair is responsible for managing three strands of activity

Managing Meetings

"How to Conduct Effective Meetings."
www.wikihow.com/Conduct-Effective-Meetings.

Many good videos are available on YouTube on running better meetings, for example:

EOS Worldwide. September 22, 2014. "How to Run an Effective Meeting–Tutorial." www.youtube.com/watch?v=u51UYseptlc.

Adamova, Elaina. April 15, 2013. "Chairing a Meeting." www.youtube.com/watch?v=oPhKhTl0Lss.

in a meeting: the people, the process, and the content. Concerning people, the chair needs to set up the group climate and ensure that the participants are comfortable with the atmosphere. The chair sets up an appropriate structure and procedures in order to promote effective group work, ensuring that everyone gets heard, no one dominates, and no one is treated badly or ignored. The chair also needs to ensure, with the minute taker, that all decisions made are recorded, and that any tasks which need to be done before the next meeting are assigned or communicated to the appropriate individual. When the discussion is under way, it is the chair's responsibility to ensure that it continues to flow smoothly by involving all members present and by not permitting one or two people to dominate the meeting. Summarizing by the chair during meetings can indicate progress or a lack of progress, refocus a discussion that has wandered off the point, conclude one point and lead into the next, highlight important points, assist the secretary if necessary, and clarify any misunderstanding.

While it is the role of the chair to run the meeting, the participation of all members is also fundamental to the meeting's success. To ensure an effective meeting, all participants should undertake any necessary preparation prior to the meeting, such as reading any materials sent along with the agenda, and note any questions that they wish to ask in order to clarify their understanding. Attendees should arrive on time, keep an open mind, listen to the opinions of others, participate in the discussion, avoid dominating the proceedings, avoid conflict situations, avoid side conversations which distract others, note down any action that is agreed upon, and after the meeting, undertake any agreed action and brief others as appropriate. The website Conducting a Meeting (www.skillsyouneed.com/ips/conduct-meeting.html) is a helpful resource.

Self-Managed Work Teams. Ross and Nilsen (2013, 221) note that self-directed work teams are different in that they do not have a supervisor, but direct their own work under the coordination of a team leader whom they select. Mark Chatfield (n.d.) of the Interaction Research Institute remarks that "a mature self-managed team, when compared to typical hierarchical management, would have measured results showing" the following:

More	Less
Enthusiasm	Individual opinion about what's important
Learning from peers	Reliance on individual abilities
Comfort knowing help is there	Panic when the workload peaks
Camaraderie	Backbiting
Shared responsibility	Protecting information
Focus on the organization	What's in it for me?
Responsibility for the team	Stress on the "supervisor"
Simple, visible measurement	Feeling unaccomplished

Virtual Teams, Conferences, and Discussions. Ross and Nilsen (2013, 222–23) suggest that libraries commonly use the capability of communications technology to allow groups to interact virtually in three different ways—virtual teams, virtual conferencing, and virtual discussion sites—listed here in order of decreasing organizational structure and increasing porousness of group membership. They go on to note that research on the differences between the interactions in face-to-face groups and virtual groups seems to indicate that when online participants "don't know each other's identities or status, they are less inhibited by the fear of being evaluated. They are therefore less likely to withhold ideas and contributions. An online decision-making group is less likely than a group that meets face-to-face to be taken over by a few dominating personalities" (p. 223). But while this same lack of inhibition can lead to more candid expression of viewpoints and more novel ideas, it can also lead to more arguments among the participants.

Virtual teams share similar characteristics with face-to-face teams, but the team members work on projects from different locations, communicating regularly by phone, e-mail, instant messaging, videoconference, or web-conferencing software. The key ingredient for successful virtual teams is having available a variety of technological tools, both synchronous and asynchronous, so that discussions and decisions don't need to be postponed until all the parties can meet. Documents need to be shared in a virtual space so that the team's resources can be accessed from wherever the team members happen to be.

Virtual conferencing (Ross and Nilsen, 2013, 227) allows "people physically located in different places to meet, using electronic communications equipment to hear, and often see, one another as they interact." In two instances, Ross and Nilsen suggest that virtual conferencing does *not* work well: when making major or very complex decisions with far-reaching consequences, and when giving bad news to employees, especially when the impact on those employees can vary. The three types of virtual conferencing that Ross and Nilsen discuss are teleconferencing or voice-only, videoconferencing, and web conferencing.

Teleconferencing typically refers to voice-only modalities. Other terms that can refer to teleconferencing are "audio conferencing," "telephone conferencing," and "phone conferencing" (*Wikipedia*, "Teleconferencing"). Because of the lack of nonverbal cues, it is important to hear all participants' voices by calling roll at the beginning of the teleconference and asking participants to identify themselves each time they speak (Ross and Nilsen, 2013, 228).

Videoconferencing uses both audio and video technologies to bring groups of people at different locations together. The addition of video brings further considerations to the mix. You should consider practicing your presentation ahead of time in order to minimize distracting behaviors that are magnified on video. Think about where you are being videoed and look for a non-distracting background, as well as a comfortable location. With multiple participants, you should have a person designated to handle technology issues, in addition to having someone moderate the flow of the conference. Be prepared for technical failures and have alternative communication strategies available, such as telephone for voice-only options. In order to keep distracting background noises to a minimum, consider asking the participants to turn off their microphones except when speaking, or you can use the software's capability to turn off microphones except when the moderator "calls" on them.

Web conferencing adds an Internet component that allows for richer engagement via your own computer terminal, which connects through the Internet and also has either a phone connection or a Voice over Internet Protocol. This allows people to view slides, a whiteboard, videos, and documents simultaneously, and may have support for chat as well as online polling. Because of the possibility to record and archive a web conference, it can be live for some attendees and asynchronous for those who view it later as a webcast or podcast. Because live attendees in a web conference are often at their own workstations, they are often multitasking and may not be as attentive as they would be in a live session. Presenters are encouraged to use

Additional Resources on Virtual and Web Conferencing

Jeff Durham. September 2, 2012. "The Art of Video Conferencing." www.worketiquette.co.uk/the-art-of-video-conferencing.html.

1VC2World. August 2, 2011. "Things to Consider When Choosing Video Conferencing." https://www.youtube.com/watch?v=CKaYXlXnWRM.

Dave Crenshaw. September 2, 2011; updated January 3, 2013. "Meeting Virtually," which is the audio and videoconferencing part of "Leading Productive Meetings." www.lynda.com/Business-Skills-tutorials/Meeting-virtually-audio-video-conferencing/ 81262/89496-4.html. (Lynda.com has a number of tutorials on videoconferencing with specific software such as GoToMeeting, FaceTime, Skype, WebEx, Lync, and a number of other popular software programs.)

the software's built-in functions to encourage asking questions via the online chat component or by polling or surveying the participants.

Virtual discussion sites (Ross and Nilsen, 2013, 230) are structured online spaces where people can have conversations in the form of "posted messages that many people will read and some will answer." Although interactive, the communication is asynchronous, with time delays between posts. The posts are usually archived and can be available indefinitely. Ross and Nilsen (p. 232) suggest that it is important in these environments to be concise and stick to the topic, avoiding remarks that could be construed as racist, sexist, or inflammatory. When responding to a request for personal assistance, you should reply directly to the individual, not to the list, and similarly, you should be aware of sending to the list or sending a command to the list moderator.

An "unconference" is a somewhat more structured format for discussing issues with colleagues. Kniberg (2016) suggests that an unconference is just an Open Space (http://openspaceworld.org/wp2/) event with some added structure to make it fit for internal organization events. The organizer sets the general theme; however, the specific topics are generated by people at the conference, with breakout groups forming dynamically based on their interest and relevance to participants. Kniberg (2016) suggests that there is only one rule for Open Space and unconferences, which is: if you aren't contributing or learning or having fun where you are now, use your two feet. In other words, we trust people to be responsible and make the best use of their time. For more information, consult "How to Run an Internal Unconference" (Kniberg, 2013).

Another idea is a professional development activity in which a small group meets in person or online at least five times a year to work on a specific question or issue. For example, see "Faculty Inquiry Groups," a document that is part of Lane Community College's Faculty Professional Development (n.d.).

Environmental Scanning. "Environmental scanning" is a very useful technique for identifying new services and programs and gathering local, national, and international news and information. Librarians responding to current trends must plan to be more flexible, more mobile when changes occur, and must engage in recognizing, talking about, and preparing for the future. One way to recognize these future possibilities and trends is to engage in environmental scanning. This involves collecting and analyzing information about the larger social, economic, and political environment that may be useful in developing organizational plans and making decisions. The primary objective is to lessen the randomness of information used in decision-making, and to alert professionals to trends and issues in the larger society that may affect the organization. Environmental scanning can assist libraries in understanding the changing needs of users and in shaping how they market their programs and services to meet those needs. Rathi, Shiri, and Cockney (2017) provide an interesting model for planning a community digital library for Canada's Northern population by utilizing evidence-based environmental scanning. The model allowed the digital library planners to gain deeper insight into the complexities of the issues and learn about the key users, project stakeholders, communities, community organizations, and libraries and information providers in the Canadian North.

In environmental scanning, colleagues within an organization or professional group agree to share anything they think would be helpful to others in the group, and they monitor specific e-mail lists, social media, and websites. LITA's "Top Technology Trends" (www.ala.org/lita/ttt) is an example of a group of librarians who are actively watching the technology environment and sharing views with their peers. Regardless of whether the environmental scanning is done by an individual or by an organized group working together, identifying these larger trends is an essential step in helping decision-makers.

Reference librarians must keep up with local, national, and international news. Not long ago this meant reading a local newspaper and listening to national newscasts to keep up with current events.

Now, however, if reading a daily paper and watching a news program every day seem like monumental chores, one can consider scanning news websites, or subscribing to a weekly newsmagazine that would summarize the top news stories. Another alternative is subscribing to news feeds via RSS (rich site summaries), which allow news aggregators to send website updates to your desktop so you don't have to visit individual sites (rss.com). News aggregators help filter and organize the content, and have become increasingly important with the growth of information. Well-known aggregators include Google News (www.news.google.com), the Drudge Report (www.drudgereport.com), and the Huffington Post (www.huffingtonpost.com), which is a combination of news aggregation and original content creation. For a list of library-related weblogs (some of which have RSS feeds), see LISWiki's "Weblogs" (2017).

Koontz and Mon (2014) suggest these guidelines for environmental scanning:

- Seek signs of change in the primary sectors: politics, technology, economy, law, society, and culture.
- Look for signals for potential events on the horizon.
- Look for forecasts by experts.
- Look for the indirect effects of events.
- Be aware that there are few guidelines on how to do scanning, but a key rule is that the categories chosen for scanning must be relevant to the organization.
- Write abstracts that summarize the environmental scanning data into scenarios, which describe the total environment in which the organization exists.

Katopol (2014) observes that environmental scanning can be challenging for librarians who are often focused on searching for definitive answers, who prefer trusted sources, and who would rather think about the present than think more broadly about events and trends in the larger society.

Organizational Reports That Are Useful for Scanning the Environment

American Libraries Direct. https://www.americanlibraries magazine.org/al-direct.

American Library Association, Office of Government Relations. "Federal Legislation." www.ala.org/advocacy/advleg/federallegislation.

Association for Library Service to Children. "ALSC Environmental Scan: The Current and Future State of Youth Librarianship." www.ala.org/alsc/sites/ala.org.alsc/files/con tent/professional-tools/2016%20 ALSC%20Env%20Scan.pdf.

Association of College and Research Libraries. "Keeping Up With . . . ," an online current awareness publication. www.ala.org/acrl/publications/keeping-up-with.

Association of College and Research Libraries, Research Planning and Review Committee. "Environmental Scan 2017." www.ala.org/acrl/sites/ala.org.acrl/files/content/pub lications/whitepapers/EnvironmentalScan2017.pdf.

Informed Librarian Online. A current awareness subscription service for professional reading. www.informedlibrarian.com.

International Federation of Library Associations. "Trend Report." https://trends.ifla.org/.

Library Information Technology Association. "Top Technology Trends." www.ala.org/lita/ttt/.

New Media Consortium. "NMC Horizon Report 2017: Library Edition for Academic and Research Libraries." https://www.nmc.org/publication/nmc-horizon-report-2017-library-edition/.

OCLC. "Membership Reports," in-depth studies and topical surveys for OCLC members. www.oclc.org/reports.

PEW Internet & American Life Project surveys. www.pewinternet.org.

Urban Libraries Council. "E-News Weekly." https://www.urbanlibraries.org/e-news-weekly-pages-33.php.

Another weakness in this regard is to rely upon a close network of people who tend to know the same things that you do. Often, more distant sources can provide access to new information that is more valuable in scanning the environment.

Individual libraries often don't have the resources to sustain a macro-level scanning project that would encompass all the factors that might have an impact on them: economics, politics, technology, and social and cultural trends. However, several organizations are scanning the larger environment and making reports available. See text box on scanning reports.

Koontz and Mon (2014) note that marketers often divide the library's environment into (1) the microenvironment, which is the library's internal environment of customers, employees, professional staff, vendors/distributors, and library stakeholders—the groups that the library can manage more proactively; and (2) the macroenvironment, which is composed of forces outside the library's control that may ultimately have greater impact upon the organization's future than internal factors. Environmental scanning focused on the macroenvironment is most closely concerned with developments in the economy. The financial trends for local, state, and federal government and for private funding directly impact the financing of libraries. In difficult economic times, library use increases but funding decreases. The state of the economy suggests that the funding of libraries will keep pace with inflation at best, and will lag behind inflation or result in actual cuts in many places. The loss of discretionary income, or a decline in the American standard of living, impacts the priorities that individuals place on libraries, particularly in view of the increasing availability of information in digitized electronic formats, and the availability of this information from alternative sources. Breakthrough developments in technology, which often result in the replacement of one type of electronic medium or device by a newer one, cannot be accurately forecasted, but they may have major implications for libraries.

Scanning the Library Field. Keeping up-to-date on the news, events, and trends in the larger social, economic, and political environment is one type of "environmental scanning." Another type, which may be more directly relevant to librarians, is that of scanning developments in the field of library and information science itself. The standard sources for keeping up in the library field include *Library Journal* and journals published by the American Library Association or its divisions, including *American Libraries, Reference & User Services Quarterly, Information Technology and Libraries, Public Libraries, College & Research Libraries,* and *Journal of Research on Libraries and Young Adults.* A listing of these journals is available at libguides.ala.org/ala-periodicals. Checking the websites of individual ALA divisions may give you more information about further resources to check. In this regard, RUSA's website is especially relevant: www.ala.org/rusa/.

Another option for keeping up-to-date is to use SDI (selective dissemination of information) services, which send you recent notice of current publications of interest for a subject profile that you select. Most database vendors provide some sort of mechanism for you to set up profiles of interest. Grants databases often have similar kinds of profiles available, so you don't need to limit yourself to just journal articles in this approach.

Some librarians have instituted "journal clubs" where individuals periodically exchange interesting articles that they have read. Young and Vilelle (2011) cite the following benefits of journal clubs: "staying current with the literature, learning new topics, identifying gaps in the literature, developing critical appraisal skills, and personal interaction." Committing to read an article and summarize it for a colleague means that you'll actually follow through and do it, and you will also benefit from hearing what other people have found interesting at the same time.

Subscribing to e-mail newsletters is another way to keep up-to-date. The advantage of this approach is that this information comes directly to your e-mail account. E-mail newsletters also eliminate the need to visit dozens of different websites in order to keep up with the latest developments and news in information technology.

Another technique to help you sort through the wide variety of information that you need in order to keep current is to use your e-mail program's ability to set up filters to automatically sort your incoming mail into specific folders. You can either set up a folder for "Keeping Up" that several items go into that you read every few days, or you can set up a folder for each newsletter or type of material. For information on setting up filters, consult WikiHow (https://www.wikihow), which has detailed instructions for creating e-mail filters on Gmail and Yahoo. Another type of "professional filter" consists of current awareness services such as Current Cites (currentcites.org), an annotated bibliography of selected articles, books, and digital documents in information technology; the Scout Report (https://scout.wisc.edu/report/current), a fast and convenient way to stay informed of valuable STEM and humanities resources on the Internet; INFOdocket (www.infodocket.com), which covers the latest information industry news and resources; and Google Alerts (https://www.google.com/alerts), which provides a tracking service for search engine results.

Depending on your institutional setting, you may need to monitor different communications from a variety of groups. Academic librarians should read campus communications (including discussion lists) and the minutes of board of trustees and faculty senate meetings, and should consider serving on campus committees that impact the library, such as those for general education and curriculum planning. For community libraries, attendance at the meetings of local city councils and county boards might be necessary. School librarians should certainly monitor the activities of their local school boards, and special librarians should read trade publications, which discuss issues and trends in the industry, and should also keep tabs on activities within the organization. The Association of College and Research Libraries' Instruction Section (acrl.ala.org/IS/) has developed a checklist of suggested groups to monitor for their possible impact on information literacy programs.

"Analyzing Your Instructional Environment" by the ACRL's Instruction Section (2010) suggests that you track whether you or someone else in your library is keeping informed by reading minutes and attending meetings, is participating in discussion and decision-making, and is taking an active role in developing projects or leading directions for the group. A similar checklist could be developed for your particular institution.

Another technique is to use alternative scenarios, which allows people to discuss and explore different alternative paths that the development of the library could take. In *The Futurist* article "Library Futures," Inayatullah (2014) notes that libraries must redefine themselves, their services, business models, and missions. He describes recent strategy sessions in Australia, with a wide variety of stakeholders, that used scenarios to develop alternate futures of the library through the use of a modified "six pillars" foresight process.

Strategies for Improving Your Active Learning Competencies. In the twenty-first century, learning is not an optional extra but an everyday process (Hoyle, 2015). Both good formal learning and effective informal learning are essential. However, employees do not view formal training as the most effective approach to meeting their learning needs. In 2015–16 the British nonprofit organization Towards Maturity (https://towardsmaturity.org/) surveyed 4,700 global knowledge workers from a wide range of businesses. Their top five preferences for learning methods were team collaboration, manager support, web search, conversations/meetings, and support from a mentor/coach/buddy. Of those surveyed, 81 percent agreed with the statement, "I am responsible for managing my development." Also, 91 percent liked to be able to learn at their own pace (Phillips, 2016).

Hoyle (2015) has developed a five-stage model for informal learning:

1. Observation
2. Imitation
3. Experience
4. Innovation
5. Articulation (explanation, which is a spur to reflection)

The learning experience must include reflection on what happened and why. Hoyle notes that the best kind of informal learning includes observation, action, feedback, reflection, and improvement. For learners, Hoyle suggests that a starting point is the learner reflecting on her experiences, her requirements for the future, and her current capabilities; and then using these reflections as a basis for planning subsequent learning.

In their book *Active Training,* Mel Silberman and Elaine Biech (2015) discuss the concept of "covering" material, and suggest that synonyms for the word "cover" include the words "hide, obscure, or block." When material is "covered" for participants, then, the individuals in the training may find the material hidden, obscured, or blocked because the individuals haven't participated in the uncovering process. The authors suggest that "active training occurs when the participants do most of the work" (p. xvi). Learning is enhanced when people are asked to do the following with their peers:

1. State the information in their own words.
2. Give examples of it.
3. Have an opportunity to reflect on the information.
4. See connections between it and other facts or ideas.
5. Practice higher-order thinking, such as analysis, synthesis, and evaluation.
6. Apply the information to case situations. (p. 3)

All of the strategies given above can also be used by individuals on their own to enhance what they glean from reading. But sharing their observations with others gives even more opportunities for reflection, as well as the opportunity to gain insights from the other participants.

Given the need for involvement in the learning process, Silberman and Biech (2015) offer further ideas for improving active learning, including demonstrations, case studies, guided teaching, group inquiry, information searches, study, groups, jigsaw learning, and learning tournaments (pp. 102–27).

In a demonstration, you include an element of showing rather than merely telling. Visual learners find this particularly helpful. So instead of talking about a concept, procedure, or set of facts, try to walk through a demonstration of the information in action. If participants are involved in the demonstration, an element of handling the materials is also added. Visiting vendor demonstrations at conferences or conventions, and inviting vendors to demonstrate their products locally are good strategies. The evangelists at Microsoft and other technology companies are only too happy to show their wares at conventions. Sometimes the application or potential of a new technology will not be immediately apparent. If having vendors demonstrate locally is not possible, you might consider having one person on staff become the "expert" in a certain topic, database, or subject and have her demonstrate the tools and techniques to others.

In a case study, a real or fictional situation is described. It normally includes enough detail for individuals or groups to analyze the problems involved. "The major benefit of a case study is that abstract information is presented concretely" (Silberman and Biech, 2015, 105).

To encourage self-discovery, guided teaching is an excellent technique. The leader asks a series of questions to tap the knowledge of the group or obtain their hypotheses or conclusions. The leader should then compare these ideas to the important points, and add those if they have not been covered in the discussion.

Going one step further, you can ask the participants to devise their own questions in order to further develop their understanding of a topic. If it is an unfamiliar topic, work examples or handouts can be given to arouse the participants' interest and curiosity and to stimulate questions. Posing a problem that the group must solve might also encourage questions. It is particularly important to allow sufficient time for the group to form some questions. The questions can be fielded either as a whole group or one at a time.

Another interesting technique is one that Silberman and Biech (2015) call the "information search" (pp. 113–15). Rather than presenting a lecture, you provide source materials such as handouts, document, textbooks, reference guides, computer-access information, artifacts, and work-related equipment, along with a worksheet. A search for information among the source materials can be conducted by either individuals or small teams. These searches can be done either cooperatively or competitively.

Another way to cover new material without lecturing is to use study groups, whose participants are asked to read a short, well-formatted handout covering the lecture material and are then placed in small groups to clarify its contents. Jigsaw learning is a variation of a study group. Rather than asking each group to study the same information, you give different information to different groups and then form new study groups composed of representatives of each of the initial groups. Every participant teaches something or brings his newly acquired knowledge to the learning task. This technique is particularly effective when the material to be learned can be segmented or "chunked" and when no one segment must be taught before the others. Each participant learns something that, when combined with the material learned by the others, forms a coherent body of knowledge or skill.

Building on the two previous techniques, and adding team competition, one can also use a "learning tournament" as an effective learning tool. This technique can be used to promote the learning of a wide variety of facts and concepts, especially if the information is dry. The participants are provided with learning material and are given time to read and study it with the knowledge that they will be

Silberman's Six Experiential Learning Approaches

1. **Role-Playing.** Typically, this is a dramatic situation in which the participants are required to confront someone else and then discuss the feelings generated by the role-playing experience.
   a. Scripting Options
      - Improvisation. Participants fill in the details themselves.
      - Prescribed roles. Participants are given a well-prepared set of instructions that state the facts about the roles they are portraying and how they are to behave.
      - Semi-prescribed roles. Participants are given information about the situation and characters, but not how to handle the situation.
      - Replay of life. Participants portray themselves in situations they have actually faced.
      - Participant-prepared scripts. Participants are given time to create a role and a chance to rehearse in preparing a role-playing vignette of their own.
      - Dramatic readings. Participants are given a previously prepared script to act out.
   b. Staging Options
      - Informal role-playing. This role-play evolves informally from a group discussion.
      - Stage-front role playing. One pair, trio, or the like can role-play in front of the group, which will observe and offer feedback.
      - Simultaneous role-play. All participants formed into pairs or trios, and simultaneously undertake their role-play.
      - Rotational role-playing. Actors in front of the group can be rotated, usually by interrupting the role-play in progress and replacing one or more of the actors.
      - Use of different actors. More than one actor can be recruited to role-play the same situation in its entirety.
      - Repeated role-playing. Reenacting the role-play allows participants to have a second chance after the initial feedback.
   c. Processing Options
      - Designated observers
      - Self-assessment
      - Open audience discussion and feedback
      - Subgroup discussion and feedback
      - Trainer observations
      - Benchmark comparison
   d. Video Feedback
      Prior to taping
      - Give adequate time for preparation before taping.
      - Lighten the mood so that the performance is as natural and relaxed as possible.
      - Consider leaving the room initially to encourage the trainees to experiment and tape each other.

(cont.)

During the taping
- Hold off on making teaching points until after recording.
- Make notes of what the trainees are doing well and what needs to be improved.

After the taping
- Give the trainees uninterrupted time to make judgments of their performance first.
- Consider creating peer support groups that watch each other's tapes and give feedback.
- Review parts of the tape you've selected with each trainee, using specific, descriptive feedback that focuses on positive performance as much as possible.

2. **Games and Simulations**
   a. The game or simulation needs to be relevant to the participants.
   b. The easiest way to create games and simulations is to mimic the format and character of well-known ones.
   c. Well-known games and simulations can be modified to suit your needs.
   d. Fun-like, contrived games can be followed by more serious, less contrived ones.
   e. The instructions for games and simulations need to be carefully thought out.
   f. Games and simulations almost always need to be discussed afterward for the experience to be effective.

3. **Observation**
   a. Design Tips
      - Provide aids to help the participants attend to and retain pertinent aspects of a demonstration they are watching.
      - When the participants are observing a role-play or group exercise, provide easy-to-use observation forms that contain suggestions, questions, and checklists.
      - Provide key questions to help the observers focus their attention.
      - Expect the observers to give constructive feedback in order to challenge them to observe carefully and apply what they have previously learned.
      - Be aware that the observers have strong vicarious experiences if what they are observing has a personal impact.
   b. Formatting Tips
      - User observers as the audience watching a demonstration, video, or role-play.
      - Assign observers to small groups to provide feedback after the small group performs.
      - Arrange the participants in a fishbowl format to form a circle around the individuals they are observing.

4. **Mental Imagery**
   a. Types
      - Visual imagery
      - Tactile imagery
      - Olfactory imagery
      - Kinesthetic imagery
      - Taste imagery
      - Auditory imagery
   b. Guidelines
      - Help the participants to clear their minds by encouraging them to relax.
      - Conduct warm-up exercises.
      - Assure the participants that it's okay if they experience difficulty visualizing what you describe.
      - Give the imagery instructions slowly and with enough pauses to allow the images to develop.
      - Invite the participants to share their imagery.

5. **Writing Tasks**
   a. Help participants to get in the mood to express themselves in writing.
   b. Make sure your instructions are clear.
   c. Allow enough time for writing.
   d. Allow enough time for feedback.

6. **Action Learning Options**
   a. In-basket assignments. Letters, memos, and phone messages are given to the participants, who are given time to write actual responses to the items.
   b. Research projects. Participants conduct research and present their findings.
   c. Field observation. Participants visit a real-life setting and observe or interview and then report their findings.
   d. Teaching projects. Have the participants teach new information to others.
   e. Task force projects. Groups generate a plan or other specific outcome that can be used by other participants in the actual work situation.

Source: Melvin Silberman and Elaine Biech. 2015. *Active Training: A Handbook of Techniques, Designs, Case Examples, and Tips.* 4th ed. Hoboken, NJ: Wiley, pp. 128-62. Copyright © 2015 by ebb associates, inc. All rights reserved.

tested on its content. Teams are formed to review the information and test each other. Then short quizzes are given on the material to each participant. A team's average score on the quiz is computed, so this encourages the team members to help others learn the material.

Additional experiential learning approaches from Silberman and Biech (2015, 128–62) are included in the text box, "Silberman's Six Experiential Learning Approaches."

If you cannot participate in a group process such as those described above, there are other alternatives to solo reading and reflection. Good online learning opportunities ask individuals to answer questions, make choices, and even offer alternative solutions, and these sites provide feedback in a variety of forms. WebJunction is probably the simplest place to start, since it aggregates online learning opportunities from MindLeaders, the University of North Texas, OCLC Western, OCLC CAPCON, and WebJunction itself (learn.webjunction.org). The course topics on WebJunction range alphabetically from Advocacy to Young Adults and Teens. Another useful website is Top 200 Tools for Learning 2017 (http://c41pt.co.uk/top100tools/), compiled by the Centre for Learning & Performance Technologies. This site includes lists for personal and professional learning, workplace learning, and education. A number of online educational programs and courses for library staff and information professionals are offered by ALA-accredited library schools, undergraduate schools, community colleges, regional library networks, and WebJunction. Reviewing the principles put forth in the "Serious eLearning Manifesto" (http://elearningmanifesto.org) should assist you in evaluating the quality of the many learning opportunities that exist online. Serious eLearning is performance-focused, meaningful to learners, and engagement-driven; and involves authentic contexts, realistic decisions, individualized challenges, spaced practice, and real-world consequences.

Participation in committee work at a local, state, regional, or national level can also be a good way to further develop your expertise, in addition to providing an opportunity to network with your colleagues. For additional information on participation, see the section in chapter 4 entitled "Develops Collaborative Relationships within the Profession to Enhance Service to Users."

Assessing Development Efforts for Leading a Life as a Learner

One of the most effective methods of assessing your lifelong learning is to keep a log or journal of all your activities in this area. In this log you record your participation in communities of practice, environmental scanning, library field scanning, and professional discussions and activities. You might be surprised at how many activities you actually participate in. On the other hand, if you do very little, then you need to review your scheduled activities and create some room for keeping up with new developments in the dynamic and ever-changing field of reference and user services.

Your log can be enriched by not just simply listing the activities, the frequency of each activity, and the time you spend on it, but the most important information you obtained from each of the various activities. Reviewing the log might lead you to decide to quit scanning some sources and try some new leads instead. You can also set some goals by starting with a list of key activities and considering the frequency with which you want to engage in them.

A good method of assessing your active learning competencies is to keep an annual list of the number of workshops, conferences, and other learning experiences, such as special projects on the job, where you have played an active role. But you should not give yourself much credit for merely attending a conference or listening to a lecture. What really counts is actively participating on a committee, attending and participating in a workshop, or even teaching the workshop. Teaching materials to others is a tremendous way to increase your knowledge and expertise. Figure 7.1, "Annual Record of Active Learning Activities," provides a form that will assist you in setting up and maintaining an annual record of your active learning activities. These records can be very helpful in updating your resume and

```
Name: _____
Activity: _____
_____
_____
Dates: _____
Time Required: _____
Purpose/Objectives of the Activity: _____
_____
_____
Describe Main Learning/Knowledge Gain from Activity:
_____
_____
_____
Future Plans (especially how you will apply the learning
to the workplace):_____
_____
_____
```

FIGURE 7.1 *Annual Record of Active Learning Activities*

displaying your expertise when you're searching for a new job.

Other techniques suggested by Silberman and Biech (2015, 320–40) for applying new skills learned in training to your job include creating job aids, realistically assessing the obstacles to applying your learning, engaging in peer consulting or peer teaching, self-monitoring, creating a contract with oneself or others, and developing an action plan by defining appropriate outcomes and steps. Creating a job aid is a realistic first step for applying your learning on the job and has several benefits. First of all, the person creating it applies what they've learned, but the job aid also provides a point-of-use way for others to benefit from it as well. Job aids include checklists, flowcharts, worksheets, and a variety of other forms that help participants remember and apply what they have learned to their current job. The process might also include setting up a meeting with the department head to discuss how your skills could be used on the job, or consciously identifying those tasks that would use the skills you learned in a training program.

"The most common obstacle [to applying new skills learned in training to the job] is a lack of support from peers, supervisors, or others on the job. Another common obstacle is the lack of time to apply new skills consciously, assess how they've been used, and get feedback from others" (Silberman and Biech, 2015, 328). One of the most helpful things you can do to avoid these problems is to conduct an obstacle assessment, in order to identify the obstacles applying to your training. It may be necessary to develop a support mechanism where someone can give you feedback on your success (or lack of success) in applying certain skills on the job. Gers and Bolin (2000) describe a training model for reference services that incorporates peer coaching as a feedback mechanism. Some programs recognize this and build feedback mechanisms into the ways they suggest implementing one's skills on the job. A good example of this is the Fish! Philosophy (www.fishphilosophy.com), which has personal application workbooks and cards that are used to give feedback to others in the group.

If groups participate in training, they can discuss in small groups their specific back-home issues. This peer consultation provides an opportunity to summarize and apply the skills they have learned and to try out their new expertise. They can also develop a plan to effectively handle change in their work unit.

"An excellent way to master new ideas and skills is to try to teach them to someone else. Teaching others is also bound to increase one's own commitment of actually using what is being taught" (Silberman and Biech, 2015, 329). Self-monitoring is another useful technique to help you apply new skills on the job. You might keep a personal diary, or use ready-made checklists, for example, the "Model Behaviors Checklist," which is available as module 3 of "ORE Online: Ohio Reference Excellence Professional Development Training" (Ohio Library Council, 2017). Through the use of self-monitoring, you become more aware of your use of a new skill and are able to evaluate your level of success in using the skill.

Individuals can also create a contract—a written expression of the intent to change one's behavior in some aspect or to undertake a particular action appropriate to the goals of the training program. The contract can be made with oneself or with others. The common elements in many of these personal contracts are the goal, the activities, and the weekly time required to meet the goal, and the incentives and reward for goal achievement. Examples of these contracts are available on the Web by searching on "personal goal contract."

Mentoring. Mentors can be a good source for getting feedback on your learning goals. Mentors provide advice, counseling, coaching, and guidance through an interactive relationship. Jenn Labin (2017) describes mentoring as a relationship-based learning process. Traditional models of mentoring have focused on a one-to-one matching model, pairing new professionals with more experienced individuals. However, models are changing (Stoudt, Birch, Chiles, Spracher, and White, 2016) and now include self-serve models (Society of Georgia Archivists, 2014) and group models or mentoring circles, such as the NEA Mentoring Program (New England Archivists, 2018). Mentoring is individually driven; you desire and foster mentoring for yourself, even when participating in a formal program. All of the models rely on individuals to identify and seek out mentoring experiences that meet their needs.

Kram and Higgins (2008) believe that the model of a single senior colleague, which is the traditional view of a mentoring relationship, no longer works. The world of work has become too complicated. A better approach is to create and cultivate a developmental network, which you can think of as your personal board of advisors. This board should consist of those who have a genuine interest in your learning and career, and its membership should change over time as your career evolves. Your success in creating a helpful personal board of advisors depends on your ability to accurately assess your needs (self-awareness) and your ability to initiate and cultivate effective relationships with others over time. Mentoring should be a relationship with mutual benefits, in which both parties learn from each other. So when establishing a mentoring relationship, consider how you might benefit the other individual. For example, a more experienced colleague might find a mentoring experience useful for developing her coaching skills, or for understanding how less experienced people or those with very different jobs see the world and establish priorities. The findings from surveys of professionals, managers, and executives show that some of the best sources of development support are personal friends, managers/supervisors, business associates, informal mentors, and spouses/life partners (Shen, Cotton, and Kram, 2015).

Kerry Ann Rockquemore (2013) suggests that mentors can play very different roles in one's personal and professional life, and she provides a mentor map (figure 7.2) for you to fill out in order to identify your areas of need and brainstorm how to fill them. The Brigham and Women's Hospital Center for Faculty Development and Diversity (2016) has developed a toolkit that includes an exercise based on the Developmental Network Model by Kathy Kram. Although both of these mentoring maps were designed with university faculty in mind, librarians in other settings will find these exercises worthwhile with a few minor adjustments made to the wording on the maps. EDUCAUSE (2018) has developed a Mentoring Information Kit that "includes resources on mentoring programs, as well as finding a mentor or becoming one. Learn all about effective mentoring and the ways it can boost your career, whether you are a mentor or a mentee."

Reflective Practices. "Reflective practice" means thinking about and questioning your practice, for example, after each reference interaction or instructional session, by asking questions like "What did I do well? What could I have done better? How might I improve in the future?" (VanScoy, 2016). Reflective practices and activities are also important in assessing your degree of competence in various areas. Press and Diggs-Hobson (2005) suggest that one of the characteristics of the culturally competent librarian is that he or she "can conduct self-assessment and is aware of how his or her own values, biases, attitudes and beliefs may affect different or minority patrons" (p. 407). Cultural self-reflection is an important process in becoming

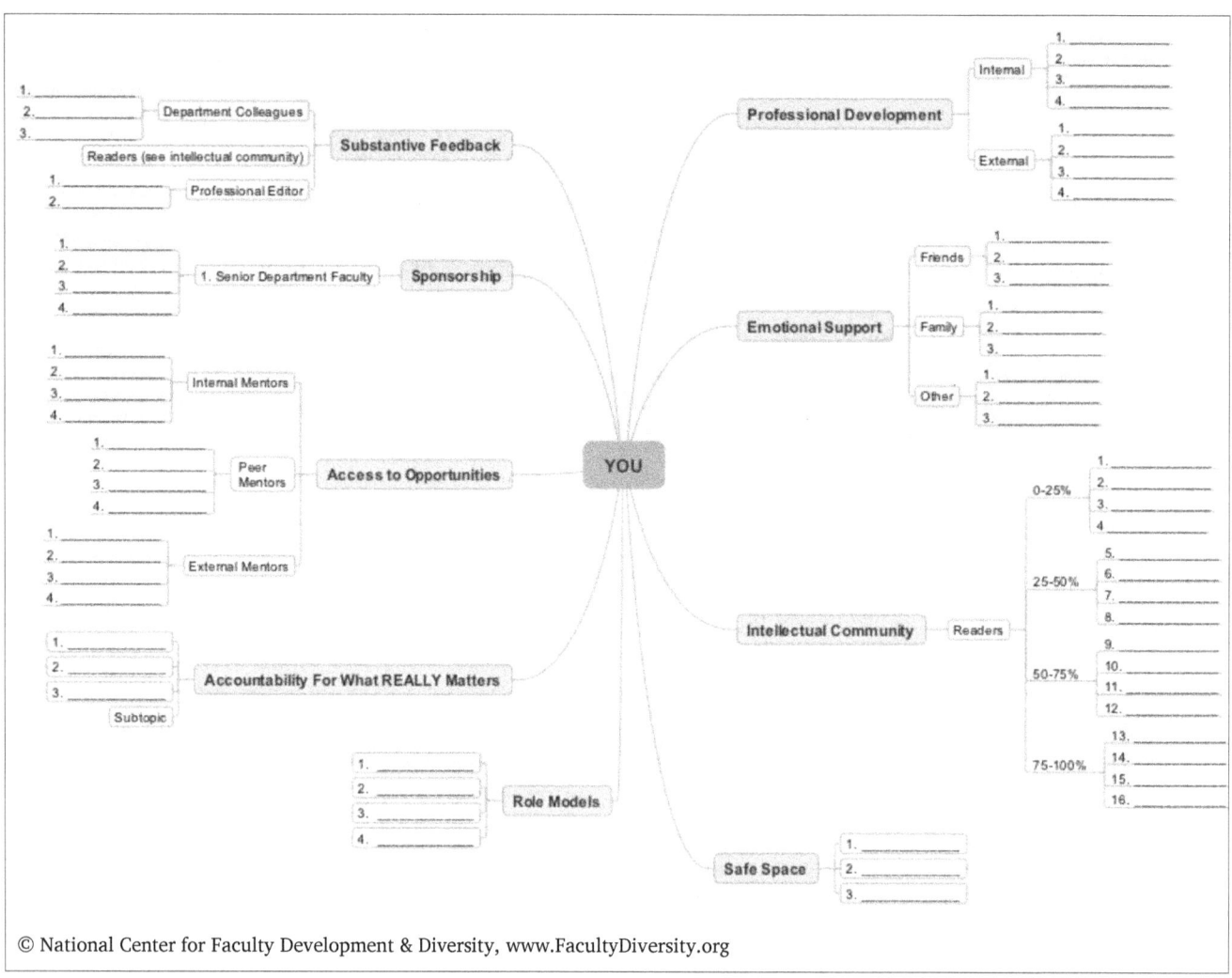

FIGURE 7.2 • *Map Out Your Mentoring Network*

culturally competent. Through a knowledge of self, individuals become aware of the unexamined cultural assumptions in their own background (Montiel-Overall, 2009). This author provides an excellent example of a reflective activity: building a cultural heritage autobiography, which serves as an initial step in developing cultural competence (p. 264). Developing cultural awareness and an understanding of one's own and others' cultural competencies form part of the "Competencies for Librarians Serving Children in Public Libraries" (Association for Library Service to Children, 2015), the "Teen Services Competencies for Library Staff" (Young Adult Library Services Association, 2018),

and "Diversity Standards: Cultural Competency for Academic Librarians" (Association of College and Research Libraries, 2012).

Self-reflection is one of the three primary methods that are useful in determining your personal development goals (White, 2017). Self-reflection is defined as an honest self-evaluation set against external standards. The other two primary methods for personal development are input from others—which includes not only formal input from managers but from other colleagues, such as mentors—and self-assessments. Self-assessments can be quite helpful in developing your self-awareness. White suggests several useful instruments—MBTI (www

.myersbriggs.org), DISC (https://discprofile.com), and the StrengthsFinder (https://www.gallupstrengthscenter.com)—for increasing your awareness of your natural tendencies and your unique strengths. An additional instrument that is very useful for personal, team, and leadership development is the "TMS Team Management Profile" (https://tmsoz.com/team-management-profile/).

As part of their goal of making leadership development accessible to everyone, Morgan, Lynch, and Lynch (2017) provide some worthwhile self-assessment instruments on a companion website for their book *Spark: How to Lead Yourself and Others to Greater Success*. The exercises that are available on the free website include Circle of Influence, Self-Awareness, Your Character, Discovering and Developing Mentors, and Developing Positive Appraisals.

DEVELOPS AND IMPLEMENTS PLANS FOR SERVICES AND RESOURCES

Competencies for Developing and Implementing Plans for Services and Resources

The typical behavioral strategies suggested by the RUSA "Professional Competencies" that demonstrate competencies related to planning for services and resources are:

- Applies knowledge of the information-seeking process to structure information services for users
- Promotes evidence-based decision-making and fiscal responsibility
- Initiates changes based on ongoing analysis of services and resources
- Retains valued, successful, and cost-effective programs and services
- Evaluates new technologies to determine if they meet user needs more effectively than current methods
- Proposes new services and programming to address identified unmet needs, taking advantage of new technologies
- Plans for the introduction of new services and programming, delineating required support and markers of success
- Allocates resources to reflect decisions made for service and programming

Development Methods for Developing and Implementing Plans for Services and Resources

Creating lists of pros and cons can be useful in helping to make decisions. For example, several sources use this technique for help in determining which type of tool is useful for gathering information in needs assessment. In *Active Training*, Silberman and Biech (2015, 29–34) present the advantages and disadvantages of techniques for gathering information.

"Force field analysis" is a method for listing, discussing, and evaluating the various forces for and against a proposed change. Using a force field analysis helps you look at the big picture by analyzing all of the forces impacting the change and weighing the pros and cons. By knowing the pros and cons, you can develop strategies to reduce the impact of the opposing forces and strengthen the supporting forces. The forces that help you achieve the change are called driving forces, and the forces that work against the change are called restraining forces. Specifically, force field analysis can determine if a proposed change can get needed support, can identify obstacles to successful solutions, and can suggest actions to reduce the strength of the obstacles. For an example, see figure 7.3.

Concept and Other Maps. Presenting information in a visual way so that relationships are highlighted is the purpose of using a concept map. The phrase "a picture is worth a thousand words" is actually based in sound pedagogical practices. A graphic organizer forms a powerful visual picture and allows the mind to "see" undiscovered patterns and relationships.

Desired State: A comprehensive information literacy program has been integrated into courses in the English Department. The Faculty and Librarians working in partnership share responsibility for the design, delivery, and evaluation of the program.

Driving Forces →	Restraining Forces ←
New department head in English who supports information literacy.	Several English department faculty who have been vocal about their opposition to giving up class time for "skills training."
The campus administration has called for an overhaul of the core curriculum courses.	A number of librarians who believe that information literacy is a passing fad and time spent on this detracts from the real mission of the library.
Two new instruction librarians who have tremendous energy, enthusiasm, and vision.	A growing student body with no real possibility of increasing library staff.
The campus instructional technology center has instructional designers and programmers who want to work with the library.	Some librarians who are willing to participate but have no experience in teaching.
The library has two well-equipped electronic classrooms.	The campus administration has been apathetic about library services.
The Library Strategic Plan includes instruction as a top priority.	The library systems staff is small and overworked. The use of the electronic classroom suffers because of this.
The library dean has some discretionary funding and wants to spend it on staff development for instruction.	

SOURCE: Karen Williams. 2006. "Worksheet for the ACRL Immersion Institute for Information Literacy." Based upon the concepts of Kurt Lewin. K. Lewin. 1943. "Defining the 'Field at a Given Time.'" *Psychological Review* 50: 292–310. Republished in *Resolving Social Conflicts & Field Theory in Social Science*, Washington, DC: American Psychological Association, 1997.

FIGURE 7.3 *Force Field Analysis*

When lists of categories, comparisons and contrasts, and pros and cons are presented in a tabular form that not only provides the information but also presents it in such a way as to make comparisons and contrasting features more readily apparent, such a tool is called a "frame." The examples above regarding pros and cons for needs analysis techniques, search conventions, and popular versus scholarly materials all use frames. Empty frames—ones in which only the row and column headings are completed and the rest are left blank for the learner to fill in—are excellent tools for learning. An empty frame is an excellent tool for helping librarians and patrons evaluate and compare web pages, for example.

One can use concept maps to plot concepts and label relationships. Examples of concept maps include hierarchies, which show both reporting structures and similarities of structures; spider maps, which show mainly breakdowns or factors of an issue; and chain maps, which show processes.

Spider or mind maps help arrange ideas logically, but they also appeal to us because the graphical nature of the drawing can let us incorporate color, symbols, and pictures into them. Mind maps help organize ideas, generate ideas, develop a memory aid, and integrate learning.

Creating a process map is a useful tool to help analyze processes. In analyzing processes, it is important to identify the critical and time-consuming processes, and analyze these processes in enough detail to find issues and opportunities for improvement. Mapping the process gives a graphical display of the work processes. A situation in which a process map might be useful would be mapping the interlibrary loan process in your library, including the decision points in obtaining materials that are not held in your library. Government documents librarians are all familiar with government process maps. One graphical example of process mapping comes from the California legislature: "How a Bill Becomes a Law" (www.leginfo.ca.gov/bi121awd.html). Nash and Poling (2009) provide an overview of process mapping and an introduction to value stream mapping, which may be preferred because of the simplicity of the map and the amount of information that can be included in a single document. And Stroud (n.d.) contrasts value stream mapping with traditional process mapping.

Strategies for Critical and Creative Thinking. Convergent thinking evaluates the quality of different ideas and chooses between them. It narrows the scope of thinking, requiring an attitude of critical judgment, constructive criticism, objectivity, and a desire to be methodical. Convergent or critical thinking is needed when a choice needs to be made. It requires an attitude of acceptance, trust, and a desire to be creative. When alternatives need to be identified, creative or divergent thinking must be used. See figure 7.4 for a comparison illustrating the differences between critical thinking and creative thinking. Several online tutorials are helpful in improving critical thinking. Searching the MERLOT II website (https://www.merlot.org/merlot/index.htm) for "critical thinking tutorials" will locate a number of these interactive resources. In these tutorials, users are introduced to the basic concepts through sets of instructions and exercises.

Brainstorming is the simplest and most widely used tool for rapidly generating ideas. Brainstorming is about solution generation rather than evaluation, and aims for quantity rather than quality.

Critical Thinking	Creative Thinking
Analytic	Generative
Convergent	Divergent
Vertical	Lateral
Probability	Possibility
Judgment	Suspended Judgment
Focused	Diffuse
Objective	Subjective
Answer	An Answer
Left Brain	Right Brain
Verbal	Visual
Linear	Associative
Reasoning	Richness, Novelty
Yes, but	Yes, and

SOURCE: From Robert Harris, "Introduction to Creative Thinking." http://www.virtualsalt.com/crebook1.htm.

FIGURE 7.4 *Comparing Critical and Creative Thinking*

IDEO's Brainstorming Rules

- Defer judgment
- Encourage wild ideas
- Build on the ideas of others
- Stay focused on the topic
- Hold one conversation at a time
- Be visual
- Go for quantity

Source: IDEO. 2018. "Effective Brainstorming Techniques." https://www.ideou.com/pages/brainstorming.

Generally, after clearly stating the problem, a time limit is specified, generally less than thirty minutes; during this time many ideas are rapidly put forth, but without evaluating or passing judgments on their feasibility. In brainstorming, free and uninhibited thinking generates many new ideas, and broadens the scope of the possibilities that are considered. Specific suggestions regarding brainstorming rules are listed in the text box below, "IDEO's Brainstorming Rules."

A variation on brainstorming is called brainwriting, in which individuals write down solutions on a piece of paper, place them on the table, and then piggyback on each other's ideas to create new ones.

"Mind mapping" is an alternative for individuals without a group. You start with a topic or issue statement placed in a circle in the middle of a blank page, and then you brainstorm each major facet of the problem or issue, placing your thoughts on lines drawn outward, adding branches as necessary and connecting lines between related ideas or similar thoughts.

Jack Foster's book *How to Get Ideas* (2007) includes a number of techniques for creative thinking, particularly ones that individuals can use in everyday life to help them become more creative. Alternatively, there are a number of innovation and creativity workshops available, including workshops from IDEO (https://www.ideo.com/), a design and innovation consulting firm in Palo Alto, California. On their website you can read more about their philosophy for innovation and about solving complex problems collaboratively, and you can access learning platforms and tools to promote creativity.

More Analytical Strategies. SWOT analysis is a tool used to help define strategies. By identifying your organization's Strengths, Weaknesses, Opportunities, and Threats, the current position of the organization is clarified, along with future directions. This type of analysis does not clearly identify problems or provide answers, but the list of strengths and weaknesses it provides can be used to evaluate and prioritize solutions.

Another analytical strategy is a fishbone diagram. A fishbone diagram can be used to help organize the output from a brainstorming or root cause analysis session. The main issue or problem is recorded as the fish's head, in the form of a question, and the fish's spines list the various aspects or categories of the problem or issue. Fishbone diagrams produce a compact, readily understood representation of the generated ideas, and they automatically structure the responses in broad categories of related ideas. Once the diagram is

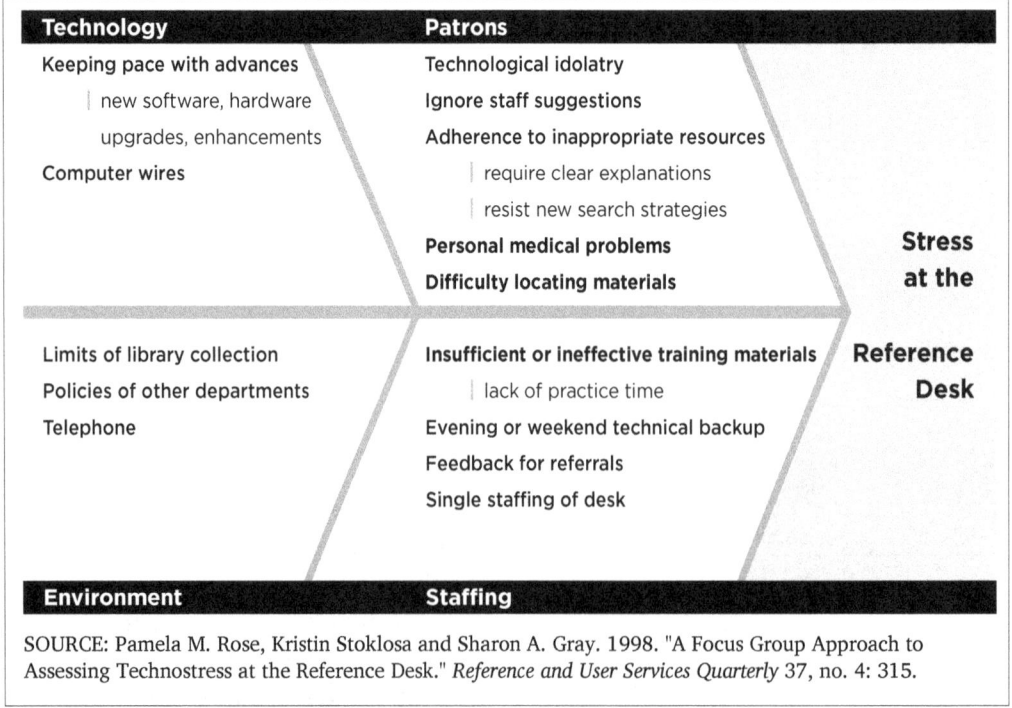

FIGURE 7.5 • *Fishbone Diagram: Stress at the Reference Desk*

complete, it provides the basis for an analysis of the categories of ideas. Figure 7.5 is a fishbone diagram documenting the factors that produce stress at the reference desk.

Yet another tool to help one analyze possible solutions is the ease/impact model illustrated in figure 7.6. Using this model, one can visually prioritize solutions based on their ease of implementation and their impact.

Determining which approach to take to solve a particular problem requires evaluative techniques; these are discussed more fully in chapter 6 on "Assessment." In addition, the Creating Minds website (creatingminds.org/) provides practical tools organized into four groups: tools for defining the creative problem, tools for creating ideas, tools for selecting ideas, and tools for implementing ideas.

Assessing Development Efforts for Developing and Implementing Plans for Services and Resources

As part of developing and implementing new services and resources, a plan for assessing the success of those services and resources should be developed. "Measuring and Assessing Reference Services and Resources: A Guide" (Reference and User Services Association, 2007a) is an excellent guide to the literature and tools that are available to assess both reference services and resources. Another very useful assessment measure is implementation fidelity—the extent to which the implementation of the service mirrors the original design. Implementation fidelity is a formative evaluation that focuses on improving the quality of the implementation by identifying potential reasons for discrepancies in the theoretical service model versus the actual implementation. Gariepy, Hodge, Doherty, and Clark's case study (2015) using implementation fidelity examined a new service model, which consolidated research assistance, circulation, and media services into one service point. As a result of the evaluation, many deficits in the new service were identified, and improvements were made to bring the new service closer to the original vision.

> This tool is great for assessing the relative value of various strategic options. It is useful for facilitating group discussions about alternative strategies. It has two dimensions: the strategy's ease of implementation and its degree of impact. This is a valuable tool for leaders who want to explore various strategic investments.
>
> To use the tool, list the options under consideration and rate each option in terms of its impact and its ease of implementation.
>
> Once each option is rated, place it in the appropriate square.
>
> **TIP:** If doing this activity as a group, allow time for the group to define what it means by "impact" and "ease of implementation" within the context of the organization. Each organization will bring different nuances of meaning to these terms.

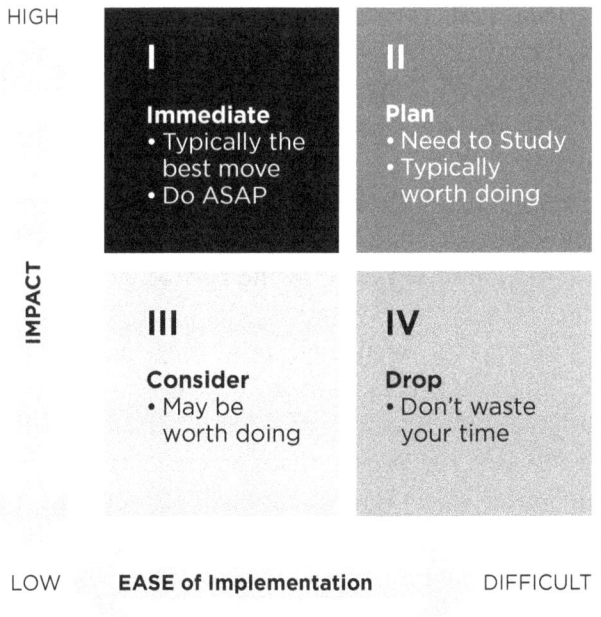

FIGURE 7.6 *Ease/Impact Model*

PLANS, IMPLEMENTS, AND EVALUATES SMALL-SCALE, INNOVATIVE EXPERIMENTS IN SERVICES AND RESOURCES

Competencies for Planning, Implementing, and Evaluating Small-Scale, Innovative Experiments in Services and Resources

The qualities which help you succeed in the workplace today are also crucial for introducing and implementing successful innovations in services and resources. The important qualities for success, according to Sweetman (2016), are:

Change—learning about change and making certain that all involved have the information needed

Collaboration—working together with people from different areas and levels of expertise, which requires knowing your stuff

Communication—knowing your audience and situation, listening carefully, and valuing diverse viewpoints and backgrounds

Manage Relationships—obtaining the best possible results by working effectively with both bosses and colleagues

Emotional Intelligence—recognizing your emotions and their impact upon your colleagues

The typical behavioral strategies suggested by the RUSA "Professional Competencies" that demonstrate competencies related to innovative experiments are:

- Identifies alternative strategies for proposed improvements
- Selects for experimentation the options determined by critical examination to be the ones most likely to succeed
- Employs experimental, small-scale projects designed to improve services and service delivery
- Evaluates results using clearly established criteria

Development Methods for Planning, Implementing, and Evaluating Small-Scale, Innovative Experiments in Services and Resources

A decision matrix can be a useful tool for developing your skills in evaluating new service ideas in detail. A matrix can help you reduce a very large number of ideas to a workable subset of ideas that can be further evaluated. In general, the process involves deciding on the detailed criteria to be used in evaluating the ideas remaining after an initial screening. The criteria could include costs, time, reliability, quality, morale, customers, legality, safety, library practices, approval process, feasibility, timeliness, and ease of implementation. A decision matrix is a list of rows and columns that allows you to evaluate and prioritize a list of options. In using a matrix, list the criteria on the left-hand side, and the ideas across the top of the matrix. Working across the columns, you can assign each idea a score out of 10 for each criterion, and then sum the ratings across criteria for each idea. Figure 7.7 is a sample decision matrix.

The simplest approach to analyzing the matrix is to add the raw scores to get an overall measure of idea quality on the various criteria. When not all the criteria are equally important, an alternative approach is to assign weights to each of the criteria so that the most important criterion is assigned the highest weight. By multiplying the raw scores by the weights, it is possible to obtain weighted scores which can then be added to produce weighted totals.

Assigning someone to the role of devil's advocate is another evaluative approach. The devil's advocate may challenge prevailing assumptions or judgments, champion an option that has been provisionally rejected, criticize a selected option, or identify risk factors that can challenge the predictions of likely future outcomes. Having someone take this role can enhance the quality of information processing in decision-making; a devil's advocate can reduce the impacts of confirmatory bias on judgments, sharpen information processing so that underlying structures are analyzed, counter subtle

Criteria	1	2	3	4
Solution Attractiveness				
Ease of implementation				
Originality				
Sustainable				
User-friendly				
Global acceptance				
TOTAL ATTRACTIVENESS				
Compatibility with Objectives and Resources				
Available funds				
Consistent with culture				
Consistent with image				
Compatible with cost control measures				
Quick to implement				
TOTAL COMPATIBILITY				

FIGURE 7.7 *Decision Matrix Example*

pressures to conform, and minimize the destructive effects of political or personally motivated actors.

Knowledge is powerful only when it is used. The early Islamic philosopher Abu Bakr said, "Without knowledge action is useless, and knowledge without action is futile" (BrainyQuote, n.d.). Knowledge application is the key to packaging knowledge to ensure widespread use, convert specialized information into practical tools, and put new knowledge into practice in the real world. The journal *Reference Services Review* often has case studies that provide models for putting new knowledge into practice, which could be replicated in other settings.

So the exploration of new technologies is not very useful unless we can try out the most promising technologies and apply them to everyday experience. Integrating new technologies into our service profiles implies that we will need to develop pilot projects, beta test software, and develop interactive tutorials to help others learn how to use the product as well. For example, an instant messenger chat service or a text messaging service for after-school homework assistance is not a high-cost investment for software, but it does require staffing and staff comfort with the technology. One would certainly need to consider having staff members put software on their staff machines in order to get comfortable with it before starting the pilot.

IDEO is a development company which is the subject of the video *Deep Dive* (Koppel, Smith, and ABC News, 1999). In his handout "Why Has IDEO Been So Innovative over the Years?" Paul Miesing (n.d.) emphasizes that IDEO has been successful because of its good skills in using enlightened trial and error. Craig Lawrence (2003) observes that a core idea for the company is the importance of prototyping, following the three "Rs": "Rough, Rapid, and Right!" The final R, "Right," refers to building several models focused on getting specific aspects of a product right. Central to this process is the idea that you learn as much from your mistakes as you do from what you get right. IDEO (2015) approaches human-centered design as a three-phase process:

1. *Inspiration*—understanding people, observing their lives, and hearing their hopes and desires
2. *Ideation*—generating tons of ideas, identifying opportunities, and testing and refining solutions
3. *Implementation*—bringing your solution to life, and maximizing its impact

A prototype is a draft version that allows you to explore your ideas before investing larger amounts of time and money in full-scale development. Prototypes can be built at any time, but you should create them as early as possible. Most often, prototyping in libraries is seen in website development, where a prototype can be anything from a series of drawings on paper, to a few images or pages that a user can click through, to a fully functioning website. A prototype is often the best way to learn how your solution works in practice by gathering feedback from users while you are still planning and designing it. It is a quick way to find out if you are on the right track with your plans and design. According to the Nielsen Norman Group (2018), prototyping results in ten times the impact if you discover a needed design change early and fix usability problems, before wasting time and money on something that doesn't work. In their discussion of service design tools, Marquez and Downey (2017, 72–75) cover various library prototypes, which can be used to test service ideas.

A pilot project is a longer-term test of your solution (IDEO, 2015), but is still a preliminary or experimental test or trial on a limited scale. A pilot project involves lower risk and a smaller commitment of time and money than full-scale implementation, while still letting you see the service or resource functioning in real-world conditions. There are three phases to a pilot: plan, run, and evaluate (Hessing, 2014). In a library environment, Rebecca Watson-Boone (2000) outlines seven steps (figure 6.2) that are very useful in implementing and evaluating a pilot project:

1. Identify the problem that needs attention.
2. Define various ways to address the problem.
3. Select the process that appears to have the greatest chance of working.
4. Set out the criteria against which to measure success.
5. Carry out the pilot project.
6. Evaluate what occurs.
7. Reflect on whether the results have solved the problem.

What is important for success in scaling up promising pilots to full implementation are planning, staff buy-in and involvement, accepting change, and knowing your limits (Koerber, 2017a). For designing pilots for scaling up in a library environment, Koerber provides this advice from Larry Neal:

1. Always focus on the needs of the end user.
2. Use the pilot as a testing lab that is flexible and organic, with opportunities to learn, experiment, adapt, succeed, and fail.
3. Document the decisions and reasons, and revise and update approaches.
4. Think about sustainability from the beginning.
5. Don't be afraid of success, which will provide great opportunities for additional partnerships and collaboration.

Assessing Development Efforts for Planning, Implementing, and Evaluating Small-Scale, Innovative Experiments in Services and Resources

A good assessment method is to fill out a form each time you read about an innovative practice, try out a new technology to improve professional practice, or experiment with a service innovation. See figure 7.8, a form that you can use to record and outline your experiments in applying your knowledge, your successes, and your failures. Analyzing a failed experiment often provides much better learning opportunities than an easy and successful innovation.

Name _____

DESCRIPTION OF APPLICATION
_____
_____
_____

List the Knowledge Competencies Being Applied
_____
_____
_____

Dates: _____ Time Required: _____

How successful was the application of knowledge?

1	2	3	4	5
Not at all	To a small extent	To a moderate extent	To a great extent	Completely

Were there organizational barriers to successful application? _____ Yes _____ No

If yes, describe what they were and how these barriers might be reduced or eliminated in the future.
_____
_____
_____

Importance of the Activity to Your Workplace

1	2	3	4	5
No importance	Minimal importance	Moderate importance	Very important	Critical importance

FIGURE 7.8 *Application of Knowledge*

conclusion

WE HOPE THE IDEAS AND PRACTICAL strategies in this book will encourage you to take a very active role in your career development. In the last two decades, the rapidly changing information environment has transformed the knowledge and skills that are needed for successful performance in reference and user services. We expect this trend to continue.

In today's environment, librarians can no longer rely upon just the basic knowledge acquired in master's programs in library and information studies, or upon development programs and resources, to achieve the full knowledge and skills that are necessary for a satisfying and enjoyable career.

Although our book does not focus primarily upon technology, it is set in the context of the rapidly changing information environment. This environment presents new and unprecedented challenges in accessing, organizing, and managing information formats and content which are continually evolving, and in satisfying the constantly changing information-seeking needs of our users in an increasingly global society. A successful and fulfilling career in this demanding environment requires lifelong learning for the self-development of one's knowledge, skills, and abilities.

We put forward the principle of self-development as the most important skill set for the future of librarians. And this self-development is your responsibility. Professional growth and development are a personal responsibility, but they should be supported by libraries and similar information organizations, as well as by the basic graduate education that is offered in library and information studies.

We encourage you to invest in yourself; you will benefit greatly from this, and so will the people you assist, advise, and instruct in meeting their immediate information needs and developing their lifelong learning skills.

You should explore not only distant professional development opportunities, but also local opportunities that offer you the chance to learn new knowledge and skills by performing challenging tasks. You should challenge your library leaders and local community leaders to provide more of these opportunities. With your learning goals firmly in mind, you can negotiate professional growth opportunities with key leaders in your organization.

And above all, you should reflect critically upon your skills, abilities, and knowledge in order to determine what you require for a personally satisfying career. We hope that this book will make a contribution on your path to a successful and rewarding career.

appendix
Professional Competencies for Reference and User Services Librarians

Written by the RUSA Professional Competencies for Reference and User Services Librarians Task Force, chair, Nancy Huling; Larayne J. Dallas; Robin Kinder; Jo Bell Whitlatch; Beth Woodard. Approved by the RUSA Board of Directors, September 7, 2017.

INTRODUCTION

As the professional organization for reference and user services, the Reference and Users Services Association (RUSA) has developed and updated a model statement of competencies essential for successful reference and user services librarians. This statement builds upon ALA's "Core Competencies of Librarianship"; Section 5 "Reference and User Services," which defines the basic knowledge to be possessed by all graduates of ALA-accredited master's programs. For each of the areas in Section 5 (A-G), a reference and user services librarian should know and be able to employ the concepts, principles, and techniques of reference and user services to individuals of all ages, cultures, and groups.

The RUSA competencies are critical to excellent reference and user services. Thus, they identify the underlying behaviors that lead to successful performance in organizations providing reference and user services to patrons. The competencies assume a basic infrastructure of competencies required by all professionals, such as skills related to communication, information technologies, digital literacy, reading, writing, and mathematics. Therefore, the RUSA competencies focus on the abilities, skills, and knowledge that make reference and user services librarians unique from other professionals. The "Guidelines for Behavioral Performance of Reference and Information Service Providers" are incorporated through specific reference into the "Professional Competencies for Reference and User Services Librarians."

In addition to the competencies detailed below, reference and user services librarians are responsible for affirming the importance of diversity issues within the broader information community; possessing awareness of their own historical, cultural, racial, gendered, and religious worldviews; and identifying where those views exclude other human experiences.

Competencies must be relevant to the particular job requirements or type of information organization. Individual organizations developing competencies need to take into consideration reference staffing models that may include collection specialists, paraprofessionals, students, and others. Individuals and organizations applying the RUSA essential competencies may wish to identify additional competency statements by consulting resources, including technology and management competencies, such as:

WebJunction's "Competency Index for the Library Field 2014," the Library Leadership and Management Association's (LLAMA) "Leadership and Management Competencies," and the Association of College and Research Libraries' "Roles and Strengths of Teaching Librarians."

DEFINITIONS

Reference and User Services Librarians: Librarians who assist, advise, and instruct users in accessing all forms of recorded knowledge. The assistance, advice, and instruction include both direct and indirect service to patrons.

Competencies: Behaviors that excellent performers exhibit consistently and effectively. A behavioral basis is necessary because effective assessment of competencies depends on observed behavior.

5A. ACCESSES RELEVANT AND ACCURATE RECORDED KNOWLEDGE AND INFORMATION

Offers Services Responsive to Individual Expressed User Needs

1. Applies "Guidelines for Behavioral Performance of Reference and Information Service Providers"
2. Recognizes, honors, and responds appropriately to diversity and cultural differences
3. Determines situational context of individual information needs
4. Engages in discussion and expresses interest in individual experiences related to information needs
5. Understands and applies laws and policies governing confidentiality and rights to privacy
6. Consults with the user to identify the most appropriate resources in the context of accuracy, authority, interest, and content level
7. Respects the right of individuals to pursue their research preferences
8. Assists the user in evaluating, managing, formatting, storing, using, or displaying information
9. Consults with the user to select appropriate technology for providing answers, balancing the nature of the information being provided with user preferences
10. Applies knowledge of state of the art information retrieval technologies and systems to assist the user in identifying and obtaining information
11. Identifies opportunities for instruction that empowers users to improve their own information-seeking abilities

Organizes and Designs Services to Meet the Needs of the Primary Community

1. Creates physical and virtual environments that encourage use of all available services

2. Designs services that reflect the demographics, cultural diversity, and special needs of the community

5B. EVALUATES, COLLECTS, RETRIEVES, AND SYNTHESIZES INFORMATION FROM DIVERSE SOURCES

Identifies and Presents Highly Recommended Sources

1. Connects users to tools that can help them identify diverse sources of information
2. Connects users to highly recommended, carefully selected sources in many formats
3. Evaluates reference tools and sources for quality, relevance, authenticity, authority, and inclusiveness
4. Identifies any bias or point of view in an information resource
5. Creates useful research guides, web pages, bibliographies, finding aids, and other appropriate tools in areas of expertise
6. Compiles and maintains information about community resources
7. Develops programming, displays, tutorials, and other specialized instructional materials reflective of the cultural diversity of the primary community

5C. INTERACTS WITH COLLEAGUES AND OTHERS TO PROVIDE CONSULTATION, MEDIATION, AND GUIDANCE IN THE USE OF KNOWLEDGE AND INFORMATION

Collaborates and Partners with the User in the Information Seeking Process

1. Engages the user in the process and in making decisions
2. Determines the user's prior knowledge and expertise
3. Consults appropriate internal and external resources

Collaborates with Colleagues to Provide Service to Users

1. Establishes shared goals and values for excellent user services
2. Facilitates team development with colleagues to improve user services
3. Shares knowledge and expertise with colleagues
4. Recognizes the unique knowledge, skills, and strengths of colleagues that can assist in responding to inquiries
5. Elicits assistance from colleagues when appropriate to enhance the user experience

Develops Collaborative Relationships within the Profession to Enhance Service to Users

1. Develops personal networks by actively participating in appropriate local, regional, state, national, and international organizations
2. Identifies and seeks out possible partners in order to expand services
3. Contributes to collaborative efforts that will benefit local users

Develops and Maintains Partnerships beyond the Library Profession to Strengthen Services to Users

1. Identifies and reaches out to potential partners who are able to contribute relevant knowledge and expertise
2. Communicates effectively with partners to ensure mutual understanding of goals, objectives, and values
3. Forms mutually beneficial partnerships to improve existing systems and to develop new products and services

5D. DEVELOPS APPROPRIATE EXPERTISE IN INFORMATION LITERACY AND INSTRUCTION SKILLS AND ABILITIES, INCLUDING TEXTUAL, DIGITAL, VISUAL, NUMERICAL, AND SPATIAL LITERACIES

Defines Information Literacy

1. Creates a personal definition of information literacy
2. Develops a shared understanding with colleagues
3. Collaborates with users and colleagues to help the institution or organization develop its own definition of information literacy

Integrates Information Literacy Concepts into the Full Range of Library Services, from Classroom Instruction to Community Programs to One-on-One Reference and Instruction

1. Helps individuals to assess their own information needs, to differentiate among sources of information, and to develop skills to effectively identify, locate, and evaluate sources
2. Adjusts communication style and methods according to learner needs and context
3. Leads or facilitates discussion of controversial or unexpected issues in a skillful, non-judgmental manner that helps individuals to learn
4. Designs interactive presentations and exploratory activities
5. Incorporates communication technologies to provide assistance to learners in and outside the classroom
6. Requests feedback from users and peers on instruction-related communication skills and uses feedback to improve individual skills
7. Develops and implements assessments that encompass the various aspects of learning in order to improve instruction

Designs and Implements Presentation and Communication Strategies to Foster Learning and Engagement

1. Makes the best possible use of voice, eye contact, gestures, and active learning methods in order to keep face-to-face instruction lively and learners engaged
2. Seeks to clarify confusing terminology, avoiding excessive jargon, and using vocabulary appropriate for level of learners
3. Presents instructional content in diverse ways (written, oral, visual, online, or using presentation software) and selects appropriate delivery methods according to learners' needs
4. Scales presentation content and learning activities to the users' needs and how people learn, adjusting to time, space, and technology available
5. Practices or refines instruction content as necessary in order to achieve familiarity and confidence with planned presentation

Creates a Learner-Centered Teaching Environment

1. Designs group instruction sessions by defining expectations and desired learning outcomes in order to determine content, sequencing the lessons and incorporating activities that facilitate learning
2. Designs instruction to best meet the common learning characteristics of individuals, including prior knowledge and experience, motivation to learn, cognitive abilities, and circumstances under which they will be learning
3. Implements active, collaborative, and other appropriate learning activities
4. Modifies teaching methods and delivery to address different learning preferences, language abilities, developmental skills, age groups, and the diverse needs of learners
5. Integrates appropriate technology into instruction to support experiential and

collaborative learning as well as to improve individual receptiveness, comprehension, and retention of information
6. Designs effective assessments of individual learning and uses the data collected to guide personal teaching and professional development
7. Reflects on practice in order to improve teaching skills and applies new knowledge of teaching methods and learning theories
8. Shares teaching skills and knowledge with other instructional staff

5E. PROMOTES AND DEMONSTRATES THE VALUE OF LIBRARY SERVICES THROUGH MARKETING AND ADVOCACY

Understands and Applies Marketing Theory and Practices

1. Practices the basic principles of marketing and applies them to library services
2. Conducts research to assess marketing landscape and to determine current position among similar and/or competing businesses and organizations
3. Identifies the strengths, weaknesses, opportunities, and challenges of library services to enhance marketing strategy
4. Identifies, analyzes, and prioritizes target markets and audiences to determine how best to promote library services that can effectively serve them
5. Determines community relationships and develops partnering models of services with groups within the community
6. Conducts periodic reviews of the community for opportunities to align needs with library services

Develops, Implements, and Evaluates an Ongoing Marketing Plan for Library Services

1. Sets measurable market goals and objectives, including brand strategy
2. Develops consistent promotion and distribution strategies to meet goals and objectives based on the analysis of target audiences
3. Participates in marketing training
4. Implements marketing efforts, maintaining records and clear communication with staff and stakeholders
5. Evaluates the effectiveness and impact of the strategies and revises as necessary

Advocates the Value of Library Services to the Primary Community

1. Engages with target audiences, connecting via the most appropriate tools and sources
2. Communicates with library users, potential users, and other stakeholders through multiple communication formats and channels
3. Maintains current awareness of communication tools and media sources used by target audiences
4. Builds relationships with partners who advocate on behalf of the library
5. Develops and maintains relationships among diverse cultural groups

5F. ASSESSES AND RESPONDS TO DIVERSITY IN USER NEEDS, USER COMMUNITIES, AND USER PREFERENCES

Assesses User Needs

1. Identifies the user population and potential user population
2. Analyzes own cultural background and assumptions, and the racial, ethnic, cultural, and other diversities of the community
3. Collects and analyzes information about users and user interactions with the library and its services, while respecting user privacy and confidentiality
4. Plans and conducts regular assessments of information needs of primary user groups, using various formal and informal methods

5. Translates assessments of user needs into a plan for services that addresses the needs and preferences of diverse user groups

Assesses Information Services

1. Creates an organizational climate of assessment
2. Develops and incorporates measures of evaluation into any new service
3. Develops service standards for new and existing information services
4. Analyzes resources available and distributes resources to service programs most effectively meeting the user needs of a designated community
5. Analyzes demographic and other information about the community to develop a wide variety of services, which meet the needs and interests of diverse communities

Assesses Information Resources

1. Maintains quality of collection resources by evaluating all formats for accuracy and currency
2. Determines authority of resources
3. Identifies any bias or point of view in an information resource
4. Evaluates new information sources appropriate for primary users
5. Consults a wide variety of reviewing sources to identify those best meeting needs of the primary community
6. Writes and distributes reviews of new information resources to appropriate online and print media

Assesses Service Delivery

1. Determines the appropriate mix of technologies and delivery channels to meet diverse user needs and preferences
2. Experiments with and evaluates changes in services to users
3. Evaluates the allocation of human and fiscal resources to ensure they are supporting priority services and delivery methods

Assesses User Interfaces for Information Resources

1. Identifies factors that impede the use of the resource
2. Evaluates format, access, and presentation aspects of resources
3. Communicates with information resource designers about usability and accessibility concerns
4. Determines if there are alternative resources that have better user interfaces and resources

Assesses Assistance to Users by Information Service Providers

1. Identifies and applies those performance measures that have been developed by the profession, for example, the RUSA "Guidelines for Behavioral Performance of Reference and Information Service Providers"
2. Consults with information service staff to develop a consensus of service standards
3. Develops measures that will be useful in assessing whether or not service standards are being met
4. Promotes a service philosophy that encourages collaboration to improve service behaviors

5G. INVESTIGATES, ANALYZES, AND PLANS IN ORDER TO DEVELOP FUTURE SERVICES

Leads a Life as a Learner

1. Devises and implements strategies to learn about emerging tools and techniques, and connects with professional communities to seek and share best practices
2. Identifies potential new services and programs through contact in the professional community, readings, and other exploration

3. Seeks opportunities to be informed, gathering news and information about the local, national, and international environment
4. Encourages discussion with colleagues that furthers reflection on services offered and on potential needs
5. Practices self-reflection, including an awareness of personal strengths and limitations
6. Maintains currency with developments in understanding how people learn and with the best ways of facilitating learning in both formal and informal settings

Develops and Implements Plans for Services and Resources

1. Applies knowledge of the information seeking process to structure information services for users
2. Promotes evidence-based decision making and fiscal responsibility
3. Initiates changes based on ongoing analysis of services and resources
4. Retains valued, successful, and cost-effective programs and services
5. Evaluates new technologies to determine if they meet user needs more effectively than current methods
6. Proposes new services and programming to address identified unmet needs, taking advantage of new technologies
7. Plans for the introduction of new services and programming, delineating required support and markers of success
8. Allocates resources to reflect decisions made for service and programming

Plans, Implements, and Evaluates Innovations in Services and Resources

1. Identifies alternative strategies for proposed improvements
2. Selects for experimentation the options determined by critical examination to be most likely to succeed
3. Employs experimental, small-scale projects designed to improve services and service delivery
4. Evaluates results using clearly established criteria
5. Adopts successful innovations on a larger scale

RESOURCES CONSULTED

American Library Association. "Core Competencies of Librarianship," 2009. www.ala.org/educationcareers/sites/ala.org.educationcareers/files/content/careers/corecomp/corecompetences/finalcorecompstat09.pdf.

American Library Association. Association of College and Research Libraries. "Roles and Strengths of Teaching Librarians," April 28, 2017. www.ala.org/acrl/standards/teachinglibrarians.

American Library Association. Library Leadership and Management Association. "Leadership and Management Competencies," 2016. www.ala.org/llama/leadership-and-management-competencies.

American Library Association. Reference and User Services Association. "Guidelines for Behavioral Performance of Reference and Information Service Providers," 2013. www.ala.org/rusa/resources/guidelines/guidelinesbehavioral.

Appendix I: "Suggested Verbs for Task Statements," pp. 25–27

Appendix II. "Verbs to Avoid Using in Task Statements," p. 28

Appendix III. "Verbs to Be Used with Caution in Task Statements," pp. 29–30 https://home.ubalt.edu/tmitch/651/PDF%20articles/Guide%20for%20Writing%20Functional%20Competencies%20(Annotated).pdf.

Association of College and Research Libraries. "Diversity Standards: Cultural Competency for Academic Libraries," 2012. www.ala.org/acrl/standardsdiversity.

Association for Talent Development. "The ATD Competency Model," 2014. https://www.td.org/Certification/Competency-Model.

Brook, Freeda, Dave Ellenwood, Althea Eannace Lazzaro. "In Pursuit of Antiracist Social Justice: Denaturalizing Whiteness in the Academic Library." *Library Trends* 64 (Fall 2015): 246–84. http://hdl.handlenet/1773/34983.

"Guide for Writing Functional Competencies." University of Baltimore, October 13, 2005.

Houston, Anne. "What's in a Name? Toward a New Definition of Reference." *Reference and User Services*

Quarterly 55 (Spring 2016): 186–88. https://journals.ala.org/index.php/rusq/article/viewFile/5927/7512.

International Federation of Library Associations and Institutions. "IFLA Statement on Digital Literacy," August 18, 2017. https://www.ifla.org/files/assets/faife/statements/ifla_digital_literacy_statement.pdf.

WebJunction. "Competency Index for the Library Field," 2014. www.webjunction.org/documents/webjunction/Competency_Index_for_the_Library_Field.html.

We thank the ALA ALCTS Cataloging Competencies Task Force (Bruce J. Evans, Chair) for permission to adapt their paragraph on diversity issues in the "Core Competencies for Cataloging and Metadata Professional Librarians to the RUSA Professional Competencies."

bibliography

Abram, Stephen. 2017. "Communicating Value and Impact through Advocacy: Dealing with the Scalability Issue in the Province of Ontario." *Public Library Quarterly* 36, no. 2: 96–122.

Allen, Michael. 2012. *Leaving ADDIE for SAM: An Agile Model for Developing the Best Learning Experiences.* Alexandria, VA: ASTD.

———. 2015. "Inside Look at SAM." ATD Links. https://www.td.org/newsletters/atd-links/inside-look-at-sam.

Alman, Susan W., and Sara Gillespie Swanson. 2014. *Crash Course in Marketing for Libraries.* 2nd ed. Santa Barbara, CA: Libraries Unlimited.

Almquist, Arne J. 2014. "The Innovative Academic Library: Implementing a Marketing Orientation to Better Address User Needs and Improve Communication." *Journal of Library Innovation* 5, no. 1: 43–54.

American Association of School Librarians. 2007. "What Is Advocacy?" www.ala.org/aasl/advocacy/definitions.

———. 2018a. "AASL Advocacy Toolkit: Educated Support for School Libraries and School Library Professionals." www.ala.org/aasl/advocacy/tools/toolkits.

———. 2018b. "AASL Standards Framework for Learners." http://standards.aasl.org/wp-content/uploads/2017/11/AASL-Learner-Framework-Spread.pdf.

American Library Association. 1989. "Presidential Committee on Information Literacy: Final Report." www.ala.org/acrl/publications/whitepapers/presidential.

———. 2008a. "ALA Strategic Planning." www.ala.org/aboutala/strategicplan.

———. 2008b. "Mission and Priorities." www.ala.org/aboutala/missionpriorities.

———. 2009. "Core Competences of Librarianship." www.ala.org/educationcareers/careers/corecomp/corecompetences.

———. 2010. "Policy Manual: A.1 Mission, Priority Areas, Goals (Old Number 1)." www.ala.org/aboutala/

governance/policymanual/updatedpolicymanual/section1/1mission

———. 2013. "Digital Literacy, Libraries, and Public Policy: Report of the Office for Information Technology Policy's Digital Literacy Task Force." https://districtdispatch.org/wp-content/uploads/2013/01/2012_OITP_digilitreport_1_22_13.pdf.

American Marketing Association. 2013. "Marketing." https://www.ama.org/AboutAMA/Pages/Definition-of-Marketing.aspx.

Association for Library Service to Children. 2015. "Competencies for Librarians Serving Children in Public Libraries." www.ala.org/alsc/edcareeers/alsccorecomps.

Association for Talent Development. 2014. "ATD Competency Model." https://www.td.org/certification/atd-competency-model.

Association of College and Research Libraries. 2010. "Value of Academic Libraries: A Comprehensive Research Review and Report," researched by Megan Oakleaf. www.ala.org/acrl/sites/ala.org.acrl/files/content/issues/value/val_report.pdf.

———. 2012. "Diversity Standards: Cultural Competency for Academic Librarians." www.ala.org/acrl/standards/diversity.

———. 2016. "Framework for Information Literacy for Higher Education." www.ala.org/acrl/standards/ilframework.

———. 2017. "ACRL Proficiencies for Assessment Librarians and Coordinators." www.ala.org/acrl/standards/assessment_proficiencies.

Association of College and Research Libraries, Instruction Section. 2010. "Analyzing Your Instructional Environment: A Workbook." https://acrl.ala.org/IS/instruction-tools-resources-2/higher-education-environment/analyzing-your-instructional-environment/.

———. 2017. "Roles and Strengths of Teaching Librarians." www.ala.org/acrl/standards/teachinglibrarians.

———. 2018. "PRIMO: Peer-Reviewed Instruction Materials Online." https://acrl.ala.org/IS/instruction-tools-resources-2/pedagogy/primo-peer-reviewed-instruction-materials-online/.

Association of College and Research Libraries, Instruction Section, Teaching Methods Committee. 2018. "Current Projects & Resources." https://acrl.ala.org/IS/is-committees-2/committees-task-forces/teaching-methods/.

Attebury, Ramirose Ilene. 2017. "Professional Development: A Qualitative Study of High-Impact Characteristics Affecting Meaningful and Transformational Learning." *Journal of Academic Librarianship* 43: 232–41.

Avery, Susan, and David Ward. 2010. "Reference Is My Classroom: Setting Instructional Goals for Academic Library Reference Services." *Internet Reference Services Quarterly* 15, no. 1: 35–51.

Bagshaw, Anna, and Phil Yorke-Barber. 2018. "Guiding Librarians: Rethinking Library Guides as a Staff Development Tool." *Journal of the Australian Library and Information Association* 67, no. 1: 31–41.

Bakhshi, H., J. Downing, M. Osborne, and P. Schneider. 2017. *The Future of Skills: Employment in 2030.* London: Pearson and Nesta. https://www.nesta.org.uk/publications/future-skills-employment-2030.

Barba, Ian, and Shelley Barba. 2011. "You Can Tell Everyone about This PHITE Club." *ACRLog: Blogging by and for Academic and Research Librarians.* https://acrlog.org/2011/06/07/you-can-tell-everyone-about-this-phite-club/.

Barkley, Elizabeth F. 2010. *Student Engagement Techniques: A Handbook for College Faculty.* San Francisco: Jossey-Bass.

Barkley, Elizabeth F., and Clair H. Major. 2016. *Learning Assessment Techniques: A Handbook for College Faculty.* San Francisco: Jossey-Bass.

Bedenbaugh, Robin A. 2016. "Marketing Is Our Game: Tackling the Library Awareness Gap." *Public Services Quarterly* 12, no. 4: 321–28.

Bill & Melinda Gates Foundation. 2015. "Global Libraries Impact and Planning Assessment Guide." www.publiclibraryadvocacy.org/wp-content/uploads/2015/06/IPA-Guide-2015.pdf.

———. 2018. "Evaluation Policy." https://www.gatesfoundation.org/How-We-Work/General-Information/Evaluation-Policy.

Blake, Barbara, Robert S. Martin, and Yunfei Du. 2011. *Successful Community Outreach: A How-to-Do-It Manual for Librarians.* New York: Neal-Schuman.

Booth, Char. 2011. *Reflective Teaching, Effective Learning: Instructional Literacy for Library Educators.* Chicago: American Library Association.

Bowles-Terry, Melissa, and Cassandra Kvenild. 2015. *Classroom Assessment Techniques for Librarians.* Chicago: Association of College and Research Libraries.

BrainyQuote. n.d. "Abu Bakr Quotes." https://www.brainyquote.com/quotes/abu_bakr_219641.

Brigham and Women's Hospital Center for Faculty Development & Diversity. 2016. "BWH Mentoring Curriculum & Toolkit." http://bwhmentoringtoolkit

.partners.org/mentoring-and-career-development/developmental-networks/.

British Columbia Institute of Technology. 2010. "Assessing Your Teaching Effectiveness." www.northernc.on.ca/leid/docs/ja_teacheffect.pdf.

Brookfield, Stephen D. 2017. *Becoming a Critically Reflective Teacher.* 2nd ed. San Francisco: Jossey-Bass.

Bruce, Christine. 2014. "Seven Faces of Information Literacy in Higher Education." www.christinebruce.com.au/informed-learning/seven-faces-of-information-literacy-in-higher-education/.

Bruce, Christine, Sylvia Edwards, and Mandy Lupton. 2006. "Six Frames for Information Literacy Education: A Conceptual Framework for Interpreting the Relationships between Theory and Practice." *Innovation in Teaching and Learning in Information and Computer Sciences* 5, no. 1: 1–18.

Burke, Jennifer E. 2017. "Top Marketing Tools to Know." *Computers in Libraries* 37, no. 7: 28–31. www.infotoday.com/cilmag/sep17/Burke—Top-Marketing-Tools-to-Know.shtml.

Butler Scientifics. 2017. "5 Kinds of Exploratory Questions You May Be Asking Yourself." www.butlerscientifics.com/single-post/2015/09/21/5-kinds-of-exploratory-questions-you-may-be-asking-yourself.

Cabello, Marcela, and Stuart M. Butler. 2017. "How Public Libraries Help Build Healthy Communities." www.brookings.edu/blog/up-front/2017/03/30/how-public-libraries-help-build-healthy-communities/.

California Community Colleges. 2016. "Online Student Readiness Tutorials." http://apps.3cmediasolutions.org/oei/.

California State University System. 2018. "MERLOT." https://www.merlot.org/merlot/index.htm.

Cameron, Lynn, Steven L. Wise, and Susan M. Lottridge. 2007. "The Development and Validation of the Information Literacy Test." *College and Research Libraries* 68, no. 3: 229–36.

Cassidy, Erin Dorris, Angela Colmenares, and Michelle Martinez. 2014. "So Text Me—Maybe." *Reference & User Services Quarterly* 53, no. 4: 300–312.

Chandler, D. E., D. T. Hall, and K. E. Kram. 2010. "A Developmental Network & Relational Savvy Approach to Talent Development: A Low-Cost Alternative." *Organizational Dynamics* 39, no. 1: 48–56.

Chartered Institute of Library Information Professionals', Information Literacy Group. 2018. "Definitions & Models." https://infolit.org.uk/definitions-models/.

Chatfield, Mark M. n.d. "Self-Directed and Self-Managed Teams." http://irism.com/selfteam.htm.

Child Development Institute. 2018. "The Ages and Stages of Child Development." https://childdevelopmentinfo.com/ages-stages/.

Clifton, Shari, Phill Jo, Jean Marie Longo, and Tara Malone. 2017. "Cultivating a Community of Practice: The Evolution of a Health Information Specialists Program for Public Librarians." *Journal of the Medical Library Association* 105, no. 3: 254–61.

Common Sense. n.d. "Give Every Child a Stake in Group Work." https://www.commonsense.org/education/teaching-strategies/give-every-student-a-stake-in-group-work.

Cornell University Library. 2017. "How to Prepare an Annotated Bibliography." http://guides.library.cornell.edu/annotatedbibliography.

Coward, C., C. McClay, and M. Garrido. 2018. *Public Libraries as Platforms for Civic Engagement.* Seattle, WA: Technology & Social Change Group, University of Washington Information School. https://tascha.uw.edu/publications/public-libraries-as-platforms-for-civic-engagement/.

Cunningham, Sojourna, Regina Mays, and Holly Mercer. 2017. "But This Is for the Library: Best Practices for Usability Testing and Library Website Design." In *The Library Assessment Cookbook,* ed. Aaron W. Dobbs, 175–76. Chicago: Association of College and Research Libraries.

Curtis, Jessica A. November 7, 2017. "The Importance of Teaching Adult Services Librarians to Teach." Public Libraries Online. http://publiclibrariesonline.org/2017/11/the-importance-of-teaching-adult-services-librarians-to-teach/.

DeLancey, Laura. 2017. "Add WebAIM and Stir: Assessing Web Accessibility for Users with Disabilities. In *The Library Assessment Cookbook,* ed. Aaron W. Dobbs, 171–72. Chicago: Association of College and Research Libraries.

Demasson, Andrew, Helen Partridge, and Christine Bruce. 2017. "How Do Public Librarians Constitute Information Literacy?" *Journal of Librarianship and Information Science.* http://journals.sagepub.com/doi/abs/10.1177/0961000617726126.

Dev, Chekitan S., and Don E. Schultz. 2005a. "A Customer-Focused Approach Can Bring the Current Marketing Mix into the 21st Century." *Marketing Management* 14, no. 1: 16–22.

———. 2005b. "Simply SIVA: Get Results with the New Marketing Mix." *Marketing Management* 14, no. 2: 36–41.

Diaz, Jose O., and Meris A. Mandernach. 2017. "Relationship Building One Step at a Time: Case Studies of Successful Faculty-Librarian Partnerships." *portal: Libraries and the Academy* 17, no. 2: 273–82.

Dobbs, Aaron W., ed. 2017. *The Library Assessment Cookbook.* Chicago: Association of College and Research Libraries.

Downey, Liana. 2016. *Mission Control: How Nonprofits and Governments Can Focus, Achieve More, and Change the World.* London: Routledge.

Doyle, Charles, ed. 2016. *A Dictionary of Marketing.* 4th ed. Oxford: Oxford University Press.

Duarte, Nancy. 2009. "Glance Test." blog.duarte.com/files/Session1%20-%20Glance%20Test.pdf.

Educators of America. 2018. "What Is Project Based Learning?" https://www.educatorsusa.org/project-based-learning.

EDUCAUSE. 2018. "Mentoring." https://www.educause.edu/careers/special-topic-programs/mentoring/.

Eisenberg, Mike, and Bob Berkowitz. 2017. "Big6 Skills Overview." http://big6.com/pages/about/big6-skills-overview.php.

Elmborg, James K. 2002. "Teaching at the Desk: Toward a Reference Pedagogy." *portal: Libraries and the Academy* 2, no. 3: 455–64.

Emerald Publishing. 2018. "How to Write . . . a Book Review." www.emeraldgrouppublishing.com/authors/guides/write/book_review.htm?part=1.

Engeszer, Robert J., William Olmstadt, Jan Daley, Monique Norfolk, Kara Krekeler, Monica Rogers, Graham Colditz, . . . Lee Williams. 2016. "Evolution of an Academic-Public Library Partnership." *Journal of the American Medical Library Association* 104, no. 1: 62–66.

Erlinger, Allison. 2018. "Outcomes Assessment in Undergraduate Information Literacy Instruction: A Systematic Review." *College and Research Libraries* 79, no. 4: 442–79.

Eury, A. Douglas, Jane King, and John D. Balls. n.d. "5 'Q.U.I.C.K.' Steps of Reflective Practice." www.teachhub.com/5-quick-steps-reflective-practice.

Everall, Kyla, and Judith Logan. 2016. "A Mixed Methods Approach to Iterative Service Design of an In-Person Reference Service Point. *Evidence Based Library and Information Practice* 12, no. 4: 178–85.

Farmer, Lesley. 2015. "Using Online Databases." https://www.merlot.org/.

———. 2016. "Searching the Invisible Web: A Learning Exercise for 99 Resources to Research & Mine the Invisible Web." https://www.merlot.org/.

Farrell, Susan. 2016. "Field Studies." https://www.nngroup.com/articles/field-studies/.

Fichter, Darlene, and Jeff Wisniewski. 2016. "Beyond Responsive Design." *Online Searcher* 40, no. 6: 65–68.

Fink, L. Dee. 2005. "What Is 'Significant Learning'?" https://www.wcu.edu/WebFiles/PDFs/facultycenter_SignificantLearning.pdf.

Finkelstein, Sydney. October 30, 2017. "Companies Should Hire Teams, Not Individuals." *Wall Street Journal,* pp. R1, R2.

Fisher, Roger, William L. Ury, and Bruce Patton. 2012. *Getting to Yes: Negotiating Agreement without Giving In.* 3rd ed. London: Random House Business.

Flom, Jason. 2014. "Peer-to-Peer Observation: Five Questions for Making It Work." http://inservice.ascd.org/peer-to-peer-observation-five-questions-for-making-it-work/.

Foster, Jack. 2007. *How to Get Ideas.* 2nd ed. San Francisco: Barrett-Koehler.

Galston, Colbe, Elizabeth Kelsen Huber, Katherine Johnson, and Amy Long. 2012. "Community Reference: Making Libraries Indispensable in a New Way." *American Libraries* 43, no. 5/6: 46–50.

Gariepy, Laura, Megan Hodge, M. Teresa Doherty, and Dennis Clark. 2015. "A Close Look in the Mirror: Evaluating the Implementation Fidelity of a Consolidated Service Point at a Research Library." In *ACRL Conference Proceedings,* 116–24. Portland, Oregon. www.ala.org/acrl/acrl/conferences/acrl2015/papers.

Garton, Janetta. 2011. "Presenting Information vs. Guiding Cognitive Processing." fusionfinds.wordpress.com/2011/10/24/presenting-information-vs-guiding-cognitive.

Gers, R., and N. Bolin. 2000. "More Than Meets the Eye: Management Support for Reference Service and Training." *Journal of Library Administration* 29, no. 1: 1–15.

Gillmor, Dan. 2010. "Mediactive." http://mediactive.com/2-0-chapter-2-becoming-an-active-user-principles/.

Godbey, Samantha. 2013. "Collaboration as an Essential Tool in Information Literacy Education 9–16: Context, Qualities and Implications." *Student Research Journal* 2, no. 2. http://scholarworks.sjsu.edu/slissrj/vol2/iss2/3.

Gottfried, John, Laura DeLancey, and Amanda Hardin. 2015. "Talking to Ourselves." *Reference & User Services Quarterly* 54, no. 3: 37–43.

Grassian, Esther. 2009. "Teach Information Literacy & Critical Thinking!" https://sites.google.com/site/teachinfolit/home.

Gustafson, Julia Chance, Zachary Sharrow, and Gwen Short. 2017. "Library Marketing on a Small Liberal Arts Campus: Assessing Communication Preferences." *Journal of Library Administration* 57, no. 4: 420–35.

Gutsche, Betha, and Brenda Hough, eds. 2014. "Competency Index for the Library Field." webjunction.org/explore-topics/competencies.html.

Hackman, J. Richard. 2012. "From Causes to Conditions in Group Research." *Journal of Organizational Behavior* 33: 428–44.

Hakala-Ausperk, Catherine. 2010. "Invest in Yourself!" *American Libraries*. http://americanlibrariesmagazine.org/features/03222010/invest-yourself.

Harding, Jane. 2008. "Information Literacy and the Public Library: We've Talked the Talk, but Are We Walking the Walk?" *Australian Library Journal* 57, no. 3: 274–94.

Heery, E., and M. Noon, eds. 2017. *A Dictionary of Human Resource Management,* s.v. "leader." Oxford University Press. www.oxfordreference.com.

Heineke, Amy J., and Jay McTighe. 2018. *Using Understanding by Design in the Culturally and Linguistically Diverse Classroom.* Alexandria, VA: ASCD.

Heinze, Jill Stover. 2017. *Library Marketing: From Passion to Practice.* Ann Arbor: Michigan Publishing, University of Michigan Library.

Hessing, Ted. 2014. "Pilot & Implementation Planning." Six Sigma Study Guide. http://sixsigmastudyguide.com/pilot-implementation-planning/.

Hicks, Deborah, and Lisa M. Given. 2013. "Principled, Transformational Leadership: Analyzing the Discourse of Leadership in the Development of Librarianship's Core Competencies." *Library Quarterly* 83, no. 1: 7–25.

Hinchliffe, Lisa Janicke. 2015. "Professional Development for Assessment: Lessons from Reflective Practice." *Journal of Academic Librarianship* 41: 850–52.

Houghton, Brigeen. 2016. "Content Marketing Your Library." *CSLA Journal* 40, no. 1: 22–24.

Hoyle, Robin. 2015. *Information Learning in Organizations: How to Create a Continuous Learning Culture.* London: Kogan Page.

IDEO. n.d. "Creative Difference." https://creativedifference.ideo.com/.

———. 2015. "The Field Guide to Human-Centered Design: Design Kit." www.designkit.org/resources/1.

Illinois Online Network. 2018. "Self-Evaluation for Potential Online Students." www.ion.uillinois.edu/resources/tutorials/pedagogy/selfEval.asp.

Inayatullah, Sohail. 2014. "Library Futures: From Knowledge Keepers to Creators." *The Futurist* 48, no. 6: 24–28.

Infopeople. 2017. "Best Search Tools Chart." https://infopeople.org/content/best-search-tools-chart.

Institute of Museum and Library Services. n.d. "Museums, Libraries and 21st-Century Skills: Definitions." https://www.imls.gov/issues/national-initiatives/museums-libraries-and-21st-century-skills/definitions.

———. 2017. "Outcome-Based Evaluations: Basics; Purposes, Webography, Presentations." https://www.imls.gov/grants/outcome-based-evaluations; https://www.imls.gov/grants/outcome-based-evaluation/basics; https://www.imls.gov/grants/outcome-based-evaluation/purposes; https://www.imls.gov/grants/outcome-based-evaluation/webography; https://www.imls.gov/grants/outcome-based-evaluation/presentations.

Institute of Museum and Library Services and Chief Officers of State Library Agencies. 2018. "Measures That Matter." http://measuresthatmatter.net/.

International City/County Management Association. 2017. "Local Libraries Advancing Community Goals, 2016." https://icma.org/documents/local-libraries-advancing-community-goals-2016.

International Federation of Library Associations and Institutions. 2018a. "Libraries and the Sustainable Development Goals: A Storytelling Manual." https://www.ifla.org/libraries-development.

———. 2018b. "Library Map of the World." http://librarymap.ifla.org/stories.

International Social Marketing Association. 2017. "Social Marketing Definition." www.i-socialmarketing.org/social-marketing-definition.

Jaeger, Paul T., Erin Zerhusen, Ursula Gorham, Renee F. Hill, and Natalie Greene Taylor. 2017. "Waking Up to Advocacy in a New Political Reality for Libraries." *Library Quarterly* 87, no. 4: 350–68.

Johnson, D. W., and F. P. Johnson. 2016. *Joining Together: Group Theory and Group Skills.* 12th ed. Boston: Pearson.

Johnston, Marcia Riefer. 2016. "Why—and How—to Map Out Your Customers' Journeys" [template]. Retrieved from http://contentmarketinginstitute.com/2016/11/map-customer-journey-template/.

Jones, Rebecca J., Stephen A. Woods, and Yves R. F. Guillaume. 2016. "The Effectiveness of Workplace Coaching: A Meta-Analysis of Learning and Performance Outcomes from Coaching." *Journal of Occupational and Organizational Psychology* 89: 249–77.

Jones, Sheri Chaney. 2014. *Impact & Excellence: Data-Driven Strategies for Aligning, Mission, Culture, and Performance in Nonprofit and Government Organizations.* San Francisco: Jossey-Bass.

Katopol, Patricia. 2014. "Managing Change with Environmental Scanning." *Library Leadership & Management* 29, no. 1: 1–7.

Kearsley, Greg, and Richard Culatta. 2018a. "ADDIE Model." www.instructionaldesign.org/models/addie/.

———. 2018b. "Andragogy (Malcolm Knowles)." www.instructionaldesign.org/theories/andragogy/.

Kenedy, Robert, and Vivienne Monty. 2011. "Faculty-Librarian Collaboration and Development of Critical Skills through Dynamic Purposeful Learning." *Libri* 61: 116–24.

Kern, M. Kathleen, and Beth Woodard. 2016. "The Reference Interview." In *Reference and Information Services: An Introduction*, ed. Linda C. Smith and Melissa A. Wong, 63–97. Santa Barbara, CA: Libraries Unlimited.

Keyes, Kelsey, and Ellie Dworak. 2017. "Staffing Chat Reference with Undergraduate Student Assistants at an Academic Library: A Standards-Based Assessment." *Journal of Academic Librarianship* 43: 469–78.

King, Nathaniel, and Kelly Lutz. 2017. "An Assessment Rubric Inspired by the Four Seasons." In *The Library Assessment Cookbook,* ed. Aaron W. Dobbs, 137–38. Chicago: Association of College and Research Libraries.

Kirkpatrick, Jim, and Wendy Kirkpatrick. 2015. "The Four Levels of Evaluation—An Update." *TD at Work* 32, no. 1502: 1–19.

Kirkpatrick Partners. 2018. "The Kirkpatrick Model." https://www.kirkpatrickpartners.com/Our-Philosophy/The-Kirkpatrick-Model.

Kissel, Francia, Melvin R. Wininger, Scott R. Weeden, Patricia A. Wittberg, Randall S. Halverson, Meagan Lacy, and Rhonda K. Huisman. 2016. "Bridging the Gaps: Collaboration in a Faculty and Librarian Community of Practice on Information Literacy." In *Information Literacy: Research and Collaboration across Disciplines,* ed. Barbara J. D'Angelo, Sandra Jamieson, Barry Maid, and Janice R. Walker. Fort Collins, CO: WAC Clearinghouse and University Press of Colorado. https://wac.colostate.edu/books/infolit/.

Kniberg, Hendrik. 2013. "How to Run an Internal Unconference." https://leanpub.com/unconference.

———. 2016. "What Is an Unconference?" *Crisp's Blog.* https://blog.crisp.se/2016/08/30/henrikkniberg/what-is-an-unconference.

Koerber, Jennifer. 2017a. "From Pilot to Permanent." *Library Journal* 142, no. 2: 18–21.

———. June 15, 2017b. "Meaningful Measures: National Initiatives Step into the Gap on the Urgent Need to Capture Outcomes." *Library Journal* 142, no. 11: 36–38.

Koontz, Christie, and Lorri Mon. 2014. *Marketing and Social Media: A Guide for Library Archives and Museums.* Lanham, MD: Rowman & Littlefield.

Koppel, Ted, Jack Smith, and ABC News. 1999. "The Deep Dive: One Company's Secret Weapon for Innovation." www.youtube.com/watch?v=JkHOxyafGpE.

Kotler, Philip. 2005. "The Role Played by the Broadening of the Marketing Movement in the History of Marketing Thought." *Journal of Public Policy & Marketing* 24, no. 1: 114–16.

Kotler, Philip, and Nancy Lee. 2007a. *Marketing in the Public Sector: A Roadmap for Improved Performance.* Upper Saddle River, NJ: Prentice Hall.

———. 2007b. "Marketing in the Public Sector: The Final Frontier." *The Public Manager* 36: 12–17.

Kram, Kathy E., and Monica Higgins. September 22, 2008. "Leadership: A New Approach to Mentoring." *Wall Street Journal.* https://www.wsj.com/articles/SB122160063875344843.

Krueger, R. A., and M. A. Casey. 2014. *Focus Groups: A Practical Guide for Applied Research.* 5th ed. Thousand Oaks, CA: Sage.

Kuhlthau, Carol C. 2004. *Seeking Meaning: A Process Approach to Library and Information Services.* Westport, CT: Greenwood.

Kuhlthau, Carol C., Leslie K. Maniotes, and Ann K. Caspari. 2007. *Guided Inquiry: Learning in the 21st Century.* Westport, CT: Libraries Unlimited.

Labin, Jenn. 2017. *Mentoring Programs That Work.* Alexandria, VA: ATD.

Ladyshewsky, Richard K. 2017. "Peer Coaching as a Strategy to Increase Learning and Development in Organizational Life—A Perspective." *International Journal of Evidence Based Coaching and Mentoring* 15, no. 1: 4–10.

Lane Community College Faculty Professional Development. n.d. "Faculty Inquiry Groups." https://www.lanecc.edu/fpd/faculty-inquiry-groups.

Law, J., ed. 2016. *A Dictionary of Business and Management*, s.v. "360° feedback." Oxford University Press. www.oxfordreference.com.

Law, Margaret, and Maria Kovacs. 2016. "Library Marketing and Advocacy Toolkit." www.inasp.info/en/training-resources/courses/173/.

Lawrence, Craig. August 1, 2003. "Right—Rapid—Rough." *Ask Magazine*. https://appel.nasa.gov/2003/08/01/right-rapid-rough/.

LearnMarketing.net. 2018. "Service Marketing Mix: Extended Marketing Mix." www.learnmarketing.net/servicemarketingmix.htm.

Lee, Nancy, and Philip Kotler. 2016. *Social Marketing: Changing Behaviors for Good.* 5th ed. Thousand Oaks, CA: Sage.

Lenkart, Joe, and Jen-chien Yu. 2017. "Specialized Reference Services at Illinois: Reference Transactional Analysis and Its Implications for Service Providers and Administrators." *Reference & User Services Quarterly* 56, no. 4: 268–76.

Library Leadership and Management Association. 2018. "Assessment Community of Practice." www.ala.org/llama/communities/assessment.

Lierman, Ashley R. 2015. "DIY Skills: Upgrading for the Teacher Librarian." *Texas Library Journal* 91, no. 3: 88–90.

LISWiki. 2017. "Weblogs." https://liswiki.org/wiki/weblogs.

Luo, Lili. 2009. "Effective Training for Chat Reference Personnel: An Exploratory Study." *Library & Information Science Research* 31: 210–24.

Lurleen B. Wallace Community College. 2018. "Information Literacy." https://www.lbwcc.edu/library/research-help/information-literacy.

Malenfant, Kara J., and Karen Brown. 2017. "Creating Sustainable Assessment through Collaboration: A National Program Reveals Effective Practices." Occasional Paper No. 31. http://learningoutcomesassessment.org/documents/Occasional_Paper31.pdf.

Mann, Karen V. 2010. "Self-Assessment: The Complex Process of Determining 'How We Are Doing'—A Perspective from Medical Education." *Academy of Management Learning & Education* 9, no. 2: 305–13.

Mansfield, Clarissa. 2015. "The Role of Stories in Library Marketing and Communications." *OLA Quarterly* 21, no. 4: 39–45.

Marquez, Joe, and Anne Downey. 2015. "Service Design: Toward a Holistic Assessment of the Library." *PNLA Quarterly* 80, no. 1: 37–47.

———. 2016. *Library Service Design: A LITA Guide to Holistic Assessment, Insight, and Improvement.* Lanham, MD: Rowman & Littlefield.

———. 2017. *Getting Started in Service Design: A How-to-Do-It Manual for Librarians.* Chicago: American Library Association.

Mattessich, P., M. Murray-Close, and B. Monsey. 2001. *Wilder Collaboration Factors Inventory.* St. Paul, MN: Wilder Research. www.wilder.org/Wilder-Research/Publications/Studies/Collaboration Factors Inventory/Collaboration Factors Inventory.pdf.

McCallum, Deborah. 2014. "6 Important Components of a Successful Online Learning Environment." https://elearningindustry.com/6-important-components-successful-online-learning-environment.

McCauley, Cynthia D. 2006. *Developmental Assignments: Creating Learning Experiences without Changing Jobs.* Greensboro, NC: Center for Creative Leadership.

McCauley, Cynthia D., D. Scott DeRue, Paul Yost, and Sylvester Taylor. 2014. *Experience-Driven Leader Development: Models, Tools, Best Practices, and Advice for On-the-Job Development.* San Francisco: Wiley.

McChesney, Elizabeth M., and Bryan W. Wunar. 2017. *Summer Matters: Making All Learning Count.* Chicago: American Library Association.

McNiff, Jean. 2017. *Action Research: All You Need to Know.* Los Angeles: Sage.

McTighe, Jay, and Grant Wiggins. 2012. "Understanding by Design Framework." https://www.ascd.org/ASCD/pdf/siteASCD/publications/UbD_WhitePaper0312.pdf.

———. 2013. *Essential Questions: Opening the Doors to Student Understanding.* Alexandria, VA: ASCD.

MERLOT II. 2018. "Learning Exercises Advanced Search." https://www.merlot.org/merlot/advSearchAssignments.htm.

Merriam-Webster Online Dictionary, s.v. "collaborate." 2008. www.merriam-webster.com/dictionary/collaborate.

Meyrink, Carla. 2015. "Sharing Our Failures in the Classroom." http://teachingexperiment.com/2015/11/sharing-our-failures-in-the-classroom/.

Mies, Ginny. 2015. "How to Create a Community Resource Guide." http://techsoupforlibraries.org/blog/how-to-create-a-community-resource-guide.

Miesing, Paul. n.d. "Why Has IDEO Been So Innovative over the Years?" https://www.albany.edu/faculty/miesing/teaching/materials/IDEO.pdf.

Miller, Ben. 2010. "Planning a Micro-Teaching Activity." http://sydney.edu.au/arts/teaching_learning/

academic_support/Planning_a_Microteaching_Activity.pdf.

Miller, Robin E. 2011. "Reference Communities: Applying the Community of Practice Concept to Development of Reference Knowledge." *Public Services Quarterly* 7: 18–26.

Mindtools. n.d. "Communication Skills." https://www.mindtools.com/pages/main/communication_skills.htm.

———. n.d. "SMART Goals: How to Make Your Goals Achievable." https://www.mindtools.com/pages/article/smart-goals.htm.

Minitex. 2015. "Minnesota Opportunities for Reference Excellence (MORE)." https://sites.google.com/a/umn.edu/more/.

Montiel-Overall, Patricia. 2009. "Cultural Competence: A Conceptual Framework for Library and Information Science Professionals." *Library Quarterly* 79, no. 2: 175–204.

———. 2010. "Cultural Competence in Web-Based Instruction: A Conceptual Framework." *International Journal of Web Based Communities* 6, no. 3: 254–68.

Morgan, Angie, Courtney Lynch, and Sean Lynch. 2017. *Spark: How to Lead Yourself and Others to Greater Success.* Boston: Houghton Mifflin Harcourt.

Nash, Mark A., and Sheila R. Poling. 2009. "Process Mapping for the 21st Century." *Quality* 48, no. 8: 24–25.

National Association of Social Workers. 2017. "Code of Ethics." https://www.socialworkers.org/About/Ethics/Code-of-Ethics/Code-of-Ethics-English.

National Council of Nonprofits. 2018. "Community of Practice." https://www.councilofnonprofits.org/tools-resources/community-of-practice.

National Research Council. 2000. *How People Learn: Brain, Mind, Experience, and School: Expanded Edition.* Washington, DC: National Academies Press. https://www.nap.edu/catalog/9853/how-people-learn-brain-mind-experience-and-school-expanded-edition.

New England Archivists. 2018. "NEA Mentoring Program." https://newenglandarchivists.org/mentoring/.

New Oxford American Dictionary, s.v. "collaborate." 2015. www.oxfordreference.com.

New York City School Library System. 2018. "Information Literacy Online Tests and Tutorials." http://nycdoe.libguides.com/InformationLiteracy/testsandtutorials.

Nielsen, Jakob. 2012. "Usability 101: Introduction to Usability." https://www.nngroup.com/articles/usability-101-introduction-to-usability/.

Nielsen Norman Group. 2018. "Topic: Prototyping." https://www.nngroup.com/topic/prototyping/.

Noonan, P., A. S. Gaumer Erickson, J. A. Brussow, and A. Langham. 2015. "Observation Checklist for High-Quality Professional Development in Education" [updated version]. Lawrence: University of Kansas, Center for Research on Learning. www.researchcollaboration.org/page/high-quality-professional-development-checklist.

North Carolina Library Association. 2018. "Help! I'm an Accidental Government Information Librarian Webinars." www.nclaonline.org/government-resources/help-im-accidental-government-information-librarian-webinars.

Oakleaf, Megan. 2009. "The Information Literacy Instruction Assessment Cycle: A Guide for Increasing Student Learning and Improving Librarian Instructional Skills." *Journal of Documentation* 65, no. 4: 539–60.

Ohio Library Council. 2017. "ORE Online: Ohio Reference Excellence (ORE) Professional Development Training." http://oreonline.olc.org/.

Online Learning Consortium. 2018. "Quality Framework." https://onlinelearningconsortium.org/about/quality-framework-five-pillars.

Owen, Tim Buckley. 2017. *Successful Enquiry Answering Every Time: Thinking Your Way from Problem to Solution.* 7th ed. London: Facet.

Oxford Dictionary of English, s.v. "manager." 2010. Oxford University Press. www.oxfordreference.com.

Pacific Library Partnership. 2018. "Examples of Successful School/Library Partnerships." www.plpinfo.org/student-success/successful-schoollibrary-partnerships/.

Palmer, Parker J. 2017. *The Courage to Teach: Exploring the Inner Landscape of a Teacher's Life.* Twentieth Anniversary Edition. San Francisco: Jossey-Bass.

Palmer, Parker J., and Megan Scribner. 2017. *The Courage to Teach Guide for Reflection and Renewal.* Twentieth Anniversary Edition. San Francisco: Jossey-Bass.

Parker, Polly, Kathy E. Kram, and Douglas T. (Tim) Hall. 2014. "Peer Coaching: An Untapped Resource for Development." *Organizational Dynamics* 43: 122–29.

Patton, M. Q. 2014. *Qualitative Research and Evaluation Methods: Integrating Theory and Practice.* 4th ed. Thousand Oaks, CA: Sage.

Pearce, C. L., C. C. Manz, and H. P. Sims. 2009. "Where Do We Go from Here? Is Shared Leadership the Key to Team Success?" *Organizational Dynamics* 38, no. 3: 234–38.

Peters, Anne, and Jan Kemp. 2014. "Ask Us Anything: Communicating the Value of Reference Services through Branding." *Public Services Quarterly* 10, no. 1: 48–53.

Pew Research Center. 2015. "Libraries at the Crossroads." www.pewinternet.org/2015/09/15/libraries-at-the-crossroads/.

Phillips, Abigail L. 2014. "What Do We Mean by Library Leadership? Leadership in LIS Education." *Journal of Education for Library and Information Science* 55, no. 4: 336–44.

Phillips, Levi. 2016. "What Can Millennials Teach Us about Supporting Learning in the Workplace?" In "The Learner Voice: Part 3." Towards Maturity. https://towardsmaturity.org/2016/11/03/learner-voice-part-3/.

Pietikainen, Virpi, Terttu Kortelainen, and Pirkko Siklander. 2017. "Public Librarians as Partners in Problem-Based Learning in Secondary Schools: A Case Study in Finland." *Information Research* 22, no. 2: 1–19.

Pinola, Melanie. 2011. "How to Create Presentations That Don't Suck." Lifehacker. https://lifehacker.com/5810271/how-to-create-presentations-that-dont-suck.

Pionke, J. J. 2017. Table of contents of "ALA Carnegie-Whitney Grant Project: Disability Resource Guide." http://guides.library.illinois.edu/alacwgdisabilitytoc.

Pionke, J. J., and Jeana Manson. 2018. "Creating Disability LibGuides with Accessibility in Mind." *Journal of Web Librarianship* 12, no. 1: 63–79.

Poll, Roswitha. 2016. Bibliography of "Impact and Outcome of Libraries." International Federation of Library Associations and Institutions. https://www.ifla.org/publications/publications-associated-with-the-s-e-section.

Potter, Ned. 2012. *The Library Marketing Toolkit.* London: Facet.

Press, Nancy Ottman, and Mary Diggs-Hobson. 2005. "Providing Health Information to Community Members Where They Are: Characteristics of the Culturally Competent Librarian." *Library Trends* 53, no. 3: 397–410.

Pretlow, Cassi, and Karen Sobel. 2015. "Rethinking Library Service: Improving the User Experience with Service Blueprinting." *Public Services Quarterly* 11, no. 1: 1–12.

Prince, Michael. 2004. "Does Active Learning Work? A Review of the Research." *Journal of Engineering Education* 93, no. 3: 223–31.

Public Library Association. 2018. "DigitalLearn.org: Available Instructional Design Training." https://training.digitallearn.org/trainings.

Puentedura, Ruben. 2015. "SAMR: A Brief Introduction." http://hippasus.com/rrpweblog/archives/2015/10/SAMR_ABriefIntro.pdf.

Purdue Online Writing Lab. 2017. "Writing a Book Review." https://owl.english.purdue.edu/owl/resource/704/01/.

———. 2018a. "Annotated Bibliographies." https://owl.english.purdue.edu/owl/resource/614/01/.

———. 2018b. "Searching Online: An Overview." https://owl.english.purdue.edu/owl/resource/558/1/.

Radnor, Zoe, Stephen P. Osborne, Tony Kinder, and Jean Mutton. 2014. "Operationalizing Co-Production in Public Services Delivery." *Public Management Review* 16, no. 3: 402–23.

Rathi, Dinesh, Ali Shiri, and Catherine Cockney. 2017. "Environmental Scan: A Methodological Framework to Initiate Digital Library Development for Communities in Canada's North." *Aslib Journal of Information Management* 69, no. 1: 76–94.

Reed, Sally Gardner, Beth Nawalinski, and Jillian Kalonick. 2013. *A Power Guide for Successful Advocacy.* Philadelphia, PA: United for Libraries (available as a free download at www.ala.org/united/powerguide).

Reference and User Services Association. 2005. Collection Development and Evaluation Section, Readers' Advisory Committee. "Taking the Guesswork Out of Non-Fiction Readers Advisory: Program Handouts." www.ala.org/rusa/sections/codes/section/codescomm/codesreadadv/codesreadadv.

———. 2007a. "Measuring and Assessing Reference Services and Resources: A Guide." www.ala.org/rusa/sections/rss/rsssection/rsscomm/evaluationofref/measrefguide.

———. 2007b. "Use, Usability, and Collection Assessment: Selected Measurement Tools and Bibliographic References." www.ala.org/rusa/sections/rss/rsssection/rsscomm/evaluationofref/measref40tools.

———. 2012. "Virtual Reference Companion." www.ala.org/rusa/vrc/.

———. 2013. "Guidelines for Behavioral Performance of Reference and Information Service Providers." www.ala.org/rusa/resources/guidelines/guidelinesbehavioral.

———. 2017. "Guidelines for Implementing and Maintaining Virtual Reference Services." www.ala.org/rusa/sites/ala.org.rusa/files/content/resources/guidelines/GuidelinesVirtualReference_2017.pdf.

Reiss, Tony. October 24, 2013. "Role of the Chair of the Meeting." http://tonyreiss.com/2013/10/24/the-role-of-the-chair-of-the-meeting/.

Relevance. 2015. "Quick Guide for Content Marketing Research." http://digital.relevance.com/hubfs/Quick_Guide_for_Content_Marketing_Research.pdf.

Reynolds, Garr. 2016. "Top Ten Slide Tips: Design." www.garrreynolds.com/preso-tips/design/.

Rockquemore, Kerry Ann. 2013. "Essay Calling for Senior Faculty to Embrace New Style of Mentoring." Inside Higher Ed. https://www.insidehighered.com/advice/2013/07/22/essay-calling-senior-faculty-embrace-new-style-mentoring.

Rogers, Emily, and Howard S. Carrier. 2017. "A Qualitative Investigation of Patrons' Experience with Academic Library Research Consultations." *Reference Services Review* 45, no. 1: 18–37.

Ross, Catherine Sheldrick, and Kirsti Nilsen. 2013. *Communicating Professionally.* 3rd ed. A How-to-Do-It Manual for Librarians. Chicago: ALA Neal-Schuman.

Ross, Catherine Sheldrick, Kirsti Nilsen, and Marie Radford. 2009. *Conducting the Reference Interview.* 2nd ed. New York: Neal-Schuman.

Ruiz, Faithe. 2017. "Recipe for Success: Add a Personal SWOT Analysis to Any Assessment Project." In *The Library Assessment Cookbook,* ed. Aaron W. Dobbs, 99–100. Chicago: Association of College and Research Libraries. (See also Ruiz's 2016 companion page: https://faitheruiz.wordpress.com.)

Saricks, Joyce G. 2005. *Readers' Advisory Service in the Public Library.* 3rd ed. Chicago: American Library Association.

Saunders, Laura. 2016. "Evaluation and Assessment of Reference Services." In *Reference and Information Services: An Introduction,* ed. Linda C. Smith and Melissa A. Wong, 212–43. 5th ed. Santa Barbara, CA: Libraries Unlimited.

Schmidt, Aaron. 2012. "Looking at Logos." *Library Journal* 137, no. 20: 20.

———. 2013. "Is Your Library a Sundial? The User Experience." *Library Journal* 138, no. 4: 21.

Scott, J., ed. 2014. *A Dictionary of Sociology,* s.v. "professions." Oxford University Press. www.oxfordreference.com.

Shank, Patti. n.d. "Learning Objectives: Why, How, and Wow!" (ATD Job Aid). https://www.td.org/job-aid-tools/writing-better-learning-objectives-job-aid.

Shapiro, Janet. n.d. "Action Planning Toolkit." www.civicus.org/view/media/Action%20Planning.pdf.

Shen, Yan, Richard D. Cotton, and Kathy E. Kram. 2015. "Assembling Your Personal Board of Advisors." *MIT Sloan Management Review* 56, no. 3: 81–90.

Silberman, Melvin, and Elaine Biech. 2015. *Active Training: A Handbook of Techniques, Designs, Case Examples, and Tips.* 4th ed. Hoboken, NJ: Wiley.

Singh, Rajesh. 2015. "Creating Engaging Library Experiences through Effective Content Marketing." *Oregon Library Association Quarterly* 21, no. 4: 49–54.

———. 2017. "Marketing Competency for Information Professionals: The Role of Marketing Education in Library and Information Science Education Programs." *Marketing Libraries Journal* 1, no. 1: 60–83.

Smith, Brenda, and Leva Lee. April 2016. "Librarians and OER: Cultivating a Community of Practice to Be More Effective Advocates." Paper presented at the 17th Distance Library Services Conference, Pittsburgh, PA. https://bccampus.ca/files/2016/04/DLS-Conference.pdf.

Smith, Risë L. 2006. "Philosophical Shift: Teach the Faculty to Teach Information Literacy." www.ala.org/acrl/publications/whitepapers/nashville/smith.

Society of Georgia Archivists. 2014. "Mentoring Program." https://soga.wildapricot.org/involvement/mentoring.

Solomon, Laura. 2016. *The Librarian's Nitty-Gritty Guide to Content Marketing.* Chicago: American Library Association.

Soules, A. 2001. "The Principles of Marketing and Relationship Management." *portal: Libraries and the Academy* 1, no. 3: 339–50.

Stock, Matt. 2009. "The Three R's: Rapport, Relationship, and Reference. *The Reference Librarian* 51, no. 1: 45–52.

Stoudt, Lynette, Caitlin Birch, Michelle Chiles, Luciana Spracher, and Darla White. 2016. "A Push in the Right Direction: Expanding Models of Mentorship." *Provenance, Journal of the Society of Georgia Archivists* 33, no. 2: 16–37.

Stroud, J. DeLayne. n.d. "More Value: Value Stream or Detailed Process Mapping?" https://www.isixsigma.com/tools-templates/process-mapping/more-value-value-stream-or-detailed-process-mapping/.

Sweetman, Kimberly. 2016. "Workplace Expectations for Today's Library." *Young Adult Library Services* 14, no. 4: 40–43.

Sze, Lian. n.d. "Basic Search." https://www.digitallearn.org/courses/basic-search.

TechSoup for Libraries. 2012. "Communication and Partnerships—Tools." www.webjunction.org/explore-topics/partnerships.html.

Texas Wesleyan Center for Excellence in Teaching & Learning. 2018. "For Students: Test of Online Learning

Success (TOOLS)." http://txwescetl.com/about-distance-ed/for-students/.

Thorpe, Angie, and Heather Bowman. 2013. "Promoting Discovery: Creating an In-Depth Library Marketing Campaign." *Journal of Library Administration* 53, no. 2–3: 100–121.

Thorpe, Clare. 2017. "Engaging Our Communities: Future Trends and Opportunities for Reference Services." *Journal of the Australian Library and Information Association.* https://doi.org/10.1080/24750158.2017.1359993.

Tofade, Toyin, Jamie Elsner, and Stuart T. Haines. 2013. "Best Practice Strategies for Effective Use of Questions as a Teaching Tool." *American Journal of Pharmaceutical Education* 77, no. 7. https://www.ncbi.nlm.nih.gov/pmc/articles/PMC3776909/.

UNESCO. 2017. "Media and Information Literacy." www.unesco.org/new/en/communication-and-information/media-development/media-literacy/mil-as-composite-concept/.

University of Illinois at Urbana-Champaign, College of Agricultural, Consumer and Environmental Sciences. n.d. "Peer Observation for Teaching Assessment." https://academics.aces.illinois.edu/files/documents/peer-observation.pdf.

University of Michigan, Center for Research on Teaching and Learning. 2016. "Introduction to Active Learning." www.crlt.umich.edu/active_learning_introduction.

University of North Carolina at Chapel Hill. 2010. "Online Learning Readiness Questionnaire." www.unc.edu/tlim/ser/.

University of Ottawa Human Resources. n.d. "Key Competencies Development Activities Guide." http://doc.hr.uottawa.ca/systems/process/halogen/dev_des_competences.pdf.

University of Sydney, Faculty of Arts and Social Sciences. 2017. "Four Lenses: Evaluation Resources." http://sydney.edu.au/arts/teaching_learning/academic_support/four_lenses_index.shtml.

University of Texas at Austin. 2018. "Community College Survey of Student Engagement (CCSSE)." www.ccsse.org/.

University of Wisconsin, Madison, Writing Center. 2017. "Academic Writing: Annotated Bibliography." www.wisc.edu/writing/Handbook/AnnotatedBibliography.html.

Urban Libraries Council. 2016. "Leadership Brief: Partners Achieving Community Outcomes." https://www.urbanlibraries.org/publications-pages-74.php.

Valentine, G., and B. D. Moss. March 2017. "Assessing Reference Service Quality: A Chat Transcript Analysis." Paper presented at the Association of College and Research Libraries conference, March 22–25, 2017, Baltimore, MD. In "At the Helm: Leading Transformation: The Proceedings of the ACRL 2017 Conference." www.ala.org/acrl/conferences/acrl2017/papers.

VanScoy, Amy. 2016. "Creating the Future of Reference Service." In *Reference and Information Services: An Introduction,* ed. Linda C. Smith and Melissa A. Wong, 837–51. 5th ed. Santa Barbara, CA: Libraries Unlimited.

Varlejs, Jana. 2016. *IFLA Guidelines for Continuing Professional Development: Principles and Best Practices.* 2nd ed. The Hague, Neth.: International Federation of Library Associations and Institutions. https://www.ifla.org/files/assets/cpdwl/guidelines/ifla-guidelines-for-continuing-professional-development.pdf.

Vaughan, Shauna. 2016. "Are Your Learning Objectives Effective?" ATD Links. https://www.td.org/newsletters/atd-links/are-your-learning-objectives-effective.

Vogt, Eric E., Juanita Brown, and David Isaacs. 2003. "The Art of Powerful Questions: Catalyzing Insight, Innovation, and Action." http://umanitoba.ca/admin/human_resources/change/media/the-art-of-powerful-questions.pdf.

Ward, David. 2003. "Using Virtual Reference Transcripts for Staff Training." *Reference Services Review* 31, no. 1: 45–56.

Watson-Boone, Rebecca. 2000. "Academic Librarians as Practitioner Researchers." *Journal of Academic Librarianship* 26, no. 2: 85–93.

WebJunction. 2017. "Health Happens in Libraries." www.webjunction.org/explore-topics/ehealth/more-info.html.

———. 2018. "WebJunction Course Catalog." https://learn.webjunction.org/course/index.php?categoryid=16; https://learn.webjunction.org/course/index.php?categoryid=51.

Wenger-Trayner, Etienne, and Beverly Wenger-Trayner. 2015. "Introduction to Communities of Practice: A Brief Overview of the Concept and Its Uses." http://wenger-trayner.com/introduction-to-communities-of-practice/.

White, Daniel W. 2017. "Invest in Yourself." *TD [Talent Development]* 71, no. 12: 64–65.

Wikipedia. September 12, 2017. "Donald Kirkpatrick." https://en.wikipedia.org/wiki/Donald_Kirkpatrick.

———. 2018a. "Information Literacy." https://en.wikipedia.org/wiki/Information_literacy.

———. 2018b. "Inquiry-Based Learning." https://en.wikipedia.org/wiki/Inquiry-based_learning.

———. 2018c. "Literacy." https://en.wikipedia.org/wiki/Literacy.

Wilkes, Bethany, and Jennifer Ward. 2016. "Building Community: Synergy and Empowerment through Staff Development and Marketing in a Small Rural Academic Library." *Collaborative Librarianship* 8, no. 4: 180–90.

World Economic Forum. 2016. "The Future of Jobs: Employment, Skills and Workforce Strategy for the Fourth Industrial Revolution." www3.weforum.org/docs/WEF_FOJ_Executive_Summary_Jobs.pdf.

Yon, Shukriah Binti Hj, and Geeta Albert. August 2013. "Developing Library Professionals: The Influence of Communities of Practice." Paper presented at the 79th IFLA World Library and Information Congress, Singapore. library.ifla.org/163/1/100-yon-en.pdf.

Young Adult Library Services Association. 2018. "Teen Services Competencies for Library Staff." www.ala.org/yalsa/guidelines/yacompetencies.

Young, Philip, and Luke Vilelle. 2011. "The Prevalence and Practices of Academic Library Journal Clubs." *Journal of Academic Librarianship* 37, no. 2: 130–36.

Zwaaf, Elizabeth. March 13, 2012. "Engaging in Professional Communities: Librarians Exchange Knowledge as Innovation Explorers." *Library Connect Newsletter* 10, no. 1. https://libraryconnect.elsevier.com/newsletters/advancing-mission-march-2012.

about the authors

JO BELL WHITLATCH has worked in three academic libraries in many areas, including collection management, acquisitions, cataloging, circulation, reference, interlibrary loan, and library management. She has also taught at San Jose State University's Graduate School of Library and Information Science, and she is a past president of the Reference and User Services Association. Her research interests and areas of special competence are information-seeking needs and behavior, user studies in libraries, the evaluation of service organizations, and the management of academic libraries. Her publications include two books, *The Role of the Academic Reference Librarian* (1990) and *Evaluating Reference Services* (2000), and articles in the *Reference & User Services Quarterly, College & Research Libraries,* the *Journal of Academic Librarianship,* and *The Reference Librarian.* She has a Ph.D. in library and information studies and an M.A. in Asian studies from the University of California at Berkeley.

BETH S. WOODARD has been an academic reference librarian for her entire career, but she developed deep interests in staff development and training and teaching when she coordinated a separate information desk staffed by graduate assistants. After training a dozen graduate assistants and then coordinating an orientation program for seventy-five graduate assistants at the University of Illinois Library at Urbana-Champaign (UIUC), she developed staff training programs, retreats, and wellness activities for the entire library—for librarians, academic professionals, and support staff, in addition to graduate and undergraduate students. She is currently teaching reference and library management at the School of Information Sciences at UIUC.

index

A

"AASL Advocacy Toolkit" (American Association of School Librarians), 98–99
Abram, Stephen, 99
access
    overview, xiv
    primary community, organizing and designing services to meet the needs of the
        competencies for, 11
        development methods for, 11–17
        development methods for, assessing, 17–22
    user needs, offering services responsive to individual expressed
        competencies for, 1–2
        development methods for, 2–7
        development methods for, assessing, 7–11
ACRL Information Literacy Immersion Program (Association of College and Research Libraries), 52
"Action Planning Toolkit" (Shapiro), xx
action plans for professional development
    Competency to Be Addressed form, xxi
    goals for, xx, xxiii–xxiv
    Library of Congress Individual Development Plan, xxii–xxiii
    overview, xx
    time frame for, xxiv
active learning, 77, 78–79, 133–137
Active Learning Techniques for Librarians: Practical Examples (Walsh and Inala), 77
Active Training (Silberman and Biech), 67, 68, 134, 141
Adamova, Elaina, 127
ADDIE (analyze, design, develop, implement, and evaluate) instructional design model, 72–73
adults, strategies for instruction to, 68
"Advocacy, Legislation & Issues" (American Library Association), 99
"Advocacy" (American Association of School Librarians), 99
"Advocacy & Issues" (Association of College and Research Libraries), 99
"Advocacy & Issues" (Library and Information Technology Association), 99
"Advocacy" (Public Library Association), 99
"Advocacy University" (American Library Association), 99
"Advocacy" (WebJunction), 98, 99
"Advocacy" (Young Adult Library Services Association), 99
advocating value of library services to primary community
    competencies for, 96, 98
    development methods for, 98–100
    development methods for, assessment of, 100
    role of instruction librarians, advocate as, 59
ALA Connect, 84
Albert, Geeta, 124
Alman, Susan W., 93
Almquist, Arne J., 88, 92
"ALSC Environmental Scan: The Current and Future State of Youth Librarianship" (Association for Library Service to Children), 131
American Association of School Librarians (AASL), 50, 96, 98, 99
American Council of Learned Societies (ACLS), 41
American Libraries Direct (AL Direct), 131
American Library Association (ALA), xiii, xvi, 40, 50, 51, 52, 64, 99, 132
    Office for Library Advocacy, 98
    Office of Government Relations, 131
American Life Project, 13
"Analyzing Your Instructional Environment" (Association of College and Research Libraries), 69, 133
Anewstip, 89
angry or difficult patrons, interacting with, 4
annotated book lists, 28
annual record of active learning activities, maintaining a, 137–138
appraisal process for assessment of librarians and staff, 118–119
approachability as aspect of reference interview, 2–4
"The Art of Video Conferencing" (Durham), 129
Aspen Institute Dialogue on Public Libraries, 43
assessment. *See also* self-assessment
    of assistance to users by information service providers
        competencies for, 116–117
        development methods for, 117–118
        development methods for, assessment of, 118–119
    of information resources
        competencies for, 106
        development methods for, 107–108
        development methods for, assessment of, 108

assessment (cont.)
  of information services
    competencies for, 105
    development methods for, 105–106
    development methods for, assessment of, 106
  overview, xv, 101–104
  of service delivery
    competencies for, 108, 110
    development methods for, 110–114
    development methods for, assessment of, 114
  of user interfaces for information resources
    competencies for, 114–115
    development methods for, 115–116
    development methods for, assessment of, 116
  of user needs
    competencies for, 104
    development methods for, 104–105
    development methods for, assessment of, 105
"Assessment Community of Practice" (Association of Research Libraries), 124
Assessment in Action program (Association of College and Research Libraries), 44
Association for Library Service to Children (ALSC), 99, 131
Association for Talent Development (ATD), 64
Association of College and Research Libraries (ACRL), 44, 50, 58, 64, 69, 84, 99, 102, 131, 154
Association of College and Research Libraries (ACRL)—Research Planning and Review Committee, 131
Association of Research Libraries (ARL), 124
Association of Specialized Government and Cooperative Library Agencies (ASGCLA), 13
Attebury, Ramirose Ilene, xxiv, xxv
Atwood, Christee Gabour, 65
audience assessment techniques, 89
Austin, Jutta, 24
Australian Library and Information Association, 64
Avery, Susan, 54

B

background knowledge probes, 55
Backward Design instructional design model, 74
Bakr, Abu, 147
Balls, John D., 77
Barkley, Elizabeth F., 55, 58
basic marketing principles, understanding and applying, 86–88
Basic Problem-Solving and Decision-Making Skills model, 102–103
BC OpenEd Librarians, 124
"Be Fearless: Public Speaking for Librarians" (WebJunction), 65
Behavioral Observation Scale (BOS), 7, 8
behaviorally based statements, competencies as, xvi
Berkowitz, Bob, 50
Biech, Elaine, 67, 134, 138, 141
Big 6 Grading Matrix, 76
Bill & Melinda Gates Foundation, 102
Bishop, Kay, 69
Blake, Barbara, 90

Bolin, N., xxv, 117, 138
book discussion groups, 17, 126
book displays, 17
book reviews, writing, 107
Booklist (Journal), 107
booktalks, 17
Booth, Char, 74
Bowles-Terry, Melissa, 55
brainstorming, 143–144
brainwriting, 144
branding strategies, marketing plan for library services and, 93–94
Brigham and Women's Hospital Center for Faculty Development and Diversity, 139
British Columbia Institute of Technology, 71
Brookfield, Stephen D., 55, 56, 64, 77
Brown, Juanita, 54
Brubaker, John, 66
Bruce, Christine, 50, 52
Burke, Jennifer, 94
Butler Scientifics, 54
BuzzSumo, 89

C

California Community Colleges, 75
Carrier, Howard S., 34
case studies
  active learning, as method of improving, 134
  on branding for libraries, 94
  marketing plans presented as, 96
Casey, M. A., 30
Caspari, Ann K., 35
Cassinelli, Collete, 69
Center for Creative Leadership's Model of Leader Competencies, xxv
"Chairing a Meeting" (Adamova), 127
characterization in fiction books, 25
Chartered Institute of Library Information Professionals' Information Literacy Group, 50
chat reference observation sheet survey, 112
checklists
  for advocacy assessment, 100
  for assessing development efforts for offering services responsive to individual expressed user needs, 7–11, 12
  for assessment of competencies in evaluation information resources, 110
  Behavioral Observation Scale (BOS), 7, 8
  for e-mail and reference transcripts of users' questions evaluation, 22
  for end-of-shift, 56
  for follow-up, 7–8, 42
  for information resources evaluation, 107, 108
  for information-seeking process (ISP) diagnosing stage self-assessment, 9
  for information services assessment, 106
  for inquiry analysis elements, 6–7
  for interest in individual's information need, 10

for interviewing skills evaluation, 12
for listening/inquiring self-assessment, 10–11, 35
for marketing assessment, 95–96, 105
for marketing evaluation, 97
for presentation skills adapted from "Proficiencies for Instruction Librarians," 67
for readers' advisory service in public libraries, 27
for roles for instruction librarians: proficiencies, 58, 59–62
for searching behaviors self-assessment, 21
for secret patron transactions evaluation, 12
Chief Officers of State Library Agencies (COSLA), 102
Child Development Institute, 69
children, strategies for instruction to, 68–69
Choice (Journal), 107
Cison, 89
"Citizens-Save-Libraries Power Guide" (United for Libraries), 99
"Civic and Community Engagement" (Urban Libraries Council), 84
Clark, Dennis, 145
classroom assessment techniques (CATs), 55–56, 66
coaching by peers, 37, 117
Coaching Ourselves, xxvi
Cockney, Catherine, 130
"Code of Ethics" (National Association of Social Workers), 5
collaboration
    collaborative relationships within the profession
        competencies for, 38, 40
        development methods for, 40–42
        development methods for, assessment of, 41, 42
    with colleagues
        competencies for, 36
        development methods for, 36–37
        development methods for, assessment of, 37–38
    defined, 34
    overview, xiv–xv, 33–34
    partnerships beyond the library profession
        competencies for, 42
        development methods for, 42–44
        development methods for, assessment of, 44–47
    with users
        development methods for, 35
        development methods for, assessment of, 35–36
Collaboration Factors Inventory (Wilder Foundation), 45
colleagues
    collaboration with
        competencies for, 36
        development methods for, 36–37
        development methods for, assessment of, 37–38
    internal communication among, 125–126
    perceptions of colleagues as perspective for evaluation of teaching, 55
College of Wooster, 94
Common Sense, 69
Communicating Professionally (Ross and Nilsen), 126
communities. *See also* primary community
    expectations and user behavior, changing, 121

    information literacy and, 69
    relationships and partnerships with, 42–47, 90
communities of practice, 123–125
"Communities of Practice for Librarians" (Institute of Museum and Library Services), 124
"Communities of Practice" (Michigan Library Association), 124
"Community College Survey of Student Engagement" (University of Texas at Austin), 58
"Community Engagement and Outreach" (Public Library Association), 84
"Community" (Institute of Museum and Library Services), 84
"Community of Practice Design Guide" (Educause), 124
comparison and contrast as technique for source identification and presentation, 28
compatible library partners, list of organizations that are, 43
competencies
    for access
        primary community, organizing and designing services to meet the needs of the, 11
        user needs, offering services responsive to individual expressed, 1–2
    for assessment
        of assistance to users by information service providers, 116–117
        of information resources, 106
        of information services, 105
        of service delivery, 108, 110
        of user interfaces for information resources, 114–115
        of user needs, 104
    as behaviorally based statements, xvi
    benefits of
        for individuals, xix
        for organizations and the profession, xix
    for collaboration
        collaborative relationships within the profession, 38, 40
        with colleagues, 36
        partnerships beyond the library profession, 42
        with users, 34
    defined, xv, 154
    for future services
        learning as life process, 122–123
        services and resources, developing and implementing plans for, 141
        services and resources, planning, implementing, and evaluating innovative experiments in, 146
    importance of, xvi
    for information literacy
        defining, 51
        integration of information literacy concepts, 53
        learner-centered teaching environment creation, 71–72
        presentation and communication strategies to foster learning and engagement, 58
    leadership, xvii–xviii
    lifelong learning and, xviii–xix, 122–123
    maintaining and enhancing, xxiv–xxv

competencies (cont.)
- for marketing and advocacy
    - advocating value of library services to primary community, 96, 98
    - marketing plan for library services, 91
    - marketing theory and practices, understanding and applying, 85
- overview, xv–xvi
- for source identification and presentation, 24
- as standards, xvi

"Competency Index for the Library Field" (Gutsche and Hough), 37, 92
"Competency Index for the Library Field 2014" (WebJunction), 154
Competency to Be Addressed form, xxi
competition assessment techniques, 88, 89
concept maps, 141–142
Conducting a Meeting (Website), 128
content marketing, 93
"Continuing Professional Development and Workplace Learning" (International Federation of Libraries), 124
coordinator as role of instruction librarians, 59
"Core Competences of Librarianship" (American Library Association), xvii
Cornell University, 44
COSLA (Chief Officers of State Library Agencies), 102
The Courage to Teach Guide for Reflection and Renewal (Palmer and Scribner), 79
The Courage to Teach (Palmer), 77, 79
Creating Minds (website), 145
Crenshaw, Dave, 129
critical and creative thinking, strategies for, 143–144
Culatta, Richard, 72
cultural awareness, 140
Cunningham, Sojourna, 115
Current Cites, 133
The Current, 51
Curtis, Jessica A., 68

D

Dallas, Larayne J., 153
data literacy, 51
decision matrix, 146, 147
DeLancey, Laura, 116
Demasson, Andrew, 52
demographic information for your primary community, 13
demonstrations as method of improving active learning, 134
Dempsey, Kathy, 84
Design Kit, 14
designing services
- assessment of, 17–22
- development methods for, 14–17
- questions to answer before starting a new service, 18
- starting, 15–16

Dev, Chekitan S., 87

development methods
- for access
    - primary community, organizing and designing services to meet the needs of the, 11–17
    - user needs, offering services responsive to individual expressed, 2–7
- for assessment
    - of assistance to users by information service providers, 117–118
    - of information resources, 107–108
    - of information services, 105–106
    - of service delivery, 110–114
    - of user interfaces for information resources, 115–116
    - of user needs, 104–105
- assessment of. *See* development methods assessment
- for collaboration
    - collaborative relationships within the profession, 40–42
    - with colleagues, 36–37
    - partnerships beyond the library profession, 42–44
    - with users, 35
- for future services
    - learning as life process, 123–137
    - services and resources, developing and implementing plans for, 141–145
    - services and resources, planning, implementing, and evaluating innovative experiments in, 146–148
- for information literacy
    - defining, 51–53
    - integration of information literacy concepts, 54–56
    - learner-centered teaching environment creation, 72–80
    - presentation and communication strategies to foster learning and engagement, 58–71
- for marketing and advocacy
    - advocating value of library services to primary community, 98–100
    - marketing plan for library services, 92–95
    - marketing theory and practices, understanding and applying, 85–90
- for source identification and presentation, 24–29

development methods assessment
- for access
    - primary community, organizing and designing services to meet the needs of the, 17–22
    - user needs, offering services responsive to individual expressed, 7–11
- for assessment
    - of assistance to users by information service providers, 118–119
    - of information resources, 108
    - of information services, 106
    - of service delivery, 114
    - of user interfaces for information resources, 116
    - of user needs, 105
- for collaboration
    - collaborative relationships within the profession, 41, 42

Index • 179

with colleagues, 37–38
partnerships beyond the library profession, 44–47
with users, 35–36
for future services
  learning as life process, 137–141
  services and resources, developing and implementing plans for, 145
  services and resources, planning, implementing, and evaluating innovative experiments in, 148–149
for information literacy
  defining, 53
  integration of information literacy concepts, 56–57
  learner-centered teaching environment creation, 80–81
  presentation and communication strategies to foster learning and engagement, 71
for marketing and advocacy
  advocating value of library services to primary community, 100
  marketing plan for library services, 95–96
  marketing theory and practices, understanding and applying, 90–91
overview, xxvi
for source identification and presentation, 29–32
developmental assignments as method of maintaining and enhancing competencies, xxiv–xxv
Developmental Assignments (McCauley), xxiv–xxv
devil's advocate evaluative approach, 146–147
Diaz, Jose O., 44
A Dictionary of Marketing (Doyle), 86
difficult or angry patrons, interacting with, 4
Diggs-Hobson, Mary, 139
Digial Polarization Initiative, 69
digital literacy, 51, 74–75
"Digital Literacy Training Tutorials for Libraries" (WebJunction), 75
DigitalLearn.org, 21, 74, 75
Dimensions of Fiction (Pejtersen and Austin), 24
disabled persons. *See* special needs populations
discussion lists on information literacy, 51
"DIY Skills: Upgrading for the Teacher Librarian" (Lierman), 77
DO-IT: Disabilities, Opportunities, Internetworking, and Technology, 14
Doherty, M. Teresa, 145
Donham, Jean, 69
Donovan, Jeremy, 64
Downey, Anne, 14, 15, 148
Downey, Liana, 14
Drudge Report, 131
Du, Yunfei, 90
Duarte, Nancy, 67
Durham, Jeff, 129

E

e-mail
  filters as method of keeping up-to-date on the library field, 132–133
  newsletters as method of keeping up-to-date on the library field, 132
  reference observation sheet survey, 113
  reference transcripts of users' questions, use of checklists to evaluate, 22
"E-News Weekly" (Urban Libraries Council), 131
ease/impact model, 145
education and training. *See* training and education
Educator Innovator, 51
Educators of America, 69
Educause, 124, 139
Eisenberg, Mike, 50
Elmborg, James, 54
Elsevier (Organization), 124
Elsner, Jamie, 54
Emerald Publishing, 107
end-of-shift checklist, 56
"Environmental Scan 2017" (Association of College and Research Libraries, Research Planning and Review Committee), 131
environmental scanning, 130–132
EOS Worldwide, 127
Erlinger, Allison, 76
Essential Questions (McTighe and Wiggins), 54
ETS (Educational Testing Service), 76
Eury, A. Douglas, 77
Evaluating Potential Partners worksheet, 45–46
Evaluating Reference Services (Whitlatch), ix
Everall, Kyla, 15
"Everyday Advocacy" (Association for Library Service to Children), 99
experiential learning approaches, 135–136
experiments in services and resources
  competencies for, 146
  development methods for, 146–148
  developmental methods, assessment of, 148–149
exploratory questions, 54

F

face-to-face communication, 126–128
"Faculty Inquiry Groups" (Lane Community College's Faculty Professional Development), 130
Farmer, Lesley, 22, 28
"Federal Legislation" (American Library Association, Office of Government Relations), 131
Federation of Ontario Public Libraries, 99
feedback and assessments as method of integrating information literacy concepts, 54–56
fiction books
  Dimensions of Fiction, 24
  perfect books, reader descriptions of, 25–26
  reader preferences, determining, 24–26
  vocabulary of appeal, 25
Fink, L. Dee, 55
Fish! Philosophy!, 138
fishbone diagrams, 144–145

"5 'Q.U.I.C.K' Steps of Reflective Practice" (Eury, King, and Balls), 77
Flom, Jason, 71
focus groups, 127
Focus Groups (Krueger and Casey), 30
focused questions, 54
follow-up
    checklists for, 7–8, 42
    improving, 7
Followerwonk, 89
force field analysis, 141, 142
formal education and training, maintaining and enhancing competencies with, xxv
formal meetings, 127–128
Foster, Jack, 144
"Four Lenses: Evaluation Resources" (University of Sydney's Faculty of Arts and Social Sciences), 55
4Ps: product, price, promotion, and place, 85–88
frame and tone in fiction books, 25
"Framework for Information Literacy for Higher Education" (Association of College and Research Libraries), 50
future, planning for the, xv
future of jobs, World Economic Forum report on the, 36
future services
    learning as life process
        competencies for, 122–123
        development methods for, 123–137
        development methods for, assessment of, 137–141
    overview, 121–122
    services and resources, developing and implementing plans for
        competencies for, 141
        development methods for, 141–145
        development methods for, assessment of, 145
    services and resources, planning, implementing, and evaluating innovative experiments in
        competencies for, 146
        development methods for, 146–148
        development methods for, assessment of, 148–149
The Future of Skills: Employment in 2030 (Bakhshi, Downing, Osborne, and Schneider), 122

G

Gallagher's Six Steps for Telling Anyone Anything, 125
Galston, Colbe, 42
games and simulations as experiential learning approach, 136
Gariepy, Laura, 145
Garton, Janetta, 66
Gers, R., xxv, 117, 138
Getting Started in Service Design (Marquez and Downey), 14–15
Getting to Yes (Fisher, Ury, and Patton), 126
Gibson, Craig, 69
"Give Every Child a Stake in Group Work" (Common Sense), 69
"Glance Test" (Duarte), 67
goals and objectives
    for action plans for professional development, xx, xxiii–xxiv
    for marketing plan for library services, 93–94, 95
    mission, goals, and values of library, making sure that new services are consistent with, 14
    SMART (Specific, Measurable, Achievable, Relevant, and Timely) goals and objectives, 95
Godbey, Samantha, 43
Google Alerts, 133
Google Analytics, 89
Google Keyword Planner, 89
Google News, 131
Google Trends, 89
Governing.com, 13
Grassian, Esther, 52, 57
group discussions, 125–128
group inquiry as method of improving active learning, 134
group leaders, questions for interviewing effective, 37
group meetings, assessment of, 41, 42
GroupHigh, 89
guided teaching as method of improving active learning, 134
"Guidelines for Behavioral Performance of Reference and Information Service Providers" (Reference and User Services Association), 2, 3, 7, 10, 18–19, 105, 106, 117, 118, 154
"Guidelines for Conducting a Focus Group" (Eliot and Associates), 127
"Guidelines for Implementing and Maintaining Virtual Reference Services" (Reference and User Services Association), 16
Guillaume, Yves R. F., 37
Gutsche, Betha, 92

H

"Habits of Mind in an Uncertain Information World" (Gibson and Jacobson), 69
Hackman, J. Richard, 123
Haines, Stuart T., 54
Hakala-Ausperk, Catherine, xx
Hall, Douglas T. (Tim), 37
Harding, Jane, 52
health information, partnerships used to improve access to, 44
HEIghten Outcomes Assessment Suite, 76
Heineke, Amy J., 74
Heinze, Jill Stover, 91, 93
"Help! I'm an Accidental Government Information Librarian" (Webinars), 41
Higgins, Monica, 139
Hilyer, Lee Andrew, 65
Himmele, Persida, 77
Himmele, William, 77
Hodge, Megan, 145
Hoff, Ron, 65
Hough, Brenda, 92
Houghton, Brigeen, 93
"How Can Your Librarian Help Bolster Brain-Based Teaching Practices?" (Mindshift), 69
How People Learn (National Research Council), 68
"How to Conduct Effective Meetings" (Wikihow), 127
"How to Create a Community Resource Guide" (Mies), 28

How to Deliver a TED Talk: Secrets of the World's Most Inspiring Presentations (Donovan), 64
How to Get Ideas (Foster), 144
"How to Run an Effective Meeting—Tutorial" (EOS Worldwide), 127
"How to Run an Internal Unconference" (Kniberg), 130
Hoyle, Robin, 133
Huber, Elizabeth Kelsen, 42
Huffington Post, 131
Huling, Nancy, 153

I

IDEO (Organization), 14, 42, 143, 144, 147–148
IFLA Guidelines for Continuing Professional Development (Varlejs), 122
"Impact Planning and Assessment Guide" (Bill & Melinda Gates Foundation), 102
Impact Survey, 13
in-person observation sheet survey, 111–112
Inala, Padma, 77
Inayatullah, Sohail, 133
Indiana University-Purdue University Indianapolis (IUPUI), 125
INFOdocket, 133
informal learning, 133–134
information
　how people look for information, understanding, 13–14
　information-seeking process (ISP), self-assessment for diagnosing stage of, 9
　presenting information to users, 17
　researching how people look for, 14
information literacy
　defining
　　competencies for, 51
　　development methods for, 51–53
　　development methods for, assessment of, 53
　　overview, 50
　integration of information literacy concepts
　　competencies for, 53
　　development methods for, 54–56
　　development methods for, assessment of, 56–57
　learner-centered teaching environment creation
　　competencies for, 71–72
　　development methods for, 72–80
　　development methods for, assessment of, 80–81
　overview, xv, 49–51
　presentation and communication strategies to foster learning and engagement
　　competencies for, 58
　　development methods for, 58–71
　　development methods for, assessment of, 71
Information Literacy Instruction Assessment Cycle (ILIAC), 76
Information Literacy Test (ILT), 75–76
information resources assessment
　competencies for, 106
　development methods for, 107–108
　development methods for, assessment of, 108

information searches as method of improving active learning, 134–135
information service providers, assessment of, 116–119
information services assessment
　competencies for, 105
　development methods for, 105–106
　development methods for, assessment of, 106
Informed Librarian Online, 131
Innovation Explorers, 124
inquiry analysis elements checklist, 6–7
inquiry-based learning, 69, 71
Inquiry-Based Learning: Lessons from Library Power (Donham, Kuhlthau, Oberg, and Bishop), 69
Inspiring Curiosity: The Librarian's Guide to Inquiry-Based Learning (Cassinelli), 69
Institute for Information Literacy's Immersion Program, 64
Institute of Museum and Library Services (IMLS), 18, 84, 102, 124
instructional design models for learning, 72–74
instructional designer as role of instruction librarians, 60
instructional methods used in all types of libraries, 57
interest (emotion)
　in individual's information need, self-assessment checklist for, 10
　reference interview, as aspect of, 2–4
internal marketing, 92
International City/Country Management Association (ICMA), 13
International Federation of Library Associations and Institutions (IFLA), 40, 94, 99, 102, 124, 131
"The International Advocacy Programme (IAP)" (International Federation of Library Associations and Institutions), 99
interviews
　awareness of your skills in reference interviews, enhancing, 2
　evaluation of interviewing skills, 12
　feedback on effectiveness of outreach efforts, questions for, 96
"Invest in Yourself!" (Hakala-Ausperk), xx
investigates, analyzes, and plans in order to develop future services (Section 5G). *See* future services
Isaacs, David, 54
iSkills Assessment, 76

J

Jacobson, Trudi E., 69
jigsaw learning as method of improving active learning, 135
Johnson, D. W., 38
Johnson, F. P., 38
Johnson, Katherine, 42
Johnston, Marcia, 88
Joining Together (Johnson and Johnson), 38
Jones, Rebecca J., 37
journals
　behavior and group dynamics, personal journal used to record information on your, 38
　for community relationship reflections, 44
　library field, as method for keeping up-to-date on the, 132
　for lifelong learning assessment, 137
　for user needs assessment, 105

K

Katopol, Patricia, 131
Kearsley, Greg, 72
"Keeping Up With . . ." (Association of College and Research Libraries), 131
Kemp, Jan, 94
Kenedy, Robert, 44
Kern, M. Kathleen, x, 4
"Key Competencies Development Activities Guide" (University of Ottawa), 38
Kinder, Robin, 153
King, Jane, 77
King, Nathaniel, 105
Kirkpatrick, Donald, 54, 73
Kirkpatrick, Jim, 117
Kirkpatrick, Wendy, 117
KMaya (Organization), 124
Kniberg, Hendrik, 130
Knowles, Malcolm, 68
Koontz, Christie, 89, 131, 132
Kostek, John, 77
Kotler, Philip, 85, 86, 87, 90–91, 92, 93, 94
Kovacs, Maria, 90
Kram, Kathy E., 37, 139
Krueger, R. A., 30
Kuhlthau, Carol C., 2, 35, 69
Kvenild, Cassandra, 55

L

Labin, Jenn, 139
Ladyshewsky, Richard K., 37
Lane Community College's Faculty Professional Development, 130
language and translation resources, 16
Law, Margaret, 90
Lawrence, Craig, 147
leadership
    management compared, xvii
    overview, xvii–xviii
    role of instruction librarians, leader as, 60–61
"Leadership and Management Competencies" (Library Leadership and Management Association), 154
"Leadership Development and Advocacy" (Public Library Association), 99
learner-centered teaching environment creation
    competencies for, 71–72
    development methods for, 72–80
    development methods for, assessment of, 80–81
learning and engagement, presentation and communication strategies to foster
    competencies for, 58
    development methods for, 58–71
    development methods for, assessment of, 71
learning as life process. *See* lifelong learning
learning tournament as method of improving active learning, 135, 137

Lee, Nancy, 86, 87, 91, 92, 93, 94
Let the Games Begin: Engaging Students with Field-Tested Interactive Information Literacy Instruction (McDevitt), 77
LibGuides Community, 28
LibQual, 13
Librarians Active Learning Institute at Dartmouth, 52
librarians and staff
    assessment of, 116–119
    future skill sets, 122
"Libraries Foster Community Engagement" (ALA Connect), 84
Library and Information Technology Association, 99
library field scanning, 132–133
"Library Futures" (Inayatullah), 133
Library Information Technology Association, 131
Library Instruction Roundtable, 64
Library Journal, 84, 107, 132
Library Leadership and Management Association (LLAMA), 84, 123, 154
"Library Marketer of the Year Award" (Library Journal), 84
"Library Marketing and Advocacy Toolkit" (Law and Kovacs), 90
Library of Congress Individual Development Plan, xxii–xxiii
Library Service Design (Marquez and Downey), 14
Library Video Network, 4, 17, 84
The Library Assessment Cookbook (Dobbs), 102
The Library Marketing Toolkit (Potter), 90, 92
Lierman, Ashley R., 77
lifelong learning
    competencies for, xviii–xix, 122–123
    development methods for, 123–137
    development methods for, assessment of, 137–141
    instruction librarians, lifelong learner as role of, 60
    overview, xviii–xix
LinkedIn, 89
LIRT News, 80
listening and inquiring
    checklist for, 10–11, 35
    reference interview, as aspect of, 4–5
"Literacy" (Wikipedia), 51
literature technique for evaluation of teaching, 57
"Local Libraries Advancing Community Goals, 2016" (International City/County Management Association), 43
local (library) organizations, 41
local (nonlibrary) professional organizations, participation in, 42–43
LOEX, 64
LOEX of the West, 64
Logan, Judith, 15
Long, Amy, 42
Luo, Lili, xxv
Lurleen B. Wallace Community College, 76
Lutz, Kelly, 105
Lynch, Courtney, 141
Lynch, Sean, 141
Lynda.com, 129

M

Major, Clair H., 55
management and leadership compared, xvii
Mandernach, Meris A., 44
Maniotes, Leslie K., 35
Mansfield, Clarissa, 94
Manson, Jeana, 29
market personas, 88–89
marketing and advocacy
    advocating value of library services to primary community
        competencies for, 96, 98
        development methods for, 98–100
        development methods for, assessment of, 100
    marketing plan for library services
        competencies for, 91
        development methods for, 92–95
        development methods for, assessment of, 95–96
    marketing theory and practices, understanding and applying
        competencies for, 85
        development methods for, 85–90
        development methods for, assessment of, 90–91
    overview, xv, 83–85
    resources for, list of, 84
"Marketing and Communications Community of Practice" (Library Leadership and Management Association), 84
Marketing and Social Media (Koontz and Mon), 89
marketing assessment checklist, 95–96, 105
marketing evaluation checklist, 97
"Marketing for the Beginner" (Association of College and Research Libraries), 84
Marketing in the Public Sector (Kotler and Lee), 91
marketing landscape, researching and assessing the, 88–89
marketing mix, 85–88
"Marketing Strategies" (Public Library Association), 84
"Marketing the Academic Library" (Association of College and Research Libraries), 84
"Marketing" (WebJunction), 84
"Marketing Your Library" (Library Video Network), 84
Marquez, Joe, 14, 15, 148
Martin, Robert S., 90
Mayer, Richard, 66
Mays, Regina, 115
McCallum, Deborah, 75
McCauley, Cynthia, xxiv, 29, 35
McDevitt, Theresa, 77
McNiff, Jean, 102
McTighe, Jay, 54, 74
Measures That Matter, 99–100, 102
"Measuring and Assessing Reference Services and Resources: A Guide" (Reference and User Services Association), 105, 145
media assessment techniques, 89
Medline, 17
"Meeting Virtually" (Crenshaw), 129
meetings
    assessment of, 41, 42
    formal, 127–128

"Membership Reports" (OCLC), 131
mental imagery as experiential learning approach, 136
mentoring as method of getting feedback on your learning goals, 139
mentoring network, 139, 140
Mercer, Holly, 115
MERLOT II, 22, 143
MERLOT system, 74
Michigan Library Association, 124
micro-teaching, 57
Mies, Ginny, 28
Miesing, Paul, 147
mind maps, 142, 144
Mindshift, 69
Mindtools (Website), 5
Minnesota Opportunities for Reference Excellence (MORE) [Website], 3–4, 6
minute paper tests, 55
mission, goals, and values of library, making sure that new services are consistent with, 14
modern library and reference services, defining and reshaping, 122
Mon, Lorri, 89, 131, 132
Monty, Vivienne, 44
Morgan, Angie, 87, 141
Moss, B. D., 35
Mozilla, 53
"The 'M' Word-Marketing Libraries: Marketing News, Tips, and Trends for Libraries" (Dempsey), 84
muddiest point technique, 55
multicultural literacy, 51
"Museums, Libraries and 21st Century Skills" (Institute of Museum and Library Services), xvii, xviii

N

narrative nonfiction, appeal factors of subgenres of, 27
National Association for the Education of Young Children, 69
National Association of Social Workers, 5
National Center for Universal Design for Learning, 72
National Council of Nonprofits, 123
National Resource Council, 68
Neal, Larry, 148
negative closure, 7
networking, 40–42
New Media Consortium, 13, 131
New York City School Library System, 74
Nielsen, Jakob, 115, 116
Nielsen Norman Group, 13, 148
Nilsen, Kirsti, 4, 5, 7, 10, 24, 54, 126, 128, 129, 130
"NMC Horizon Report 2017: Library Edition for Academic and Research Libraries" (New Media Consortium), 131
"No Attention Means No Learning" (Kostek and Stewart), 77
nonprofit organizations and communities of practice, 123–124
nonverbal stance during reference interviews, 3
North Carolina Library Association, 41
numerical literacy, 51

O

Oakleaf, Megan, 76–77
Oberg, Diane, 69
objectives and goals. *See* goals and objectives
observation as experiential learning approach, 136
"Observation Checklist" (Noonan, Gaumer, Erickson, Brussow, and Langham), 71
OCLC (Online Computer Library Center), 13, 131
Office for Library Advocacy - American Library Association, 98
Office of Government Relations - American Library Association, 131
on-the-job learning
    competencies, as method of maintaining and enhancing, xxiv–xxv
    information services, as development method for assessing, 105–106
    user needs, as development method for assessing, 104
1VC2World, 129
online learning
    assessment of, 31–32
    options for, 137
    PRIMO selection criteria for, 31–32
    technology and online learning environments, 74–75
Online Learning Consortium, 75
"Online Learning with RUSA (Marketing)" (Reference and User Services Association), 84
"Online Student Readiness Tutorials" (California Community Colleges), 75
Open Space, 130
"ORE Online: Ohio Reference Excellence Professional Development Training" (Ohio Library Council), 138
ORE Online (Website), 3, 4
organizational reports useful for environmental scanning, 131
organizing or chunking content as aspect of reference interview, 5–7
outcome-based evaluation, 18

P

Pacific Library Partnership, 43
pacing in fiction books, 25
Palmer, Parker J., 77, 79
Parker, Polly, 37
Partnership Evaluation rubric, 47
partnerships and collaboration. *See* collaboration
Partridge, Helen, 52
patron involvement as aspect of reference interview, 5
Patton, M. Q., 30
peer coaching, 37, 117
peer observation as method of assessing your teaching efforts, 71
peer review of chat transcripts, 18
peer technique for evaluation of teaching, 57
"Peer-to-Peer Observation: Five Questions for Making It Work" (Flom), 71
Pejtersen, Annelise Mark, 24
Pejtersen and Austin's Dimensions of Fiction, 24
perfect books, reader descriptions of, 25–26

permission form for recording interactions with library staff (sample), 35
personal experience perspective for evaluation of teaching, 55
personal journal used to record information on your behavior and group dynamics, 38
Peters, Anne, 94
PEW Internet, 13
PEW Internet & American Life Project surveys, 131
PHITE (Present Hypothesis in Team Environment) Club, 66
Pierce College, 56
pilot projects, 148
Pinola, Melanie, 66
Pionke, J. J., 29
Potter, Ned, 86, 88, 90, 91, 92, 94
A Power Guide for Successful Advocacy (Reed, Nawalinski, and Kalonick), 98
presentation and communication strategies to foster learning and engagement
    competencies for, 58
    development methods for, 58–71
    development methods for, assessment of, 71
Presentation Basics (Rosania), 65
Presentation Feedback Form, 70
presentation skills adapted from "Proficiencies for Instruction Librarians," checklist for, 67
"Presentation Skills" (American Library Association), 64
Presentation Skills Training (Atwood), 65
Presentations for Librarians: A Complete Guide to Creating Effective, Learner-Centred Presentations (Hilyer), 65
presenting information to users, 17
Press, Nancy Ottman, 139
Pretlow, Cassi, 88
primary community
    advocating value of library services to
        competencies for, 96, 98
        development methods for, 98–100
        development methods for, assessment of, 100
    demographic information for your, 13
    organizing and designing services to meet the needs of the
        competencies for, 11
        development methods for, 11–17
        development methods for, assessing, 17–22
    who your users are, learning, 13
    who your users can be, learning, 13
PRIMO: Peer-Reviewed Instruction Materials Online Database, 16, 74
PRIMO selection criteria for online learning, 31–32
Prince, Michael, 77
problem-solving groups, 126–127
Process for Seven Steps in Practitioner Research model, 103–104
process maps, 142–143
Professional Competencies for Reference and User Services Librarians (Document)
    Accesses relevant and accurate recorded knowledge and information (5A)

primary community, organizes and designs services to meet the needs of the, 154–155
user needs, offers services responsive to individual expressed, 154
Assesses and responds to diversity in user needs, user communities, and user preferences (5F)
assistance to users by information service providers, assesses, 158
information resources, assesses, 158
information services, assesses, 158
service delivery, assesses, 158
user interfaces for information resources, assesses, 158
user needs, assesses, 157–158
definitions, 154
Develops appropriate expertise in information literacy and instruction skills and abilities, including textual, digital, visual, numerical, and spatial literacies (5D)
information literacy, defines, 156
integrates information literacy concepts into full range of library services, 156
learner-centered teaching environment, creates a, 156–157
learning and engagement, designs and implements presentation and communication strategies to foster, 156
Evaluates, collects, retrieves, and synthesizes information from diverse sources (5B), 155
Interacts with colleagues and others to provide consultation, mediation, and guidance in the use of knowledge and information (5C)
colleagues, collaborates and partners with, 155
partnerships beyond the library profession, develops and maintains, 155
professional relationships for, 155
users, collaborates and partners with, 155
Investigates, analyzes, and plans in order to develop future services (5G)
learner, leading life as a, 158–159
services and resources, develops and implements plans for, 159
services and resources, plans, implements, and evaluates innovations in, 159
overview, 153–154
Promotes and demonstrates the value of library services through marketing and advocacy (5E)
marketing plan for library services, develops and evaluates an, 157
marketing theory and practices, understanding and applying, 157
primary community, advocates value of library services to the, 157
resources consulted for, list of, 159–160
sources, identifies and presents highly recommended, 155
text of (complete), 153–160
professional discussions and activities, 125–128

professional organizations
lists of, 40, 41
local organizations, 41
participation in, 40–42
in specialized subject areas, 41
"Proficiencies for Assessment Librarians and Coordinators" (Association of College and Research Libraries), 102
project-based learning, 69
Project SAILS (Standardized Assessment of Information Literacy Skills), 75
promotion strategies, developing, 94
prototypes, 148
"Public Awareness Tools and Resources" (American Library Association), 99
public libraries as information literacy providers, 52–53
Public Library Association (PLA), 74, 75, 84, 99
published reviews, questions for the analysis of, 107
Puentedura, Ruben, 75
Purdue Online Writing Lab, 22, 107

Q

Qualitative Research & Evaluation Methods (Patton), 30
"Quality Framework" (Online Learning Consortium), 75
"Quick Guide for Content Marketing Research" (Relevance), 89

R

Radford, Marie, 5, 7, 24, 54
Rails (Organization), 43
rapport during reference interviews, 3
Rathi, Dinesh, 130
READ (Reference Effort Assessment Data) scale, 105
reader preferences, determining, 24–26
Reader's Advisory Service in the Public Library (Saricks), 27
readers' advisory services, 27–28
reference activity counts sheet for various delivery methods, 114
Reference and User Services Association (RUSA), xiii, 40, 84, 132, 153
reference and user services librarians defined, 154
Reference Electronic Database Questionnaire, 109, 116
"Reference Interview Evaluation Sheet" (Ward), 22
Reference Services Review, 147
reference text project rubric, 19–20
reflective practices, 77–79, 139–141
Reiss, Tony, 127
relationships, maintaining and enhancing competencies with, xxv. *See also* collaboration
Research and Statistics (RSS) Committee of RUSA, 104
Research Planning and Review Committee - Association of College and Research Libraries, 131
resource guides for source identification and presentation, 29
Reynolds, Garr, 67
Rockquemore, Kerry Ann, 139
Rogers, Emily, 34
role-playing as experiential learning approach, 135–136
"Roles and Strengths of Teaching Librarians" (Association of College and Research Libraries), 154

roles for instruction librarians: proficiencies checklist, 58, 59–62
roles of library staff and future skill sets, reviewing, 122
Rosania, Robert J., 65
Ross, Catherine Sheldrick, 4, 5, 7, 10, 24, 54, 126, 128, 129, 130
Ruiz, Faithe, xxiv

S

Sam Houston University, 18
SAM (Successive Approximation Model) instructional design model, 73–74
SAMR Model, 75
San Jose State University, 107
Saricks, Joyce G., 17, 24, 27, 28
Say It in Six: How to Say Exactly What You Mean in Six Minutes or Less (Hoff), 65
SCARF model for successful peer coaching, 37
Schmidt, Aaron, 94, 115
school library media specialists and academic librarians, partnerships between, 43
school-library partnerships, 43–44
Schultz, Don E., 87
Scout Report, 133
Screaming Frog, 89
Scribner, Megan, 79
SDI (selective dissemination of information) services, 132
search
    behaviors
        assessment of, 21–22
        checklist for, 21
    strategies, updating, 16–17
Search Engine Watch, 16
secret patron transactions
    evaluation of, 12
    use of, 10
Seeking Meaning (Kuhlthau), 2
self-assessment
    checklists
        for listening/inquiring, 10–11, 35
        for searching behaviors, 21
    of collaboration skills, 37–38, 39
    development methods assessment, xxvi, xxvii
    information-seeking process (ISP), self-assessment for diagnosing stage of, 9
    of presentation of information on web pages, 29, 30
self-examination as method of improving teaching skills, 64–65
self-leadership, 33
self lens technique for evaluation of teaching, 56
self-managed work teams, 128
SEMrush, 89
"Serious eLearning Manifesto," 137
SERVE (Smile, Eye Contact, Recognize, Voice, Exceed) rubric, 105–106
service blueprinting, 88
service delivery assessment
    competencies for, 108, 110
    development methods for, 110–114
    development methods for, assessment of, 114
service delivery evaluation competencies assessment sheet, 115
services and resources
    developing and implementing plans for
        competencies for, 141
        development methods for, 141–145
        development methods for, assessment of, 145
    planning, implementing, and evaluating innovative experiments in
        competencies for, 146
        development methods for, 146–148
        development methods for, assessment of, 148–149
7Ps (service marketing mix), 86–87
Shank, Patti, 72
Shapiro, Janet, xx
Share Tally, 89
shared-leadership, 33–34
sharing teaching stories, 79–80
Shiri, Ali, 130
Silberman, Melvin, 67, 134, 138, 141
Silberman's six experiential learning approaches, 135–136
simulations and games as experiential learning approach, 136
Singh, Rajesh, 85
SMART (Specific, Measurable, Achievable, Relevant, and Timely) goals and objectives, 95
Sobel, Karen, 88
social marketing, 87–88
social media and marketing plan for library services, 94
Society of American Archivists, 41
Solomon, Laura, 88, 93
source identification and presentation
    competencies for, 24
    development methods for, 24–29
    development methods for, assessment of, 29–32
spaces and service delivery, offering flexibility in, 122
Spark: How to Lead Yourself and Others to Greater Success (Morgan, Lynch, and Lynch), 141
spatial literacy, 51
special needs of users, understanding, 16–17
special needs populations
    accessibility for, 116
    language and translation resources, 16
    source identification and presentation for, 28–29
    web accessibility for, 13–14
specialized database questionnaire as method of assessment of information resources, 109
specialized subject areas, professional organizations in, 41
spider maps, 142
spontaneous questions, 54
staff of library
    assessment of, 116–119
    future skill sets, 122
standards, competencies as, xvi
"Standards of Professional Excellence for Teacher Librarians in Australia" (Australian Library and Information Association), 64

Stewart, Amanda, 77
story line in fiction books, 25
Stroud, J. DeLayne, 143
student engagement techniques, 62–63
Student Engagement Techniques (Barkley), 58, 62
student lens technique for evaluation of teaching, 56–57
student's eyes perspective for evaluation of teaching, 55
study groups as method of improving active learning, 135
style in fiction books, 25
Successful Community Outreach (Blake, Martin, and Du), 90
Summer Matters: Making All Learning Count (Wunar and McChesney), xvii
supervisors and others, assessment by, xxvi, xxviii
surveys
    service delivery, surveys as method of assessing, 110–113
    user interfaces for information resources, surveys as method of assessing, 116
    on who your users are, 13
    on who your users can be, 13
Swanson, Sara Gillespie, 93
Sweetman, Kimberly, 146
SWOT (Strengths, Weaknesses, Opportunities, and Threats) analysis, 89, 144

T

target markets, 89–90
"Taxonomy of Significant Learning" (Fink), 55
teacher as role of instruction librarians, 61
teaching faculty, collaboration with, 44
Teaching Methods Committee (Association of College and Research Libraries), 69
teaching partner as role of instruction librarians, 61–62
technology
    and online learning environments, 74–75
    service profiles, integrating new technologies into, 147
Techsoup for Libraries (Organization), 43
teleconferencing (voice-only), 129
telephone reference observation sheet survey, 112–113
10 Steps to Successful Virtual Presentations (Turmel), 65
Texas Tech University, 66
text message reference services, rubric for assessment of, 19–20
textual literacy, 51
theory perspective for evaluation of teaching, 55
Thiagarajan, Sivasailam, 65
Thiagi's Interactive Lectures: Power Up Your Training with Interactive Games and Exercises (Thiagarajan), 65
"Things to Consider When Choosing Video Conferencing" (1VC2World), 129
Thorpe, Clare, 121, 122
time allocation in a class session, 81
time frame for action plans for professional development, xxiv
Toastmasters International, 43
Tofade, Toyin, 54
"Top Technology Trends" (Library Information Technology Association), 131
Top 200 Tools for Learning, 137

Total Participation Techniques: Making Every Student an Active Learner (Himmele and Himmele), 77
Towards Maturity, 133
training and education
    applying new skills learned in training to your job, techniques for, 138–139
    formal education and training, maintaining and enhancing competencies with, xxv
    lifelong learning
        competencies for, xviii–xix, 122–123
        development methods for, 123–137
        development methods for, assessment of, 137–141
        instruction librarians, lifelong learner as role of, 60
        overview, xviii–xix
translation and language resources, 16
"Trend Report" (International Federation of Library Associations), 131
trends assessment techniques, 89
Turmel, Wayne, 65

U

unconferences, 130
UNESCO, 50
United for Libraries: The Association of Library Trustees, Advocates, Friends, and Foundations, 98, 99
Universal Design for learning guidelines, 72, 73
University of California at Berkeley Library, 16
University of California at Berkeley Library guides, 16
University of Illinois LibGuides project, 29
University of Kansas Libraries' Reference Services, 18
University of Michigan's Center for Research on Teaching and Learning, 77
University of Oklahoma Health Sciences Center Library, 123–124
University of Ottawa, 38
University of Sydney's Faculty of Arts and Social Sciences, 55
University of Tennessee Libraries, 92
University of Washington, 14
Urban Libraries Council, 44, 84, 131
usability of information resources, 115–116
Usability.gov, 29
Usability.gov: Improving the User Experience, 14
user collaboration
    competencies for, 34
    development methods for, 35
    development methods for, assessment of, 35–36
user interfaces for information resources assessment
    competencies for, 114–115
    development methods for, 115–116
    development methods for, assessment of, 116
user needs, offering services responsive to individual expressed
    competencies for, 1–2
    development methods for, 2–7
    development methods for, assessing, 7–11
user needs assessment
    competencies for, 104

user needs assessment (cont.)
  development methods for, 104–105
  development methods for, assessment of, 105
user testing as method of evaluating information resources, 115–116
USER (Understand, Structure, Engage, Reflect) instructional design model, 74

V

Valentine, G., 35
Value of Academic Libraries, 100
values, mission, and goals of library, making sure that new services are consistent with, 14
Vaughan, Shauna, 72
1VC2World, 129
videoconferencing, 129
Vilelle, Luke, 132
"Virtual Reference Companion - Marketing" (Reference and User Services Association), 84
"Virtual Reference Companion" (Reference and User Services Association), 16, 18
virtual reference services
  assessment of, 18
  designing, 16, 18
virtual teams, conferences, and discussions, 128–130
visibility as aspect of reference interview, 2–4
visual literacy, 51
vocabulary of appeal for fiction books, 25
Vogt, Eric E., 54
voice-matching during reference interviews, 3

W

Walsh, Andrew, 77
Ward, David, 54
Ward, Jennifer, 92
Watson-Boone, Rebecca, 148
Watts, John, 104

WAVE Validator, 116
web accessibility for special needs populations, 13–14
web-based tools, assessment of, 30–31
web conferencing, 129–130
"Web Literacy" (Mozilla), 53
web pages
  self-assessment of presentation of information on, 29, 30
  usability of your library's web pages, improving, 14
Weber, Max, xvi
WebJunction, 4, 5, 15–16, 17, 28, 52, 65, 75, 84, 85, 92, 98, 99, 137, 154
Webquest, 16
Western Oregon University, 94
what's the principle? technique, 55
Whitlatch, Jo Bell, ix, 153
who your users are, learning, 13
who your users can be, learning, 13
"Why Has IDEO Been So Innovative over the Years?" (Miesing), 147
Wiggins, Grant, 54
Wilder Foundation, 45
Wilkes, Bethany, 92
WILU (Workshop for Instruction in Library Use), 64
Woodard, Beth, ix, 4, 81, 153
Woods, Stephen A., 37
workshops on information literacy, 52
World Almanac, 16
World Economic Forum report on the future of jobs, 36
Writing for the Web, 13
writing tasks as experiential learning approach, 136

Y

Yon, Shukriah Binti Hj, 124
"You Can Do It: A Recipe for Designing Web-Based Instruction" (WebJunction), 75
Young, Philip, 132
Young Adult Library Services Association, 99

CPSIA information can be obtained
at www.ICGtesting.com
Printed in the USA
LVHW060922140620
658006LV00006B/90